Contribution and Collaboration:
The Work of Petra Andrejova-
Molnár and her Contemporaries

Koenig Books

THE COLLECTI
SHIP OF MODE

SEAN KELLER

VE AUTHOR-
RNISM

Interwar European modernism reminds us of a possibility that seems lost: the possibility of architecture as a collective practice, a shared exploration. For the architects who aligned themselves with the *Congres Internationaux d'Architecture Moderne* (CIAM), similarities of form were not—as they are often taken to be today— signs of brand encroachment, but indications that one was contributing to the great remaking of the world. Not that there were no personalities—and "heroic" ones too—but even the stars (as we would say) spent much of their time advancing the cause of the collective effort of modern architecture, urbanism, and design. We could speak of these architects working semi-privately, each producing modulations of the collective vocabulary, personalized to greater and lesser extents but never fully individuated.

Which is to say that modernism *was* a style. But notice how important that style—that constellation of aesthetic choices— was to the sense of a collective project. See how the style was not an autonomous formal code but how it marshaled social aspirations as well (admittedly mixed, and sometimes inchoate, but never cynical). See too how that style—that way of handling material, form, color, and line—is tied to time: how it once, for the CIAM generation, embodied a time that was coming; and how it now, for us, embodies a time past. Though here it would be truer to say that much modernism

before 1945 saw itself not only as a new, emerging architecture but simultaneously as a summation, or restatement, of all past architectures. (It is on this issue that the more radical modernisms of the Futurists and hardcore Constructivists diverged from the dominant Werkbund- Bauhaus mode).

Complementing its treatment of time, modernism in architecture and design also saw itself drawing on craft cultures and ways of building from around the world, and drawing these into a new trans-cultural vocabulary. This unity was to be attained through form—through basic geometric organizations that were supposed to be common to all arts everywhere. Though developed to solve the crises of industrialized Europe, modern architecture saw its vocabulary of intersecting planes and volumes presaged throughout world history.

So, if modern architecture was a style it was surely an international(-ist) one. CIAM, modeling itself more or less explicitly as a socialist organization, sought to spread modern architecture throughout the world. Central Europe might have been its center of gravity, but it was intended to arise everywhere in conjunction with technological development. On this point we can distinguish early twentieth-century modernism from the contemporary architecture of globalization, propelled as it is by a neo-liberal search for targets of opportunity. International-style modernism

was not (or not only) spread by opportunism but
by design, as part of a plan, as a self-proclaimed movement.

Yet, if the geographical and political aspirations of interwar modernism were vast, the architectural concerns could also be modest to a degree that, again, seems mostly lost today. All of the CIAM architects were concerned with research into, and construction of, *Existenzminimum* housing. Viewed alternately as a key component of the socialist revolution, or as the means of avoiding this revolution—Le Corbusier's famous "architecture *or* revolution"—the provision of new, technologically advanced, and scientifically planned housing for the world's workers was arguably the foundational premise of international modernism. As an ideological commitment, the concern for economy of means often extended even into private free-standing houses where it was not required (we could say it was part of the style). Compare the relatively modest scale of interwar modernist houses to the excessive showpieces of contemporary practices. Clear organization, high-quality construction, good light and air were proposed to be adequate for all.

Against all of this one might object: what about those (male) heroes of "Heroic Modernism"? Yet how real were they, with their invented names ("Le Corbusier," "van der Rohe") and their costumes (the cape, the glasses, the cigar) and their costume parties? With their doctored photographs, pasted-up collages, and canvas mock-ups? (Cutting and gluing the past, present, and future into the shapes they desired.) Their little, self-important, self-published journals, written by themselves (perhaps under multiple pseudonyms) and a few friends? All of those buildings—and even cities for millions—designed for people and technologies and opinions that didn't (yet) exist?

For what was modern architecture if not the summoning up of a new world with new ways of living, seeing, and building? This world had to be projected before it could be legislated and built, projected through drawing, model making, photography, and writing. The incredible, magical fact is the extent to which this summoning worked. Those odd journals, grainy photos, and miniature buildings did somehow remake the world.

And what too about the myth that the architect makes architecture? Isn't the architect really more like an organizing force—perhaps even an imaginary one—wrapping around, or running through, a flow of people, material, images, money, space, and time? Trying to cajole and compel all of the hands that sign contracts, write checks, draw details, dig holes, lay bricks, paint walls, manufacture fixtures, take photographs, and write reviews to construct something they may never have seen before. Like most myths, the story of the architect making architecture is both literally untrue and yet not false. For there is (or may be)

a sensibility and intelligence
guiding the production but, given
the complexity of realizing any
project, who could say where
the architect stopped or started?
Or if, perhaps, he or she were
ever there at all?

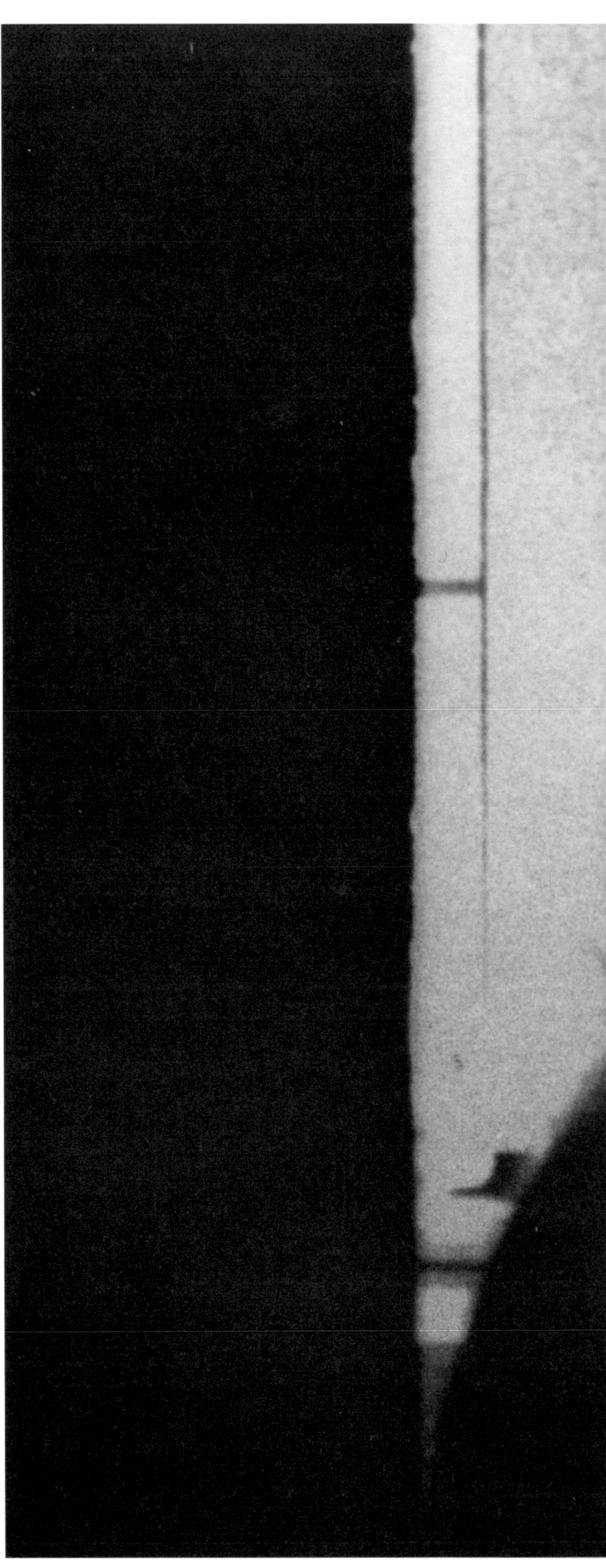

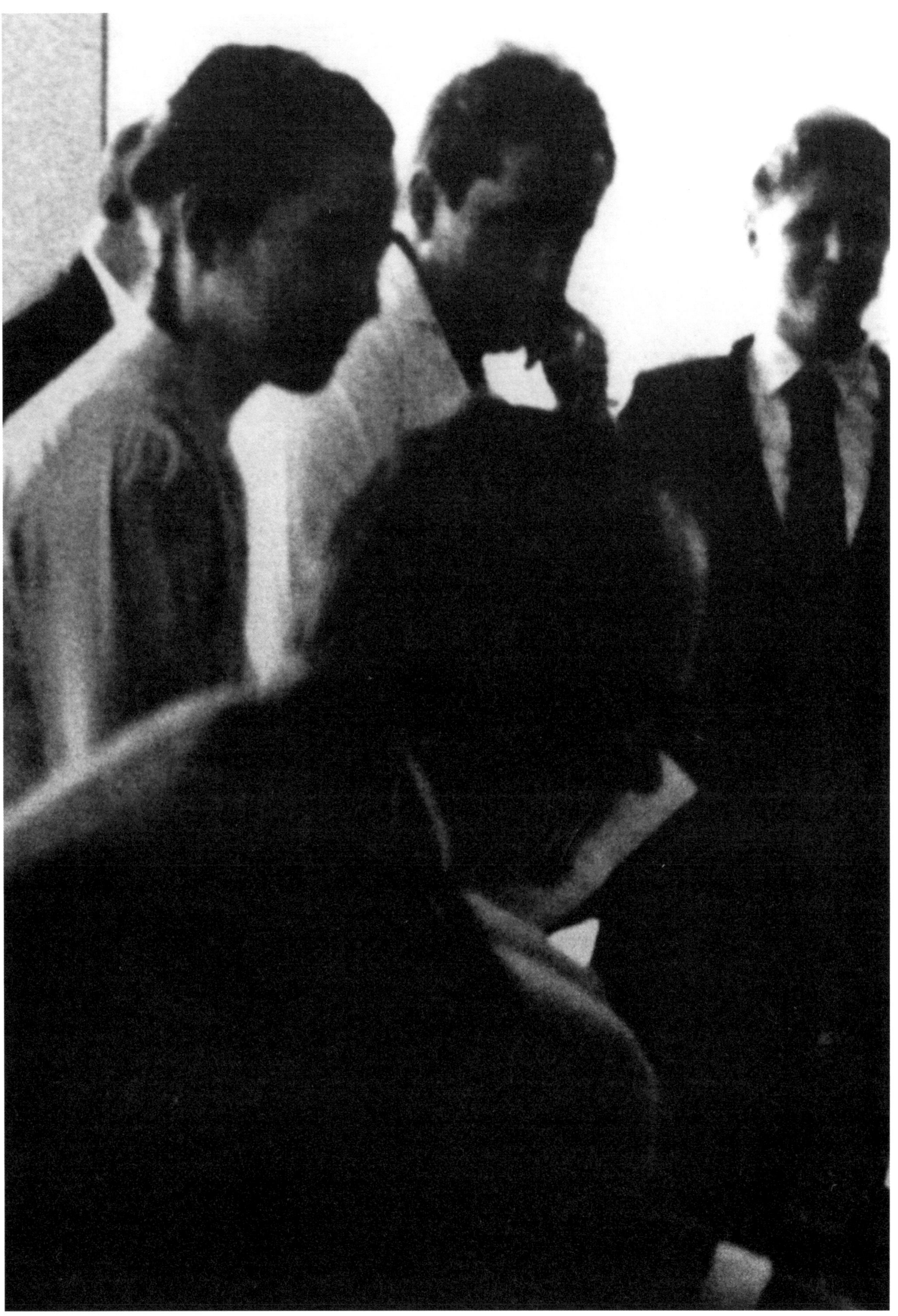

IN COLLABORA
ANDREJOVA-M
HER CONTEMP

J.A. GIBSON

TION: PETRA
OLNÁR AND
ORARIES

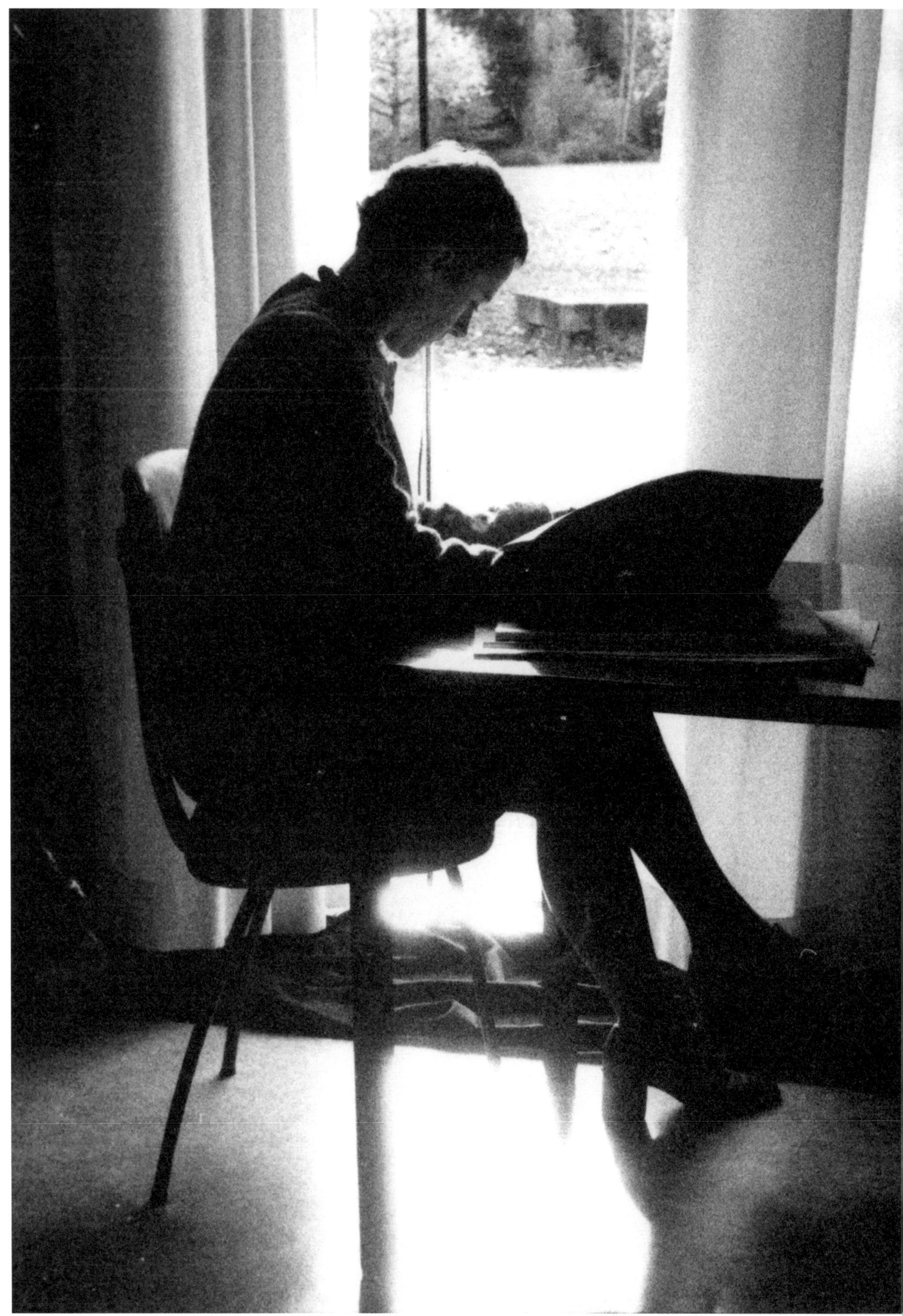

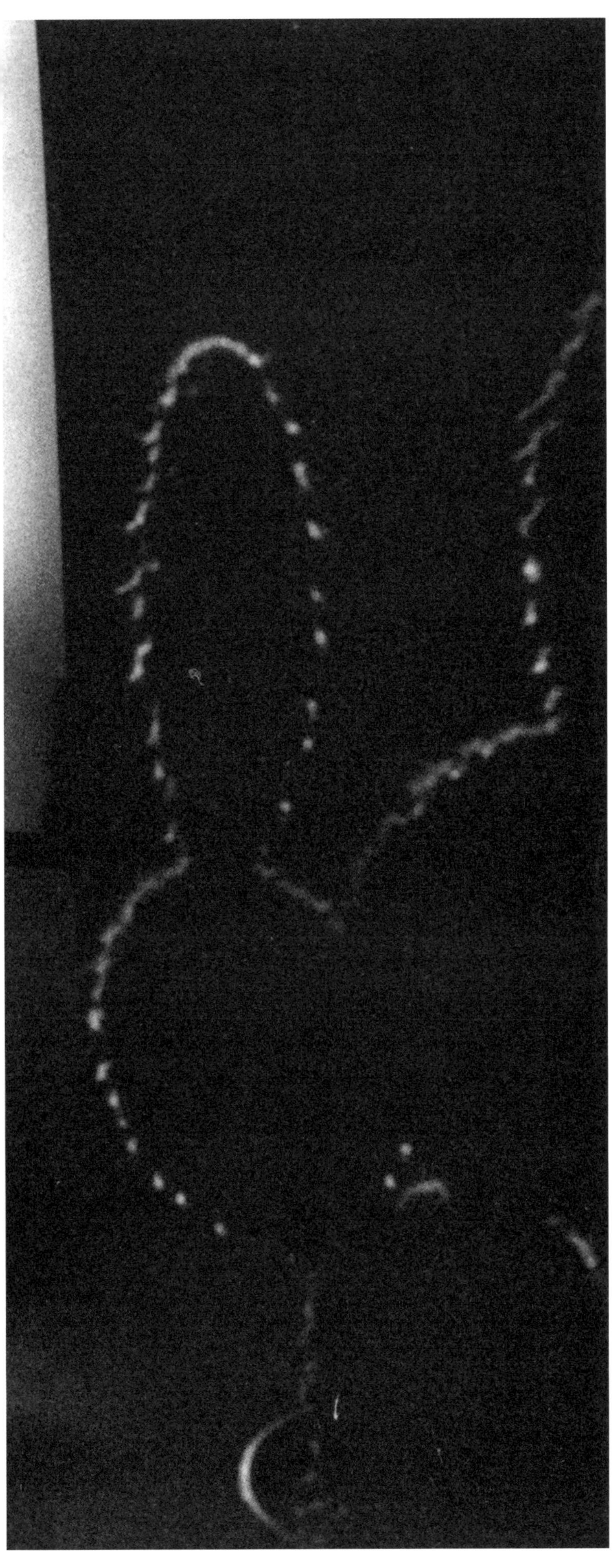

The architect Petra Andrejova-Molnár—better known as P.A.—was an integral part of the fertile architectural communities that flourished throughout Eastern Europe in the 1920s. Enthusiastic about possibilities for political renewal, P.A. and her contemporaries were dedicated to design as a means to promote progressive ideas. Collaboration and collective practice were hallmarks of the epoch, yet this egalitarian approach has arguably obscured the individual achievements of architects such as P.A., whose contributions have largely remained unrecognized. As a rare female participant in the male-dominated dialogues of the period, P.A. not only found the establishment of her own architectural office to be challenging, but was subsequently neglected by historians who considered her work marginal.
In recent years, particularly since the fall of Communism, archival material has become more readily available and the breadth of P.A.'s contributions and influence have become apparent. Not a peripheral player in the least, Petra Andrejova-Molnár emerges as a central yet overlooked figure of her generation.

Petra Jozefina Andrejova was born in Zlín (Moravian Czechoslovakia) in 1898 to an educated, bourgeois family whose connection to the thriving Czech textile industry encouraged a recognition of Petra Andrejova's early aptitude for design. By the mid-1920s she had studied at both the School of Decorative Arts in Prague and the Academy of Fine Arts in

Vienna where in 1919 she initially became interested in architecture. Throughout the 1920s she traveled extensively and sought out like-minded architects, designers, typographers, and artists in Germany, Austria, Hungary, and Czechoslovakia, soon developing a broad network of colleagues across the region. In the interwar period she worked consistently, becoming well known both for her individual projects such as the influential *Hotel Nord-Sud*, but also for her editorial and design role in several publications of the 1920s and 1930s in Prague and Brno. After having attempted unsuccessfully to set up her own architectural office in Brno in the mid-1930s, she left the city for several years in Budapest and Vienna. By this point the political situation in Europe was beginning to feel threatening and she fled Austria shortly after the Nazi Anschluss of 1938. She settled in France where she remained until after the liberation of Paris by Allied forces in August 1944. Her precise activities in France remain unknown—it has been suggested that she was involved in leftist politics although there is little concrete evidence—but it appears likely that she was in contact with artists Robert and Sonia Delaunay; the interior designer Jean-Michel Frank, and the architect Robert Mallet Stevens. By 1945 she had permanently relocated to the United States where, after a nearly nine-year hiatus, she began once again to design, albeit in a radically different context from her formative years in Eastern Europe.

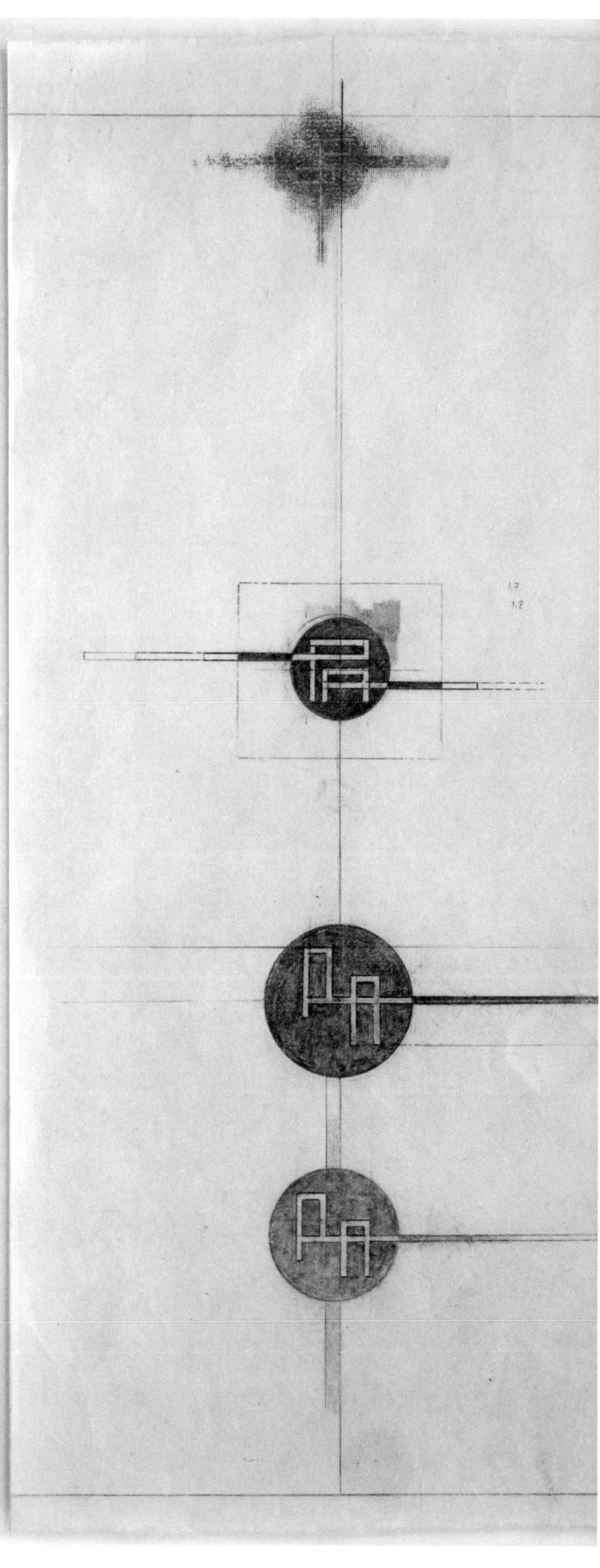

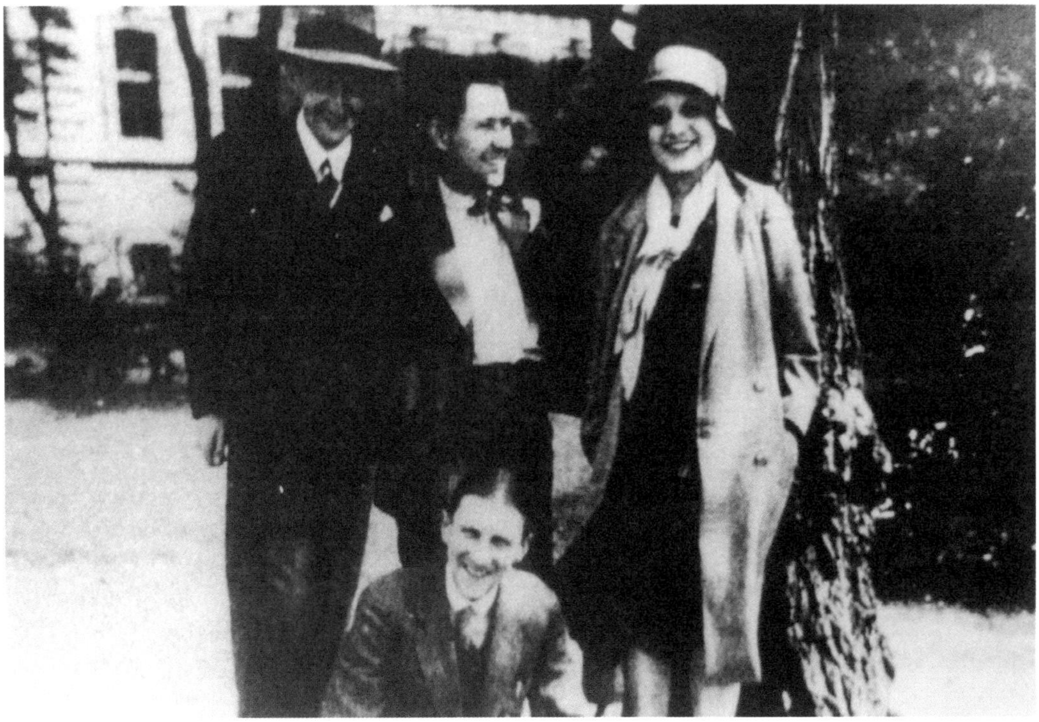

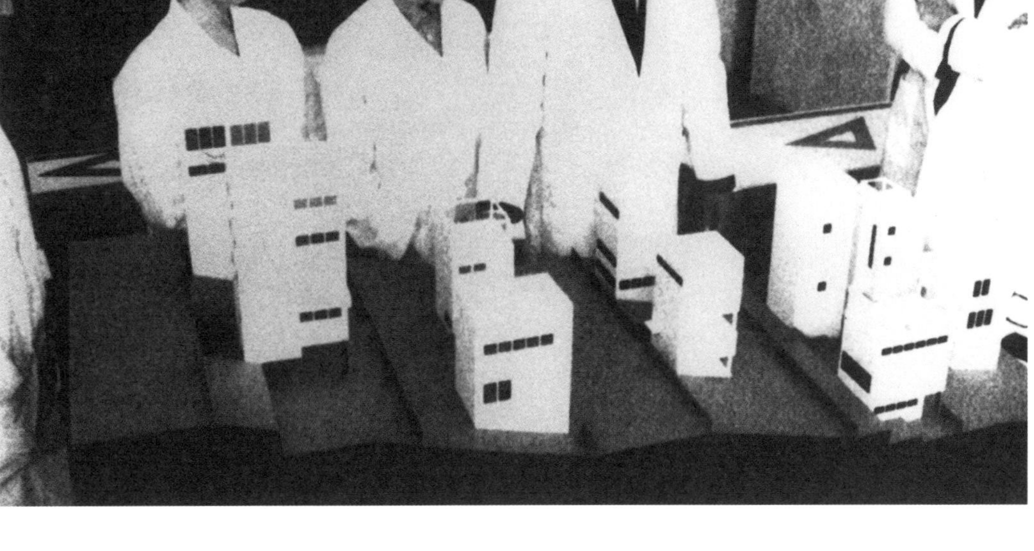

6–7
Design Studio
with Farkas Molnár
and Pal Ligeti,
Technical University
Budapest, 1928

10–11
House on Csatárka
Street, Budapest,
ca. 1931

12–13
Design for
monograms, ca. 1922

Petra Andrejova-
Molnár with Karel
Teige, Brno, 1931

Studio of Bohuslav
Fuchs, Brno, ca. 1928

THE CZECHOSLOVAK
PARIS 1925: A LABOR
DESIGN IDEAS

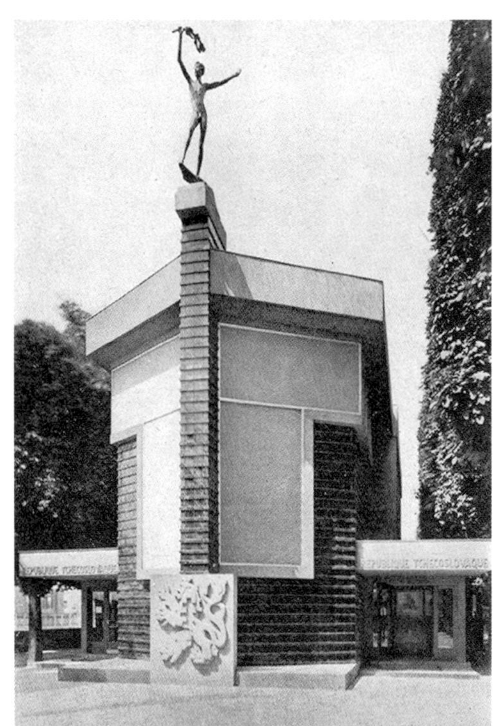

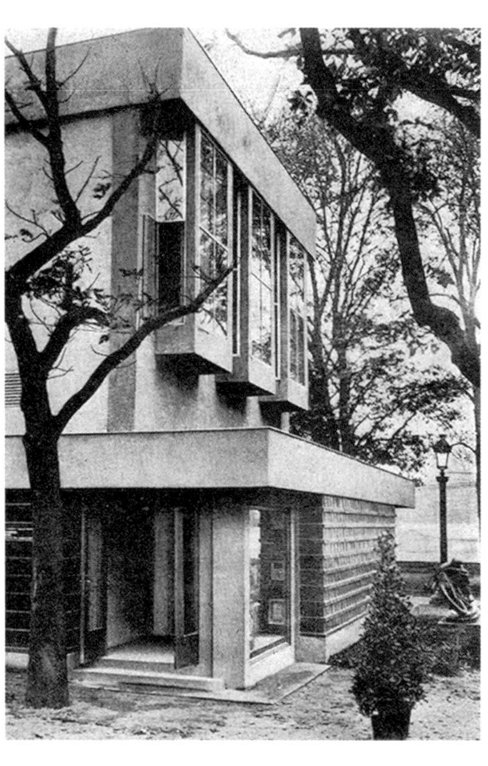

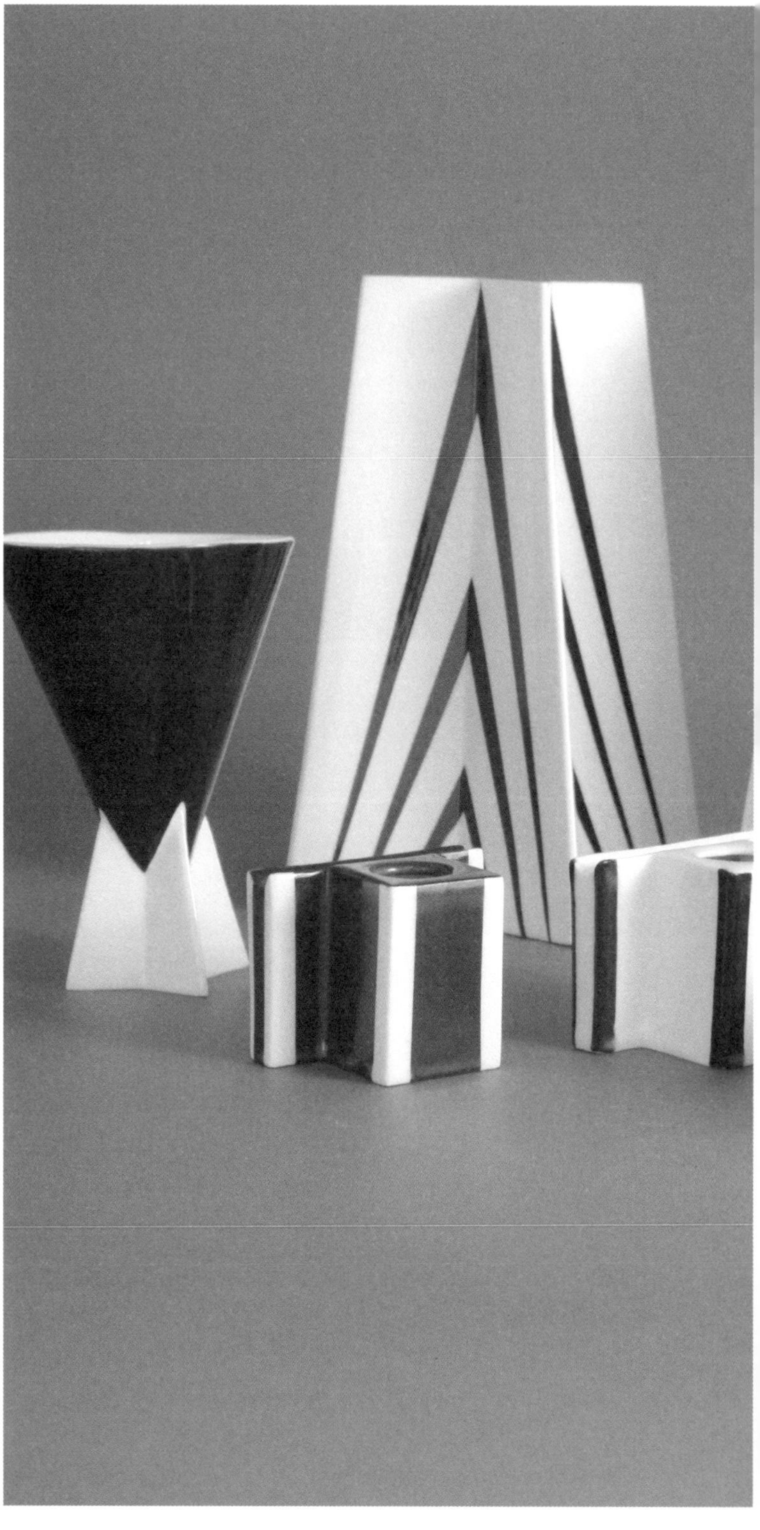

Czechoslovakian
Pavilion façade,
and rear entrance,
Paris 1924–25

Various designers,
cubist ceramic
vases, ashtray and
inkwell, exhibited
at Czechoslovakian
Pavilion, 1918–22

16–17

Petra Andrejova-
Molnár and Josef
Gočár, entrance hall,
Czechoslovakian
Pavilion, Paris 1924–25

Petra Andrejova-
Molnár, pedestal for
ceramic display, 1925

Petra Andrejova-
Molnár, Josef
Gočár, interior for
a modern woman,
Czechoslovakian
Pavilion, 1924–25

IAN PAVILION, ATORY FOR NEW

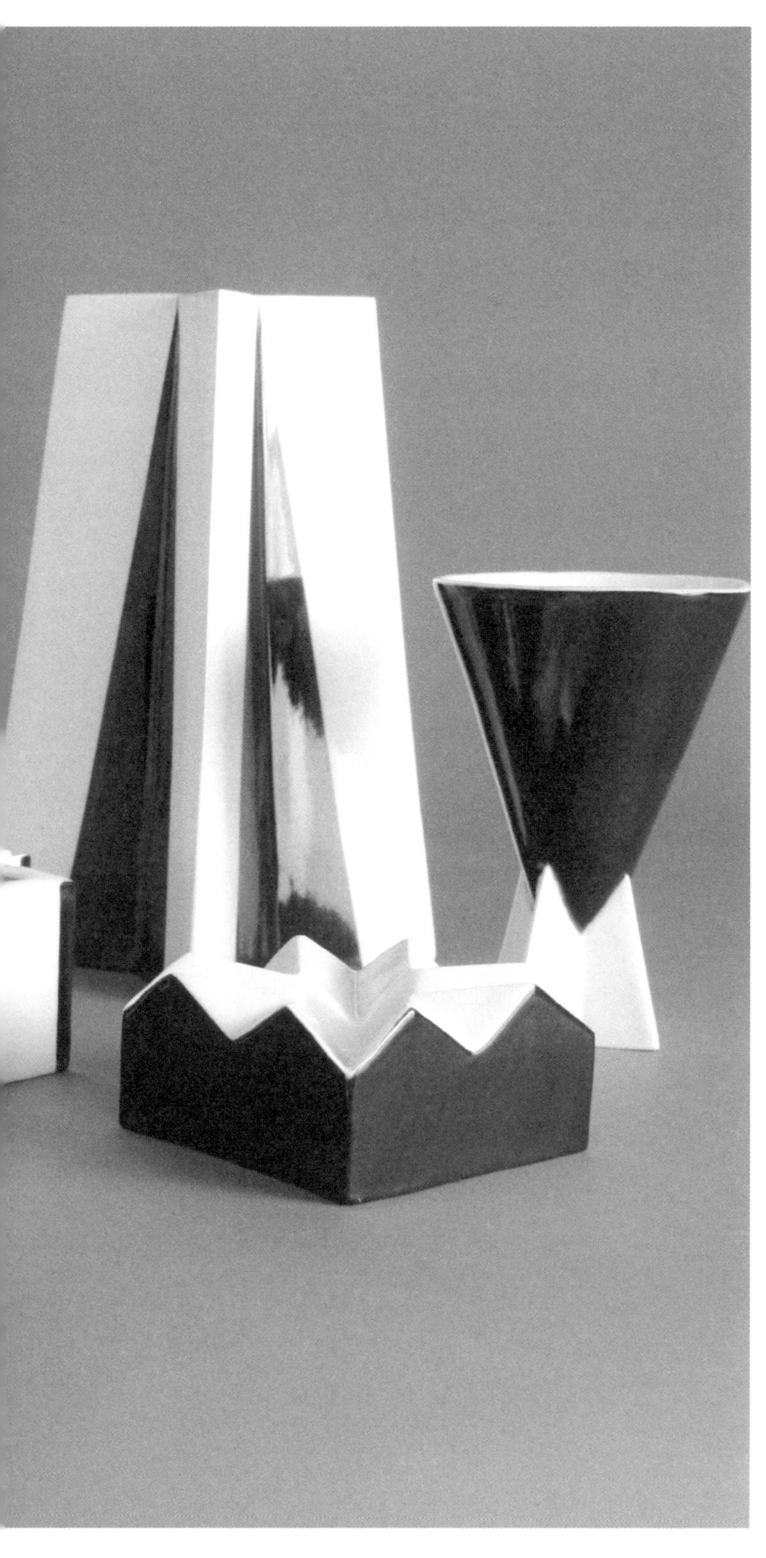

Designed by Josef Gočár, the Czechoslovak Pavilion at the 1925 International Exposition of Modern Industrial and Decorative Arts in Paris bridged traditional design and an avant-garde aesthetic. While the pavilion's exterior was inspired by abstracted nautical forms, its interior rooms combined self-conscious references to folk art and the Renaissance alongside geometric Cubism. In its balance between history and regionalism on the one hand, and modernist internationalism on the other, the pavilion registers the competing aesthetic influences of this period in Czechoslovakia.

This tension can be understood to have resulted from generational differences: the pavilion's furniture, for example, was designed by Gočár's teacher, the architect and interior designer Jan Kotěra, himself a student of Otto Wagner, whose work stood on the boundary between late nineteenth-century design and the beginnings of modernism. With the participation of Kotěra, Gočár, and their younger colleagues, the pavilion effectively presents a genealogy of early Eastern European modernism comprising three generations of Czech architects each leaning progressively further toward a twentieth-century aesthetic.

The connections formed by the junior architects who worked on the project, many of whom would go on to have distinguished careers, are an important legacy of the Czechoslovak pavilion and the collaborative atmosphere produced what P.A.

later called a "laboratory for new design ideas."[1] Participating young architects included Farkas Molnár, Jósef Fischer, Jaromír Krejcar, Bohuslav Fuchs, and P.A., who had just completed her studies and was still known only as Petra Andrejova. P.A.'s involvement originated with Pavel Janák, who had been her professor at the School of Decorative Arts in Prague. The friendships she made during the pavilion's design would be instrumental in the development of her career. By 1927, for example, she was employed by Fuchs in the design of his influential *Hotel Avion* in Brno, and the following year she worked with Krejcar on his *Machnač Sanatorium* in Trenčianske Teplice. Moreover, during the pavilion project P.A. grew closer to Farkas Molnár whom she had first met in 1922. He would become her intellectual and romantic companion until his death in 1945.

Working under Gočár and Janek, PA was assigned to many aspects of the pavilion design and, although precise records of her involvement have not survived, her characteristic desire for efficient simplicity of form can be seen in a number of the pavilion elements. Perhaps her greatest known contribution was the terra-cotta *brise soleil* which projected from either side of the building. Angular interlocking forms created symmetrical perforated shade walls which provided partial shadow while simultaneously delineating an exterior terrace. While her full design was curtailed and remained

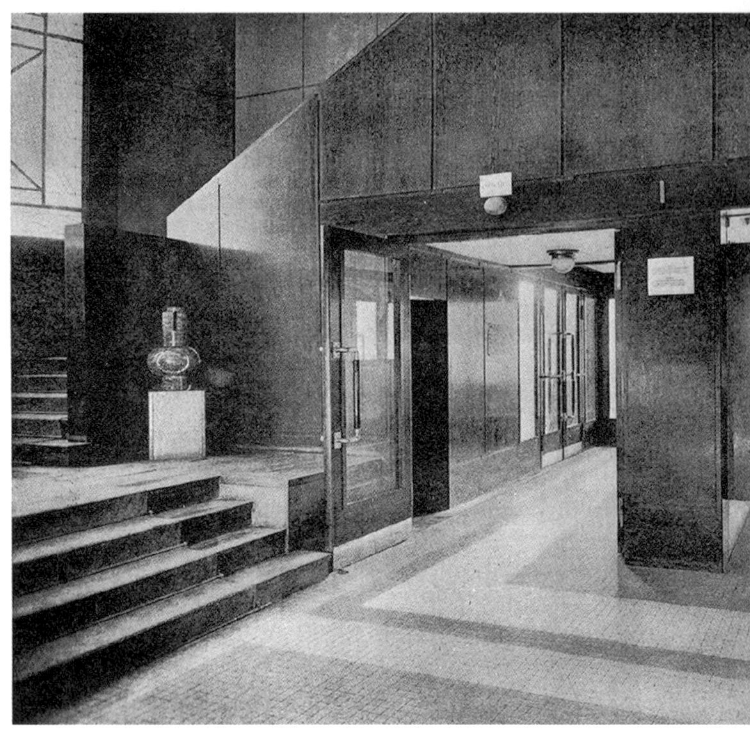

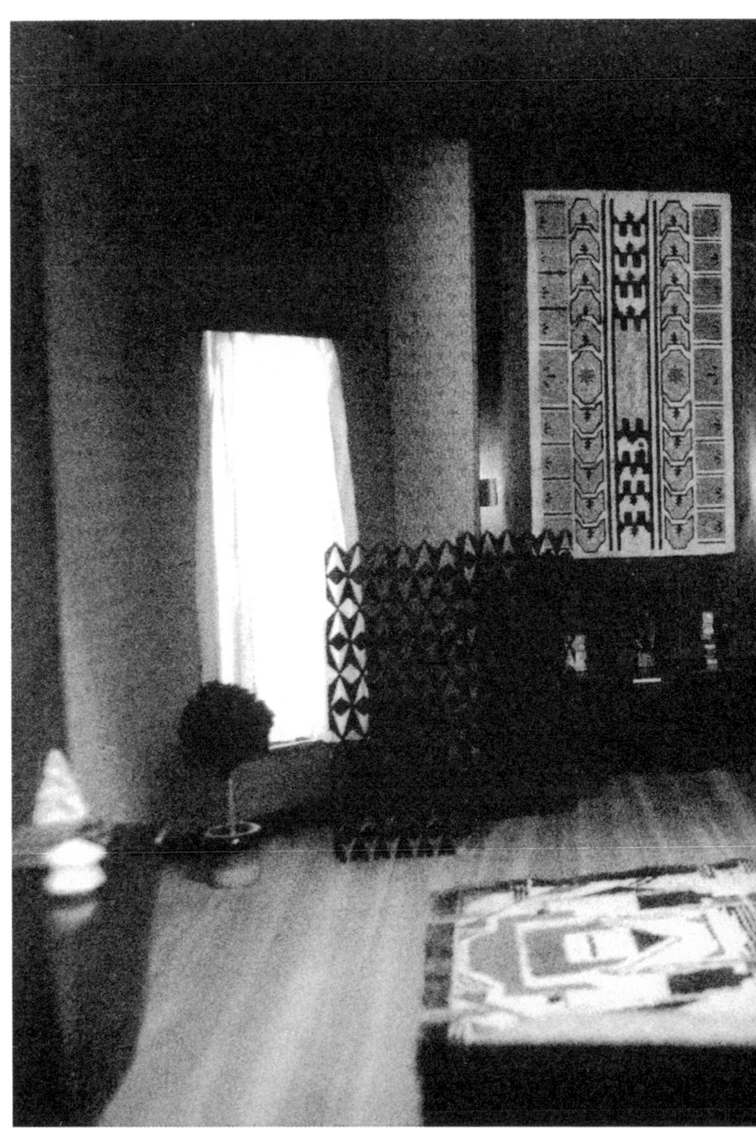

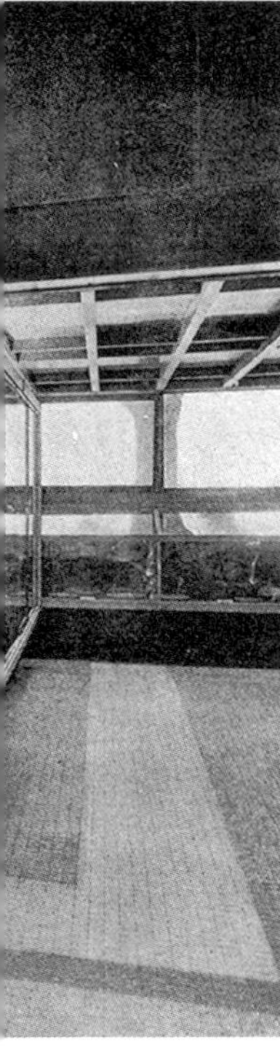

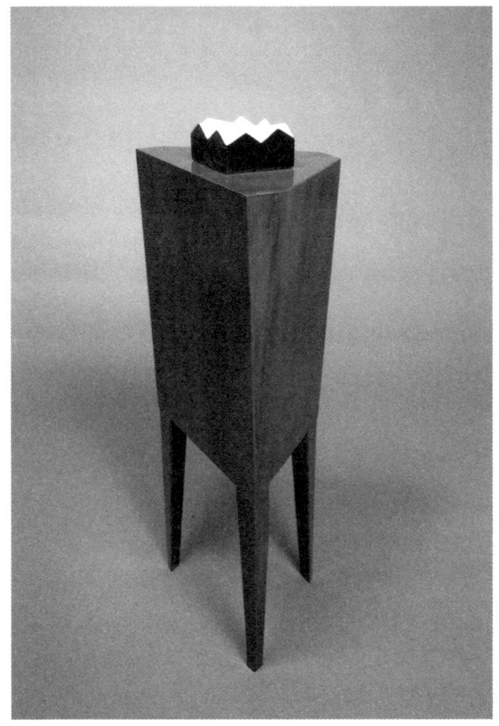

unrealized, this interest in fluid relationships between interior and exterior space would preoccupy P.A. for the remainder of her career. In addition, perhaps because her early studies in Vienna had been in textile design, or perhaps because textiles were still considered "feminine" design work, P.A. was largely entrusted with the tapestries for two interiors—the "Room for a Modern Man" and its companion, "Room for a Modern Woman"—which featured furniture by Jan Kotěra. Despite references to Czechoslovakian folk art, P.A.'s designs remain abstract and their geometry complements Kotěra's interest in "space and construction" and his move away from "form and decoration."[2] Finally, P.A.'s hand can be seen in crucial elements of the exhibition design such as the small shelves and mirrors she conceived for the "Room for a Modern Woman," and the pedestals on which Czech ceramics by Vlastislav Hofman, Pavel Janak and others were displayed. Here too P.A. presented simplified geometries, pared down forms which echo the ceramics' angular planes.

ENDNOTES
1. Petra Andrejova-Molnár interviewed by Anna Novak, *The Architectural Review*, April 1951.

2. Jan Kotěra, "O novém umění" [On New Art] in *Volné směry* [Free Directions] vol. 4, 1900: p.189-95.

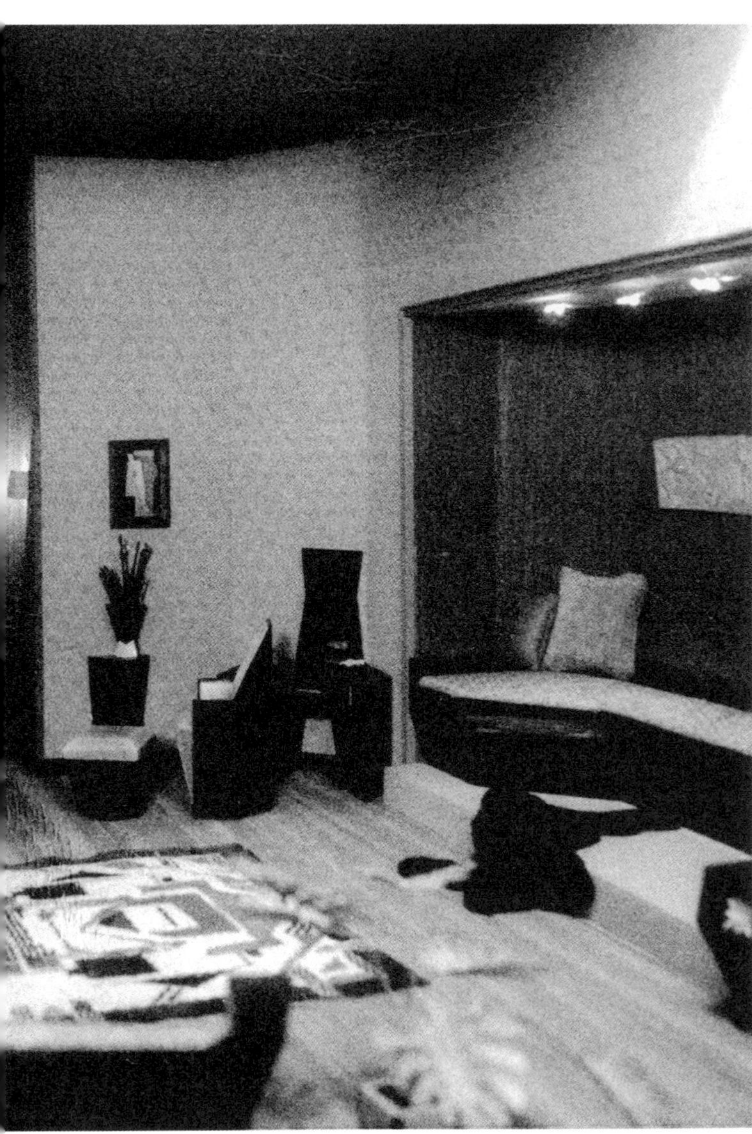

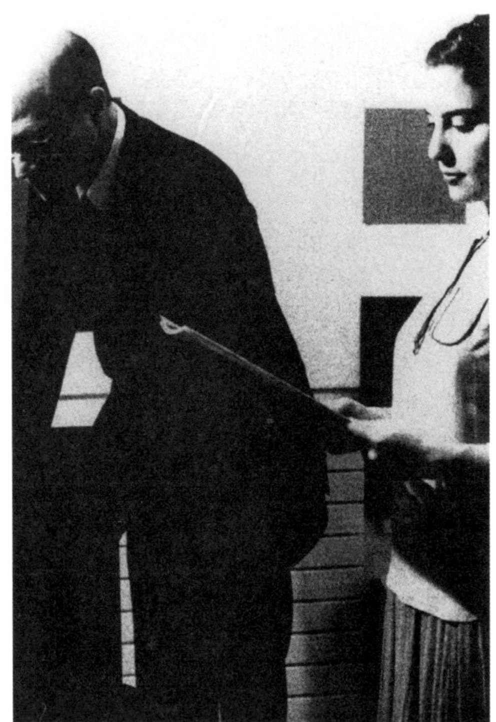

18–19

P.A.-Molnár at the
office of Professor
Jaromír Krejcar,
Prague, 1938

Ladislav Sutnar, cover
design, Výtvarné
Snahy, VS5X, Prague,
1928–29

Latislav Sutnar, cover
design, Výtvarné
Snahy, VSX2, Prague,
1928–29

Petra Andrejova-
Monlnár, design for
storefront Žijeme,
first project, Brno,
1924–25

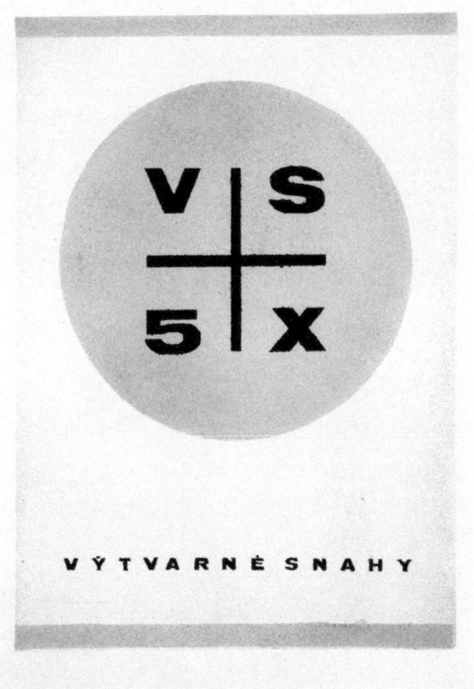

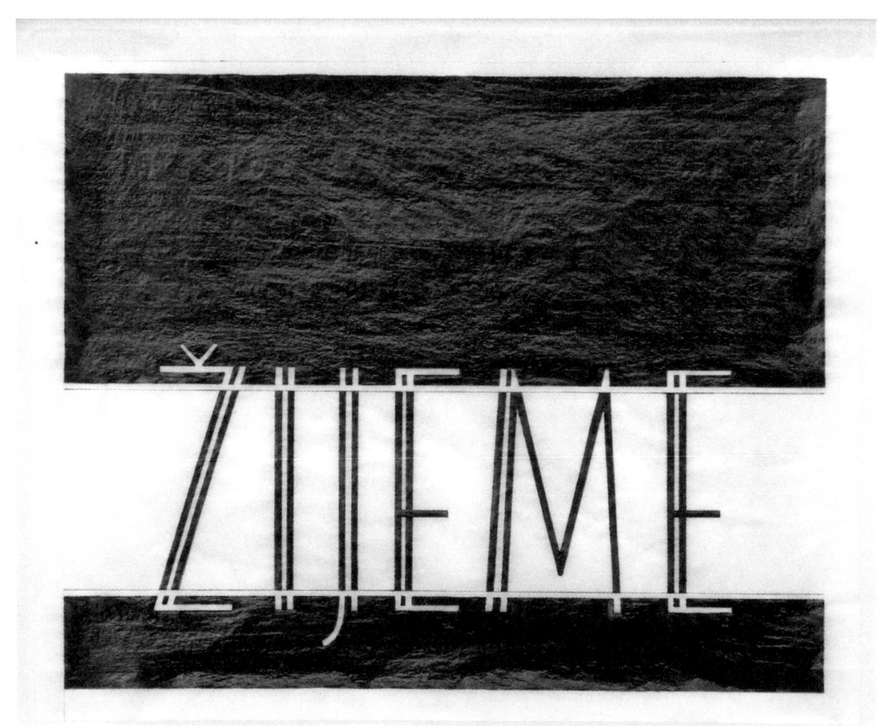

ESIGN: BETWEEN
TERNATIONALISM

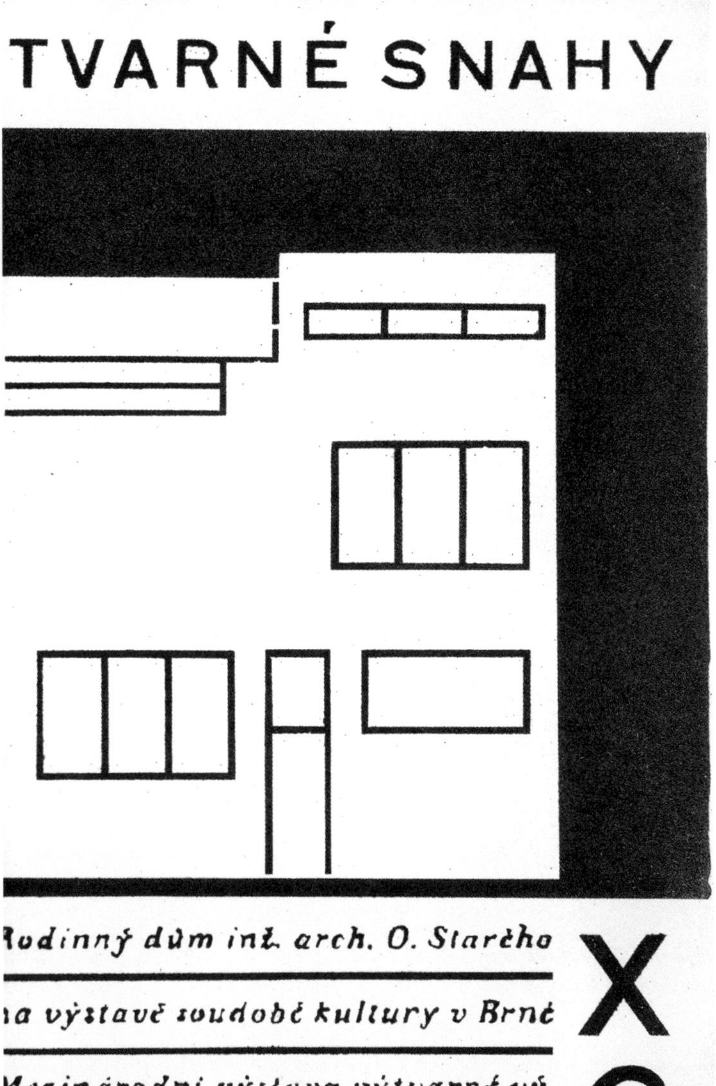

Between 1921 and 1935, numerous architecture and design periodicals were established to disseminate international developments while at the same time focusing on regional styles. Through publications such as *Volné směry*, *Stavba*, and *ReD*, Eastern European audiences could read about Frank Lloyd Wright, Le Corbusier, Charlotte Perriand, Robert Mallet-Stevens, Theo Van Doesburg, the Bauhaus, and other contemporaries. Brno and Prague—the location of *Volné směry*, affiliated with the Mánes Union of Fine Arts—were active centers of print media and the proliferation and cross-pollination of such journals bear witness to an energetic and politically engaged community dedicated to sharing ideas about aesthetics, technology, and politics.

Petra Andrejova-Molnár was an active participant in the debates of her era, including those that took place in the pages of the newly established journals. On the editorial board of the magazines *Byt* and *Stavba* (the revue published by the Club of Architects at the Technical University of Prague), she is thought to have played a key role in their design. Additionally, P.A's influence can be seen in the increased coverage given to avant-garde Western European architects and debates about the new internationalism.

P.A.'s involvement with architectural journals only increased after she met the graphic designer and typographer Karel Teige, a leader of the Czech avant-garde movement Devětsil which was founded in Prague in 1920 and later expanded to include a Brno chapter. Through the magazine *ReD* (*Revue Devětsilu*) as well as various other publications and anthologies, Teige greatly influenced the group's theoretical stance (and propensity for manifestos). Teige and P.A. were kindred spirits, interested in Functionalism, technology, and politics; and having met in the late 1920s through Jaromír Krejcar, the two became frequent interlocutors.[1]

Teige was enthusiastic about P.A.'s activities in Brno, particularly the community that developed around her *Žijime* shop project. In the late 1920s Brno was one of Europe's major hotbeds of modern architecture: in 1925 Bohuslav Fuchs built the *Café Zeman*, his first Functionalist structure, and then the *Hotel Avion* in 1928; in 1928 Mies van der Rohe built the *Villa Tungendhat*. The same year saw the *Nový Dům* (New House) development: sixteen houses built by nine architects as part of 1928s Exhibition of Contemporary Culture.

In this context P.A. established *Žijime*—roughly translated as "living"—a small shop and community meeting place for which she designed the storefront, signage, and interior. As a shop, *Žijime* was run by P.A.'s colleague Hana Kučerová-Záveská and sold decorative objects by local Czech designers—including Bohuslav Fuch's AKA interior accessories—as well as a small selection of furni-

ture.[2] But its more important role was as a meeting place for the Brno design community between 1927 and 1930. P.A. and Kučerová-Zaveska hosted readings, lectures, and political discussions at which both local and international architects met to talk about the developments of their day. The editorial teams from *Byt* and *Stavba* were known to use the storefront space and P.A. made efforts to provide a wide range of contemporary publications for sale in the shop itself.

ENDNOTES
1. It is not known what P.A. thought of Karel Teige's critique of Le CorbusierKarel Teige, "Mundaneum," *Stavba* 10, 1929: pp. 145-55.

2. Petra Andrejova-Molnár, Letter to Hana Kucerova-Zaveska, August 27th, 1928. Box 1, Folder 7. Petra Andrejova-Molnár papers. Brno City Museum: Brno Archives, Czech Republic. Accessed 10 February, 2013.

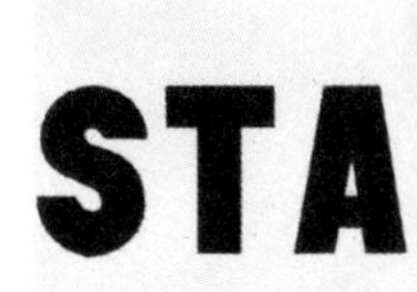

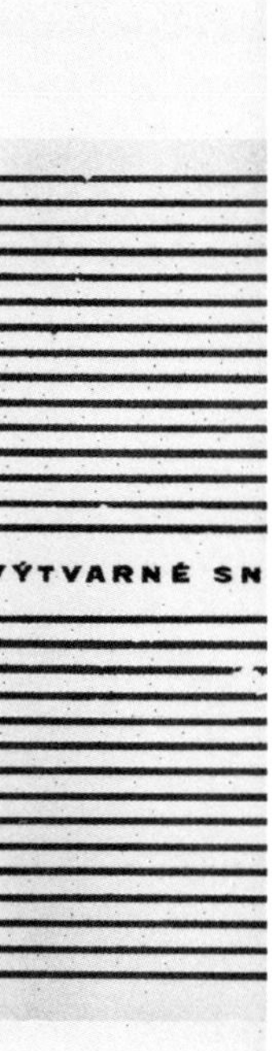

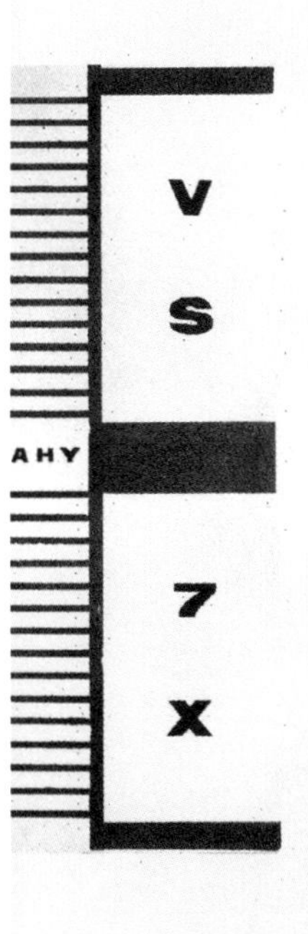

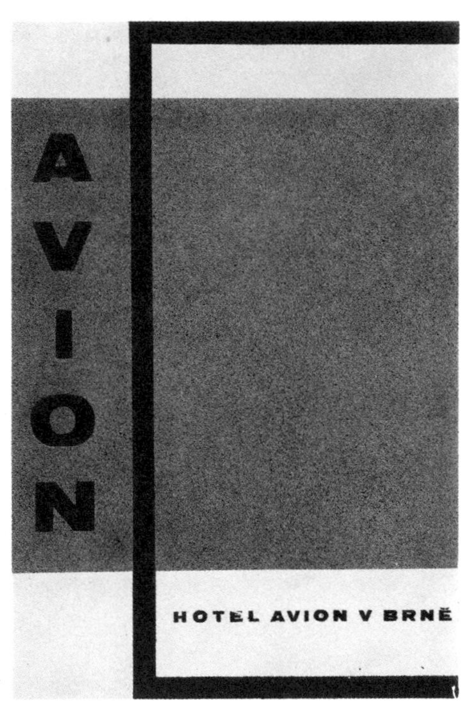

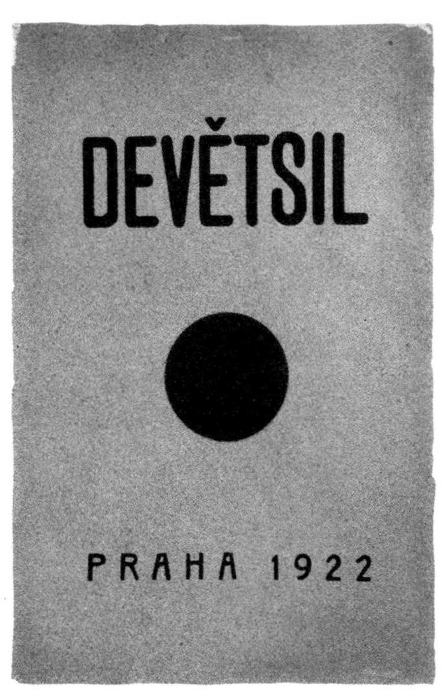

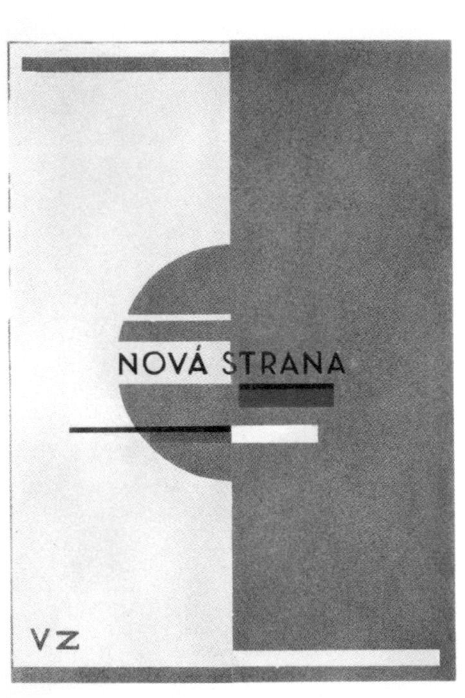

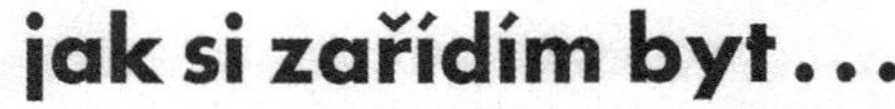

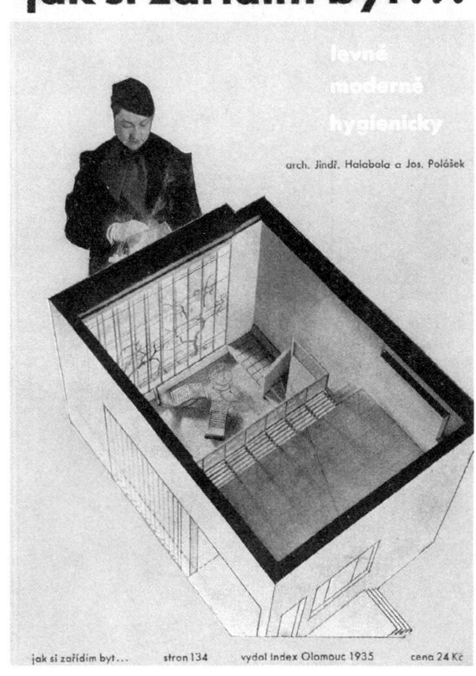

20–21

Unknown designer, cover design, Stavba VIII, Vol 8, 1932

Josef Zamazal, Bohuslav Fuchs, logo design, *Hotel Avion*, Brno, 1928–29

Karel Teige, cover design, *Devětsil*, Prague, 1922

Jindrich Halabala and Jos Polásek, cover design, Jak si zařídím byt… 1935

Petra Andrejova-Molnár, cover design, Nová Strana, Vol. 2, Brno, 1928

Unknown designer, cover design, Výtvarné Snahy, VS7X, Prague, 1928–29

P.A. and many of her contemporaries were drawn to the design
of modular and communal
housing; apartment complexes,
hotels, and sanatoria all provided
opportunities to think though the
problems of efficient, modern,
collective dwellings. By the late
1920s, architectural groups such
as the Czechoslovak CIRPAC
(International Committee
for the Resolution of Problems
in Contemporary Architecture)
had begun to propose "hotel
style" dwellings as an alternative
to conventional bourgeois apartments. Such dwellings included
collectivized service facilities and
minimum residential areas and
often took the efficient design
solutions of established collective
housing types (hotels, dormito-
ries, sanatoria) as their models.[1]

In 1927, P.A. was ap-
proached by Bohuslav Fuchs
to join his office for the design
of the Avion Hotel in Brno.
Emphatically Functionalist in
approach, the hotel is a narrow
urban building designed with
efficient stacked floors and open,
fluid spaces. Fuchs used reinforced concrete to create an
interior segmented by galleries
and lit by expanses of glass and
skylights. Although the hotel's
fifty guest rooms, café, and
restaurant are spatially separate,
their service areas are intercon-
nected. The efficient sophistica-
tion of Fuchs's *Avion* inspired
several contemporary hotel
designs such as Pavel Janák's
Hotel Juli of 1933 as well as P.A.'s
own *Hotel Nord-Sud* of 1932.

The *Nord-Sud* was P.A.'s
first independent large scale

HOTELS AND SANAT
FOR COLLECTIVE HO

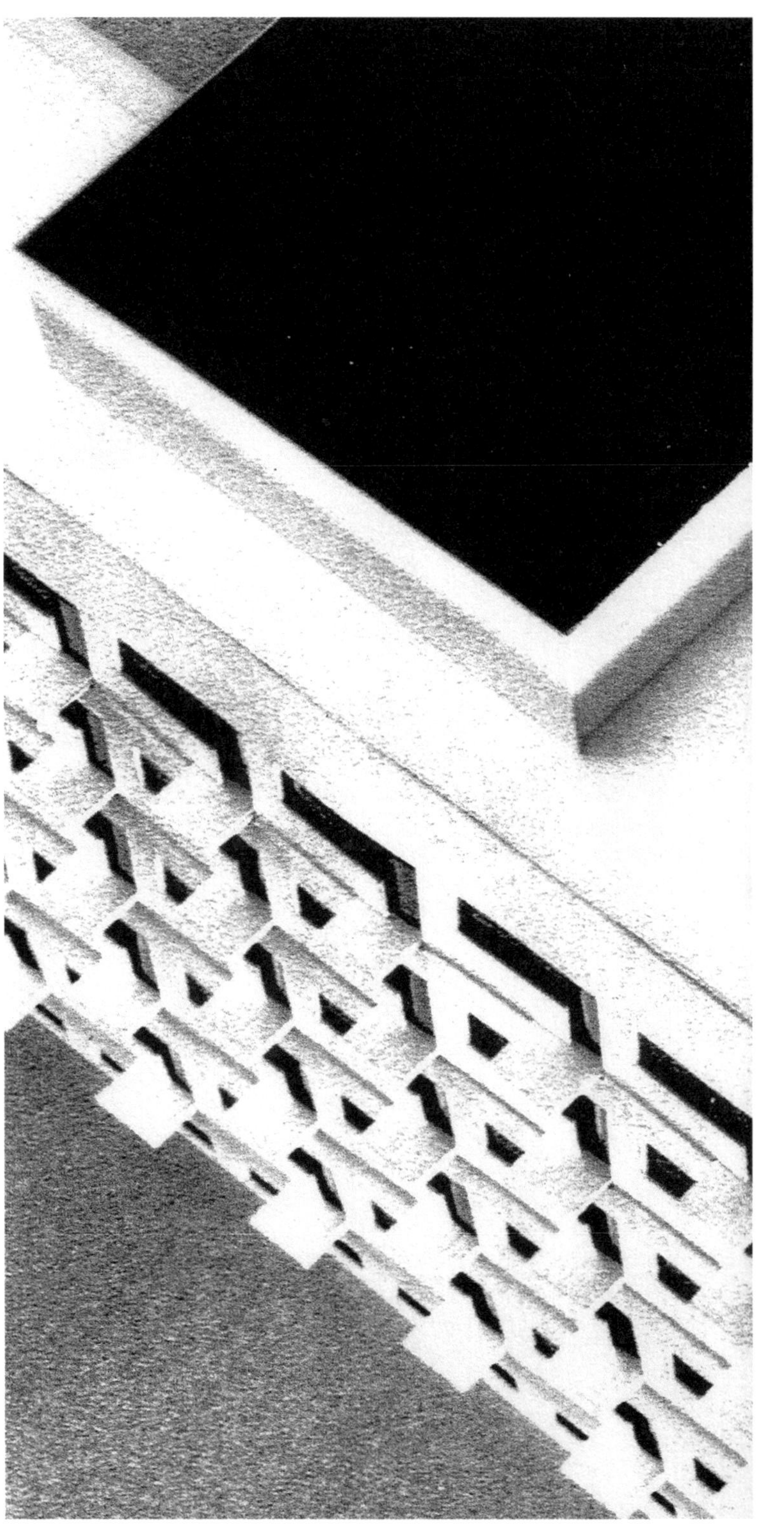

ORIA: PROTOTYPES USING

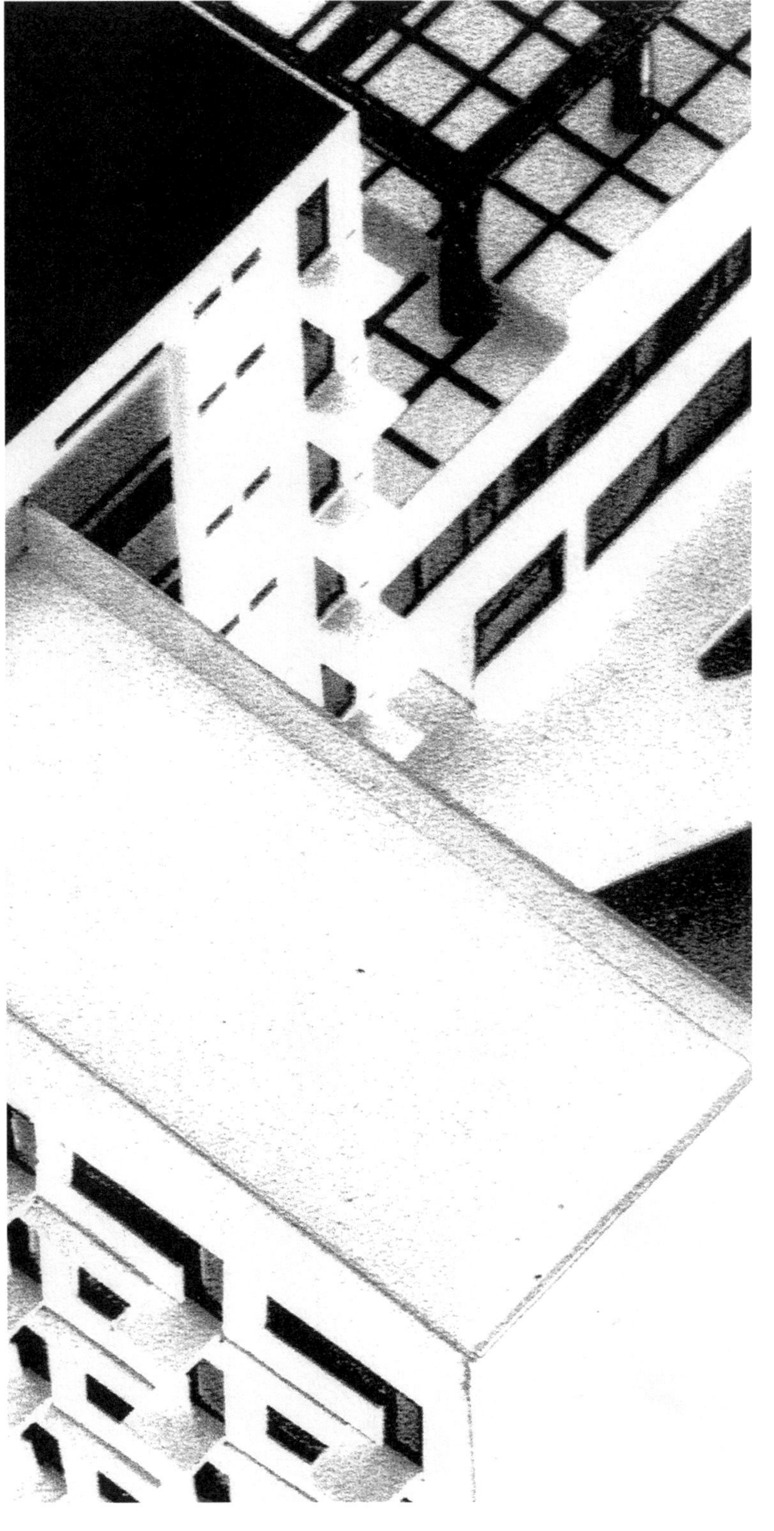

construction. Located on the Adriatic coast of Yugoslavia, the hotel was destroyed in the Second World War, but from extant plans and photographs it is clear that P.A. adapted the techniques she had developed while working for Fuchs, adjusting her design principles to take advantage of the hotel's seaside location.[2] The hotel itself was intimate, with fourteen bedrooms and two suites it had a capacity of approximately thirty-five guests. Perhaps because of its proximity to the ocean—and P.A.'s fascination with the efficient, streamlined design of ocean liners during this period—both the cabin-like bedrooms and the design of the hotel as a whole retained a nautical influence. P.A.'s custom furniture for the guest rooms, lobby, and dining areas was composed of floating horizontal planes that reiterated the hotel's cantilevered design. Throughout the hotel, her interest in lighting could be seen in the wall sconces which similarly echoed her design principles on smaller scale. The remarkable rectilinear shade walls at the *Nord-Sud* seem an extension of the *brise soleil* P.A. had designed in 1925 for the Czech pavilion in Paris. As in her earlier work, the relationship between interior and exterior space was a priority for P.A.: the hotel included an open air third floor café as well as numerous terraces separated from the interior by glass walls. The importance of transparency can be seen in the careful positioning of the hotel in such a way that

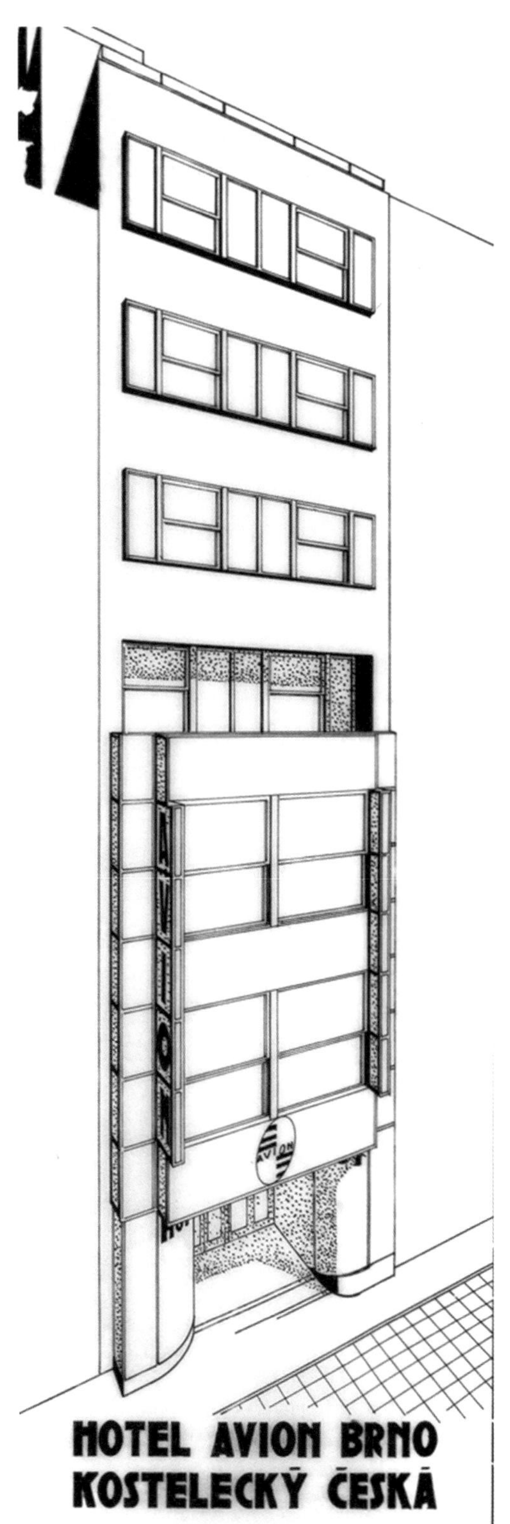

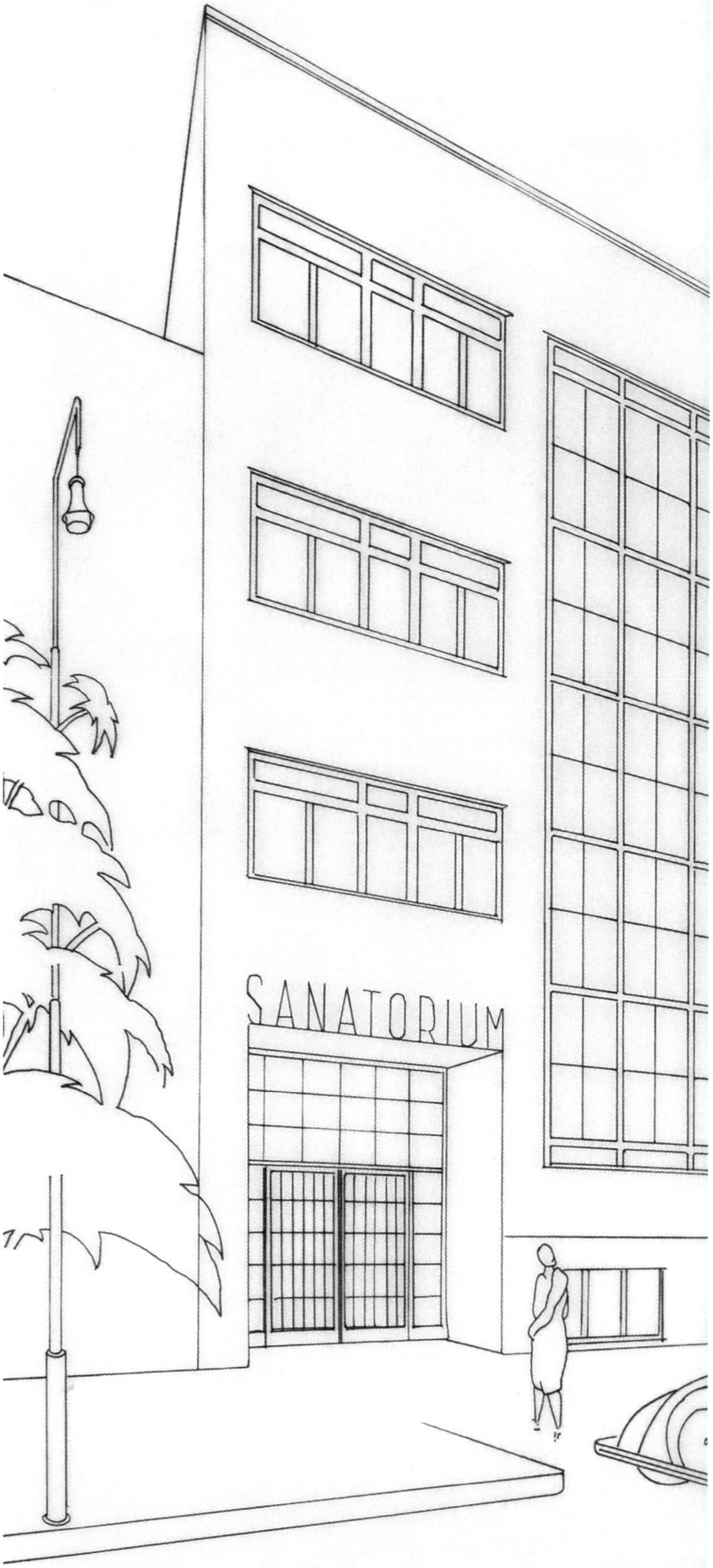

22–23

Jaromír Krejcar,
model, view of terrace
colonnade and south
balconies, Sanatorium
Machnáč, 1930–32

24–25

Bohuslav Fuchs,
alternative project for
Hotel Avion of Miroslav
Kostelecky, 1926–27

Jan Víšek, project for
Silhan Sanatorium,
perspective view,
Brno-Veveri, 1929–35

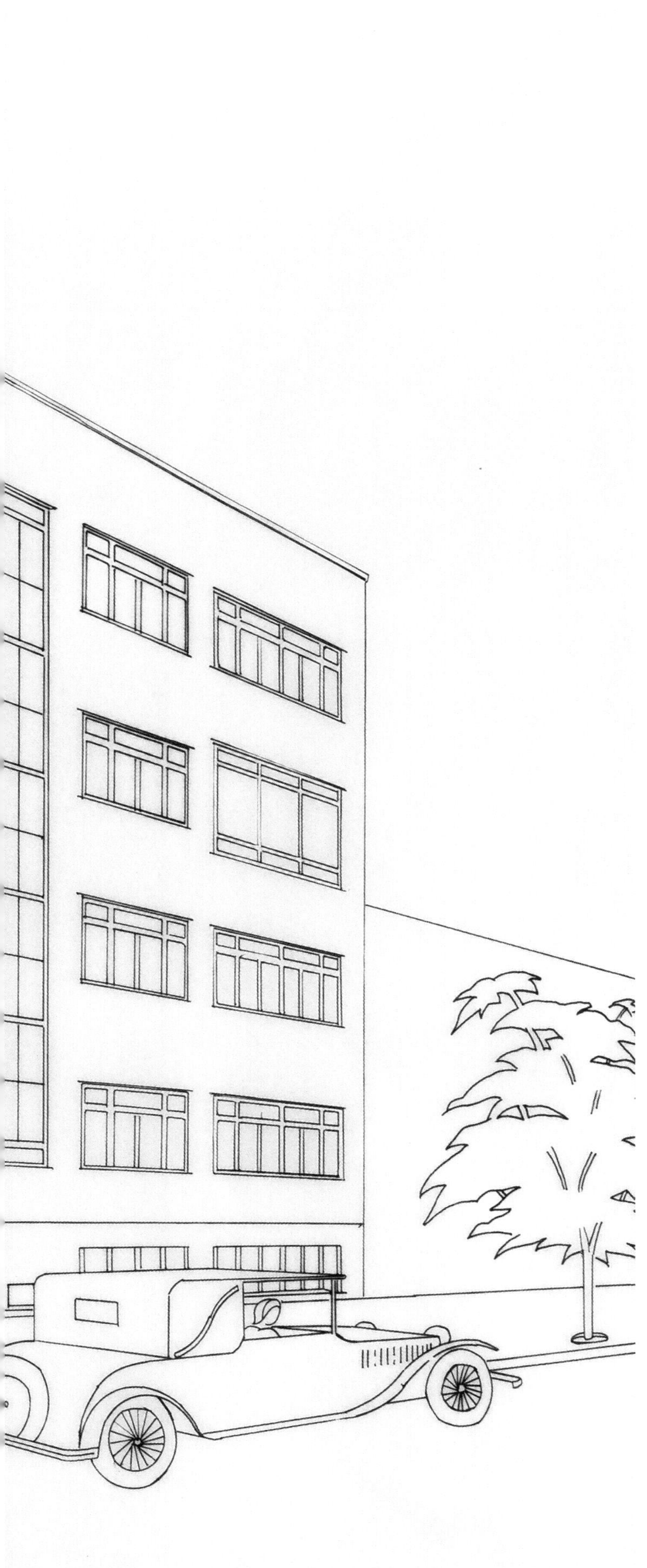

guests would have unobstructed views of the surrounding land and seascape.

Almost immediately upon the completion of the hotel P.A. was asked by Jaromír Krejcar to work on his 1932 *Machnáč Sanatorium* in Trenčianske Teplice (Slovakia). In contrast to the narrow *Hotel Avion* (which had replaced a one-story guest house) and the intimate design of the *Nord-Sud*, the sanatorium was an expansive structure, the largest building in the Slovak health system at the time. Built of reinforced concrete, the *Machnáč* consisted of two attached wings: a five-story residential block containing bedrooms and a two-story social wing with a foyer, a restaurant, and a lounge. Similar to both the *Hotel Avion* and the *Hotel Nord-Sud*, the Machnáč's common areas were efficiently designed to produce open, fluid spaces. The residential wing likely owes its careful arrangement of cabin-like rooms and corridors to P.A.'s experience with the *Nord-Sud* and her hand can perhaps also be seen in its open-air roof terrace and in the design of simple brass wall sconces similar to those she had produced for the *Nord-Sud*.

The hotels and sanatoria with which P.A. was involved in the late 1920s allowed her to put into practice ideas about spatial organization and efficient housing. As she observed in 1950, "Hotels became test cases for the design of practical, modular residential space combined with open public areas."[3] The enthusiasm for new building technologies and open public spaces of such projects echoed Karel Teige's assertion that, "Factories, train stations, viaducts—not palaces, castles, and temples—are the forms and building tasks of the new era. What matters in this new era is to build simply and economically; to reject everything illogical, uncomfortable, and superfluous; to master light, air, and spatial freedom."[4]

ENDNOTES

1. See Karel Teige, *The Minimum Dwelling* (Cambridge Mass.: MIT Press, 2002): pp. 103-104.

2. See E.R. Alden, "Idealism and Interwar Internationalism between Brno and Budapest: P.A. and her Contemporaries." *Between Brno and Budapest: the Work of Petra Andrejova-Molnár and her Contemporaries,* Exhibition Catalogue. (The Architectural Association: London, UK, 1976).

3. Petra Andrejova-Molnár interviewed by Anna Novak, *The Architectural Review*, April 1951.

4. Karel Teige, *Modern Architecture in Czechoslovakia and Other Writings*, trans. Irena Murray and David Britt. (The Getty Research Institute: Los Angeles, CA, 2000): p. 92.

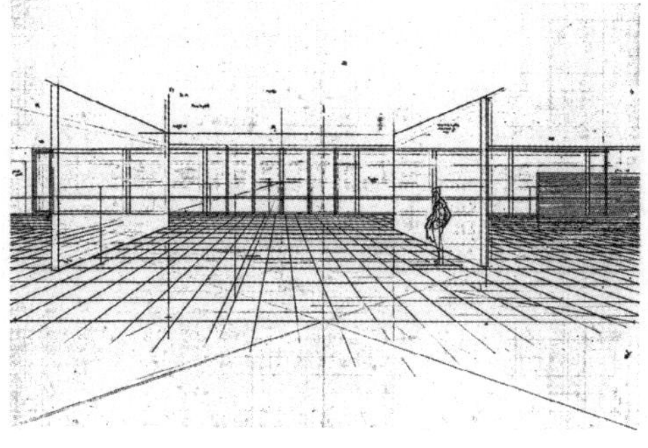

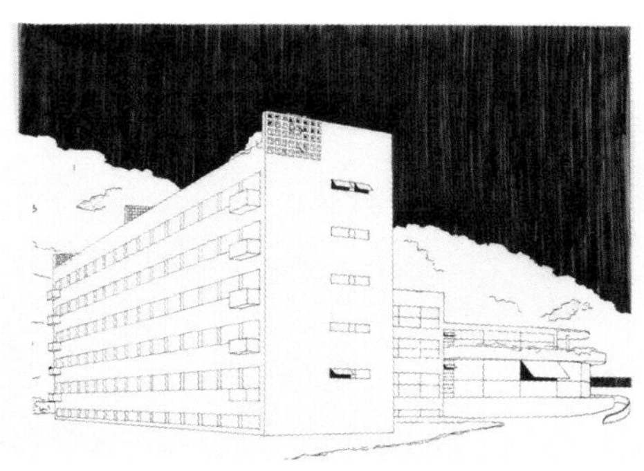

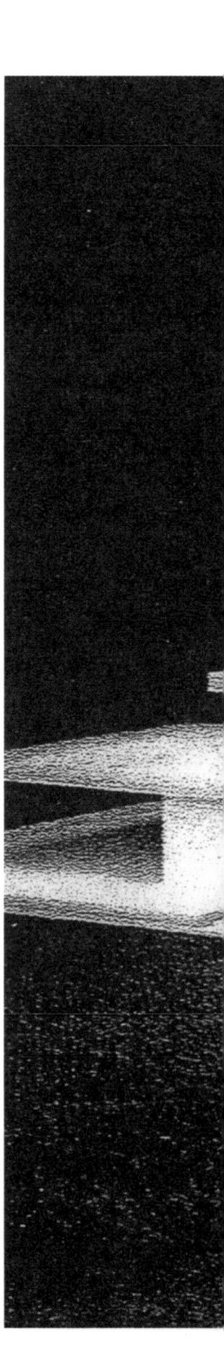

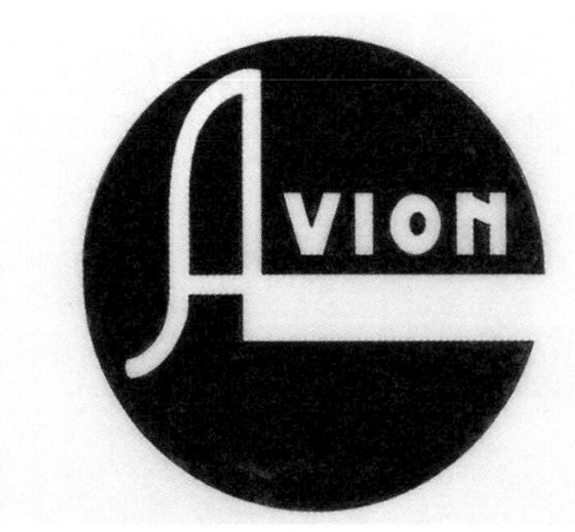

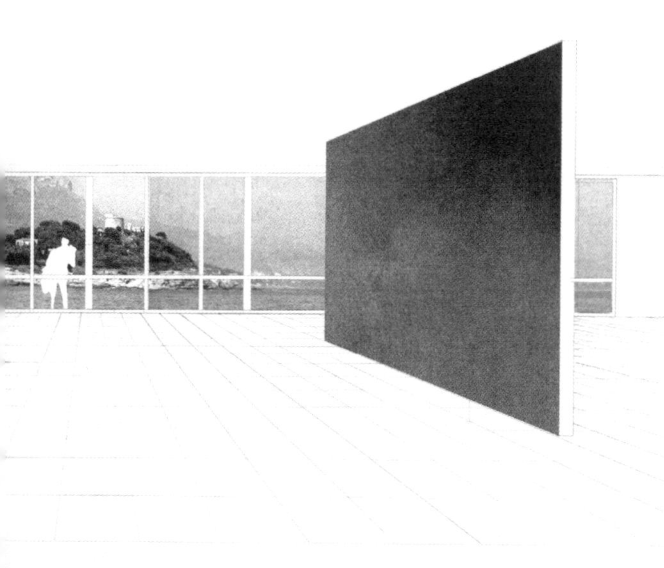

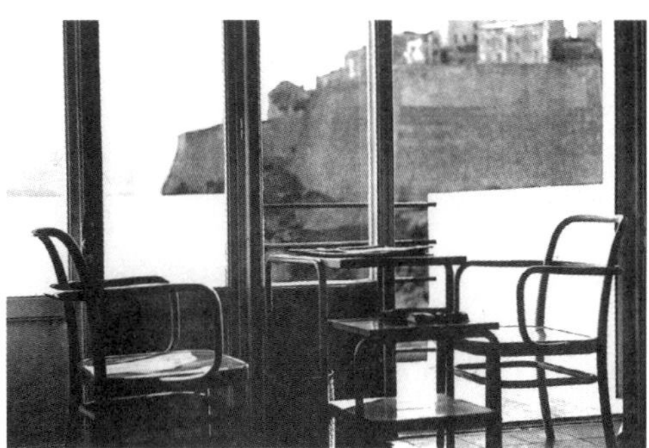

Petra Andrejova-Molnár, view from interior; perspective drawing of lobby; view of lobby, *Hotel Nord-Sud*, 1932–34

Jaromír Krejcar, alternative competition entry for a sanatorium, Trenčianské Teplice, 1930

Emanuel Hrbek, logo design, for the *Hotel Avion*, 1926–27

Petra Andrejova-Molnár, model, north view, *Hotel Nord-Sud*, 1932–34

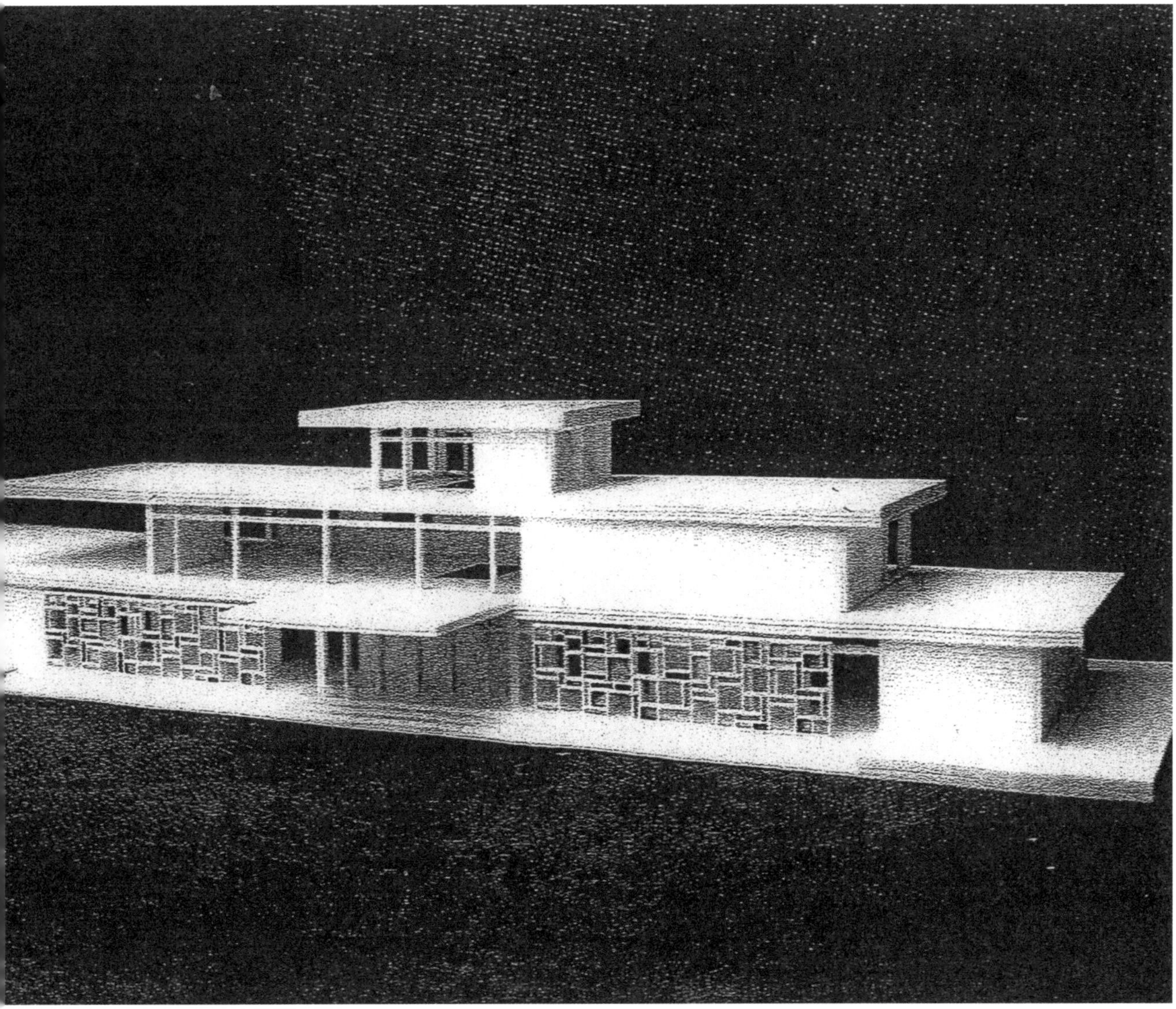

Housing shortage was a major problem in the years after the First World War and, by the mid-1920s, had become an urgent question for modern architects. Brno saw a number of experimental designs for efficient housing: in 1928 the *Nový Dům* (New House) colony, built under the aegis of the Czechoslovak Werkbund, showcased designs by nine architects in a suburban setting. The Werkbund was also responsible for the *Baba Housing Estate* in Prague of 1932-1936. Both projects involved many of P.A.'s colleagues and she would have been intimately familiar with the designs and construction. She also would have been aware of the second annual conference of CIAM held in Frankfurt-Am-Main in 1929 which was focused on the theme of "the minimal dwelling." While apartments, hotels, and sanatoria addressed the question of larger communities, architects were also interested in the design of efficient single residences. With CIAM's call for "minimal dwellings" foremost in her mind, P.A. embarked on her *Studio Efficiency*. She initially began the project in 1938, sketching several variations of the studio, each tailored to an individual client. P.A.'s prototypes all included workspaces and were conceived as country rather than urban houses. Although she finalized her design in 1938, it was not built until P.A. had moved to the United States where, in the early 1950s she redesigned and supervised the Studio's construction for an American client.

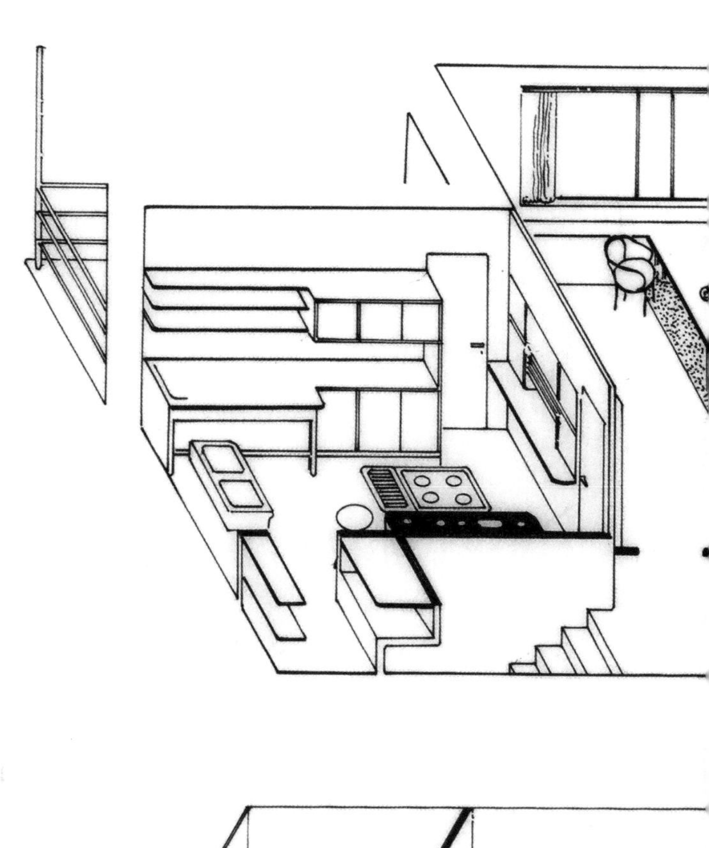

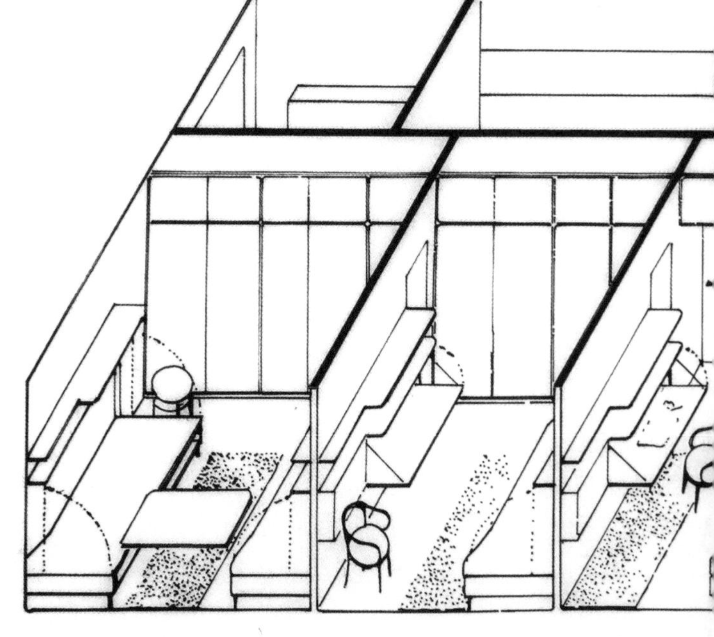

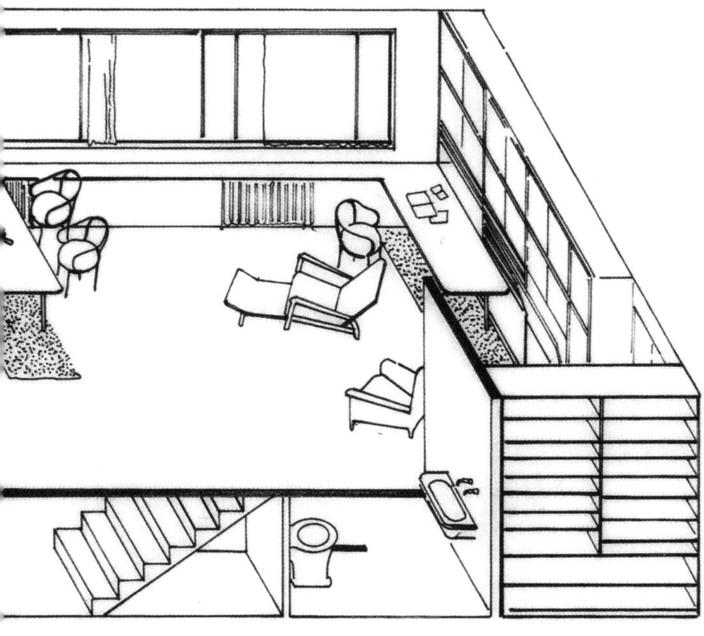

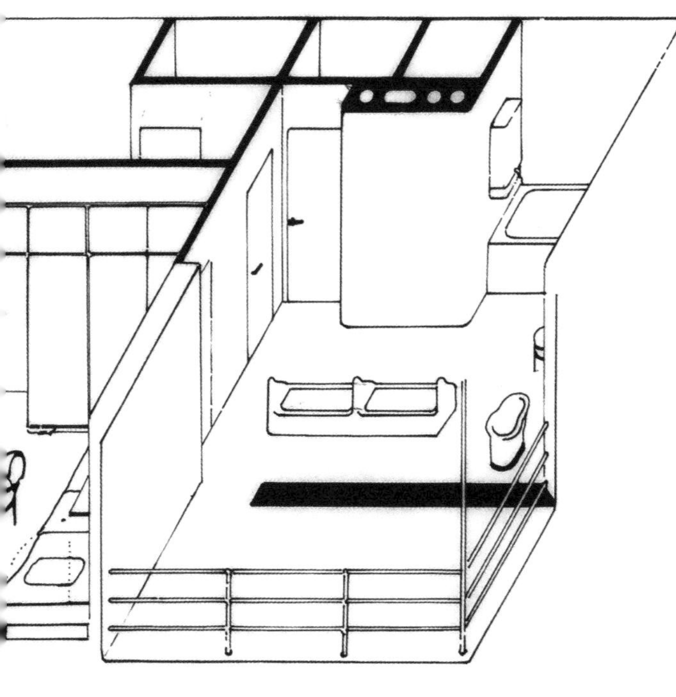

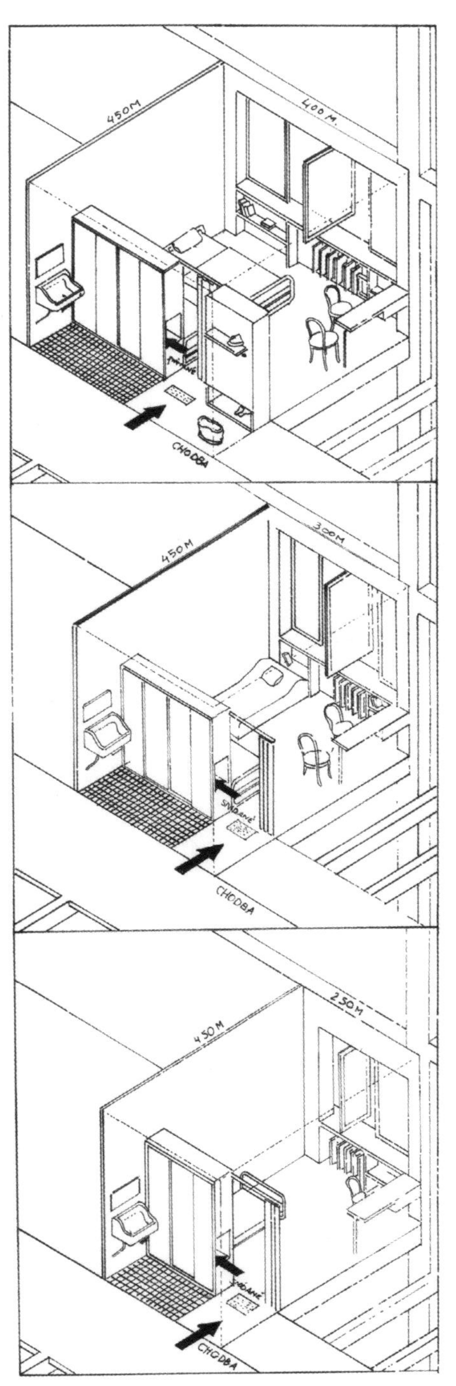

28–29
Ladislav Žák, design
for minimum dwelling,
a. kitchen, living room
and toilet b. sleeping
cabins and bathrooms,
Brno, 1920

Jaromír Krejcar,
alternative competition
entry for a sanatorium,
Trenčianské Teplice,
1930

30–31
Petra Andrejova-
Molnár, façade
drawing and floor-plan,
studio efficiency
for the countryside,
1938–56

Planned for a wooded countryside location, the *Studio Efficiency's* design—like the *Hotel Nord-Sud*—pays great attention the surrounding landscape. The interior is a mere 70sq feet but, despite its small size, the high ceilings and P.A.'s characteristic interest in fluid crossovers between the interior and exterior spaces give the impression of a much larger building. Constructed of wood on a concrete base, *Studio Efficiency* comprises both living and working areas—partitioned by bookcases—that can be easily transformed for different purposes. P.A. remained preoccupied by the divisions between the house and its surroundings: a long built-in counter extends from the kitchen to the outdoors, physically and visually connecting the interior to the exterior space while serving the activity of outdoor dining on the terrace which wraps around the entire building.

The *Studio Efficiency* was the culmination of P.A.'s remarkable career in Europe. Between her participation in the Czechoslovak pavilion in 1925 and her departure from Vienna in 1938 she was at the center of Eastern Europe's dynamic architectural community. She took an active part in the dialogues and debates of her period surrounding communal housing and efficient dwellings. P.A. was enthusiastic about collective production and took many opportunities to work with her fellow designers, but she was also fiercely self-sufficient and determined to forge an architectural

career on her own terms. It is from this balance between collectivity and individuality that P.A.'s interwar work emerges.

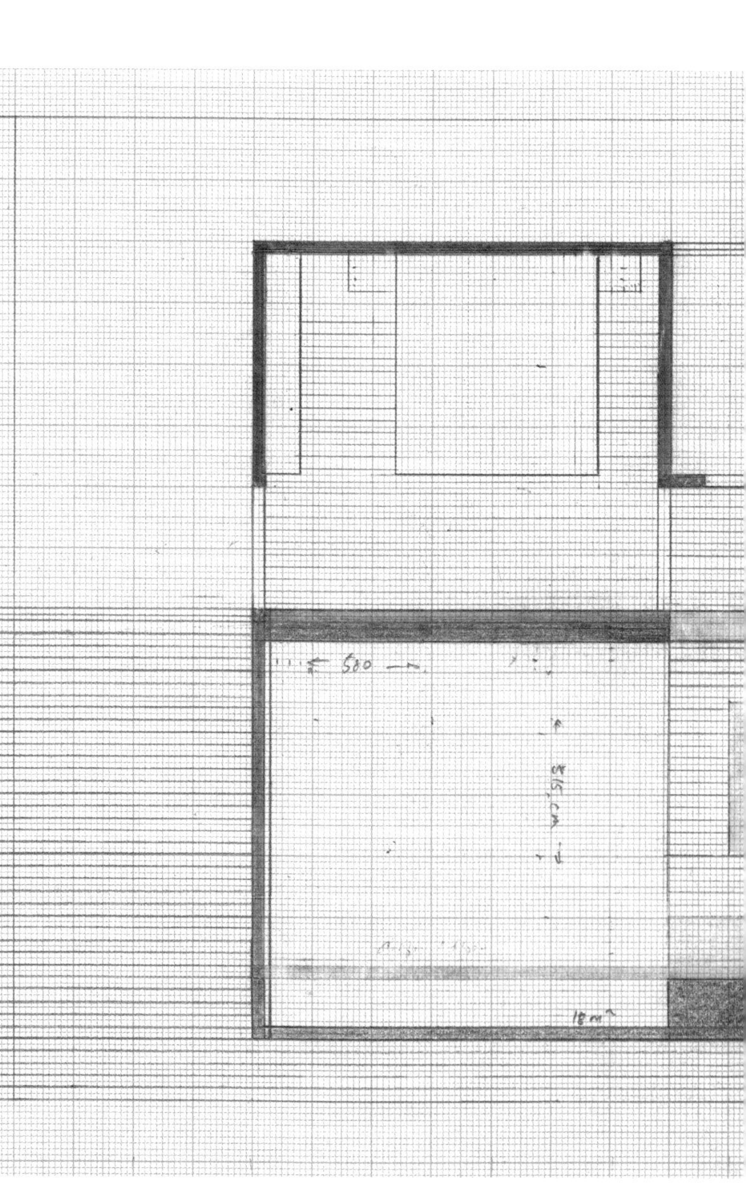

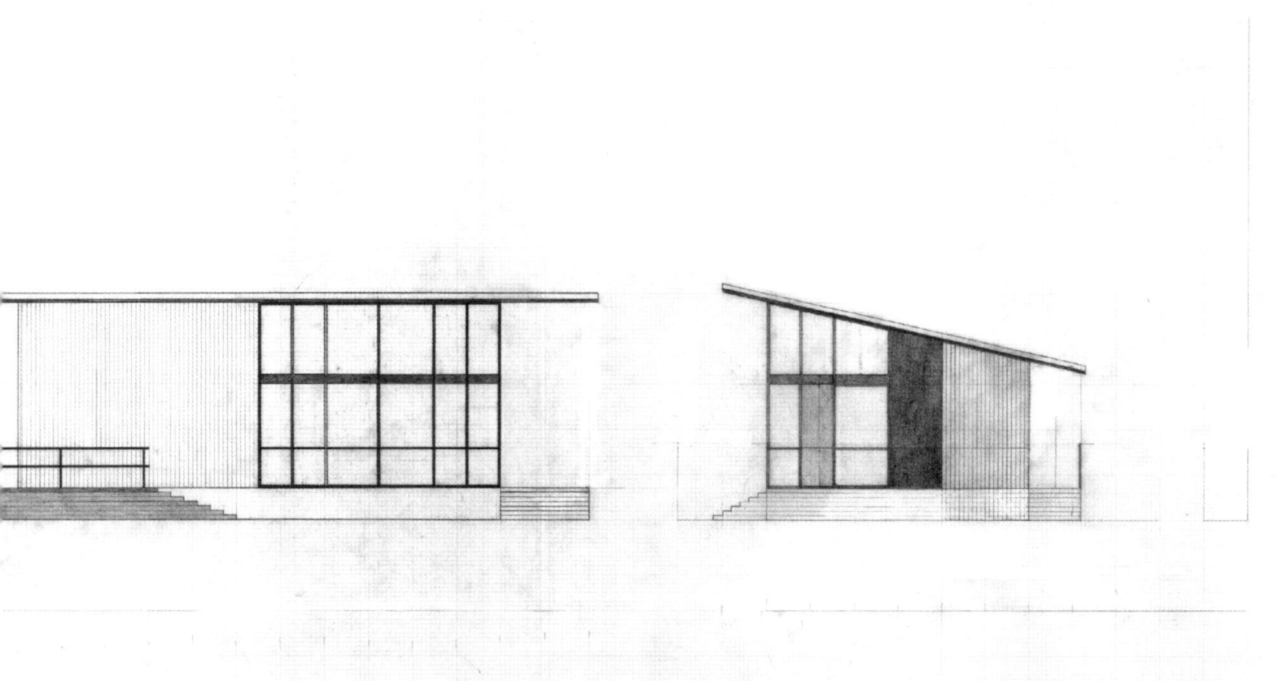

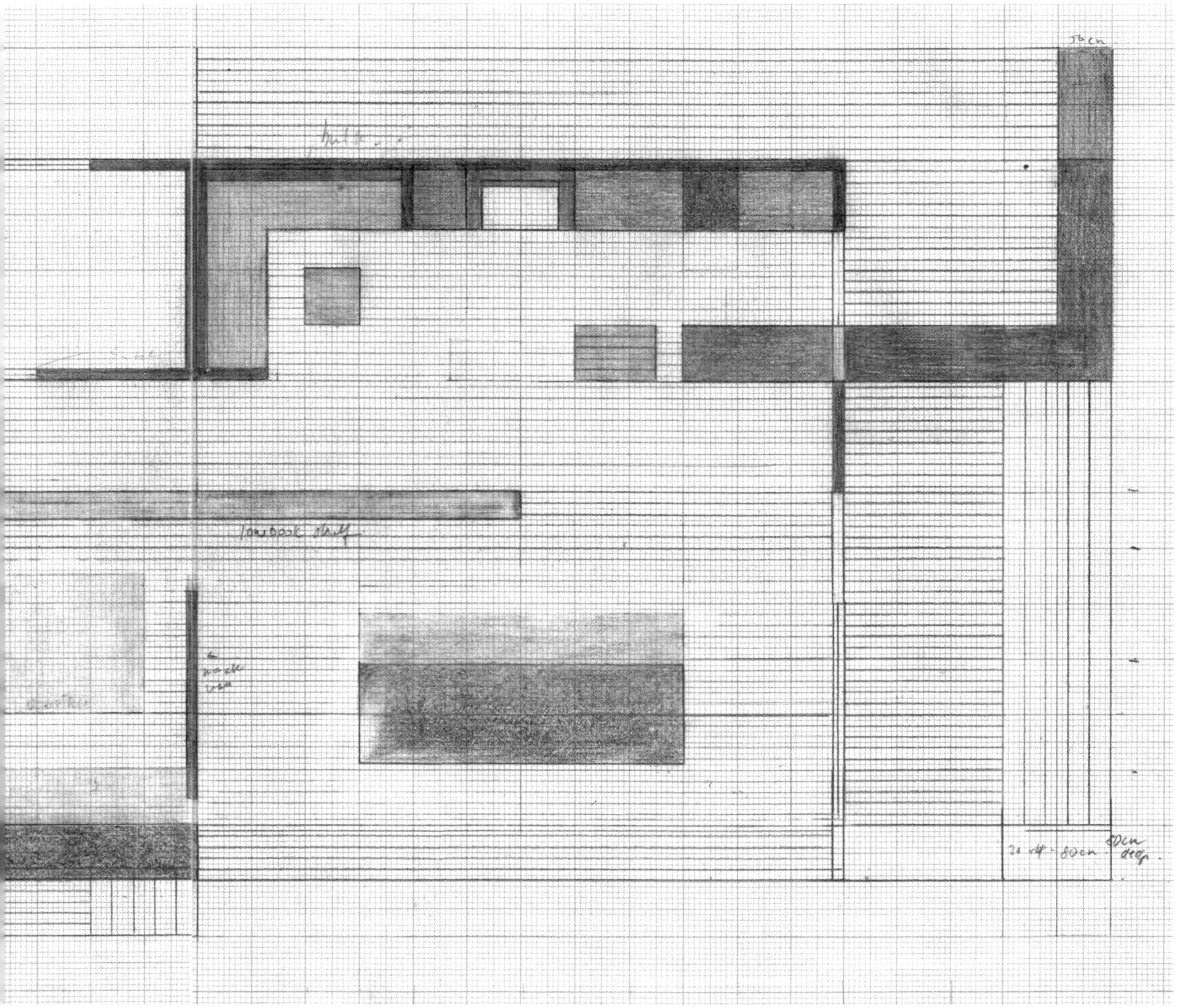

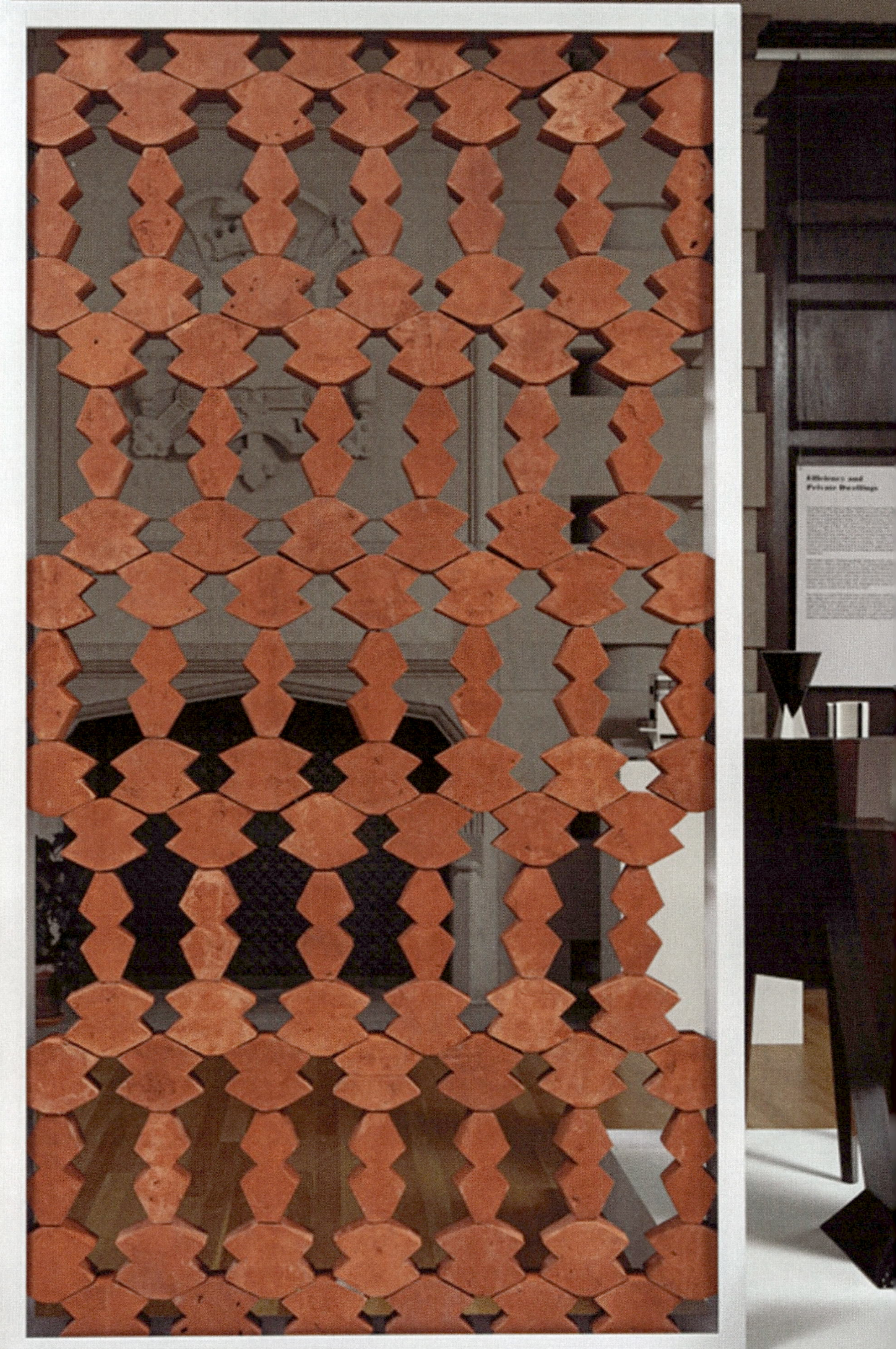

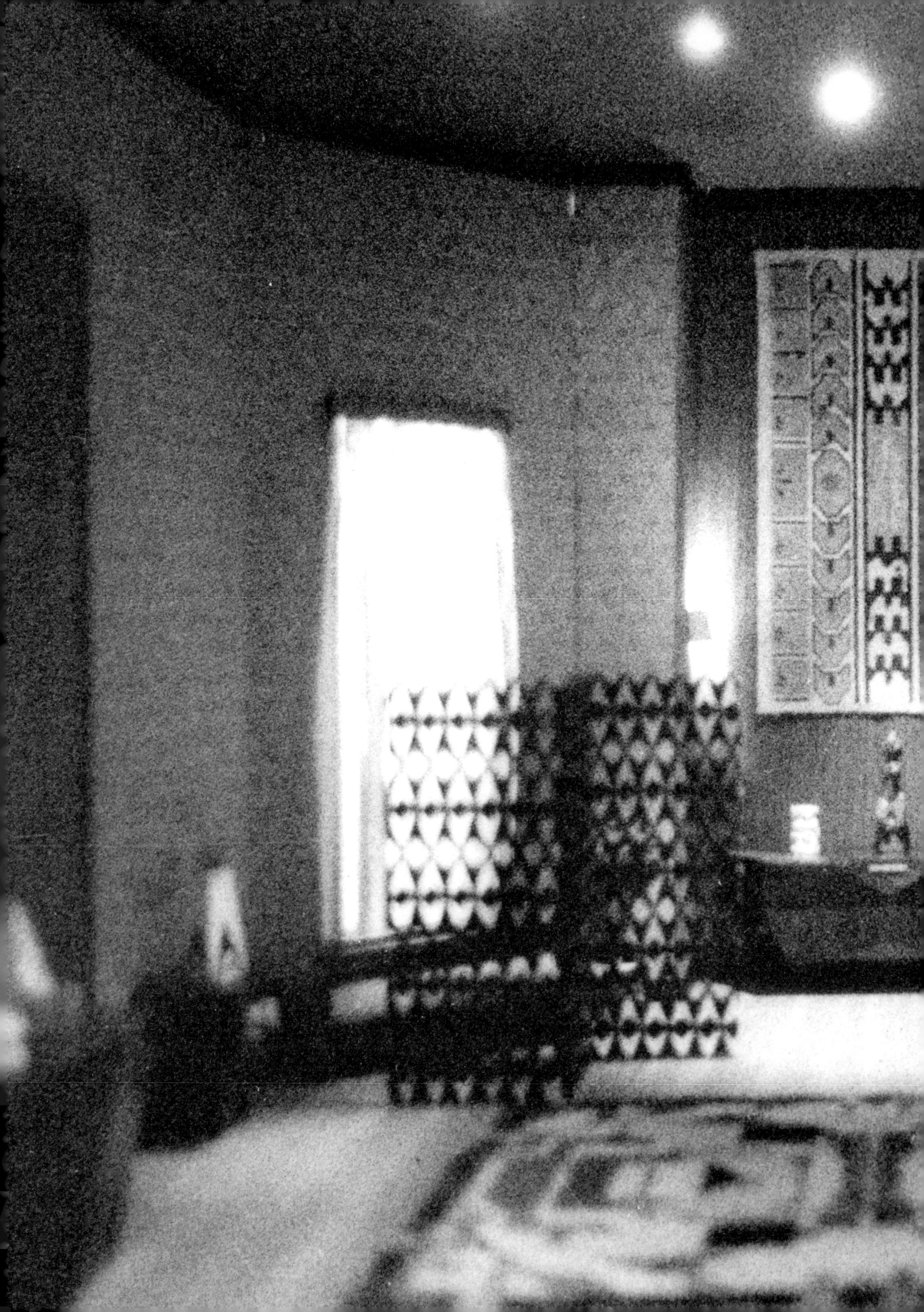

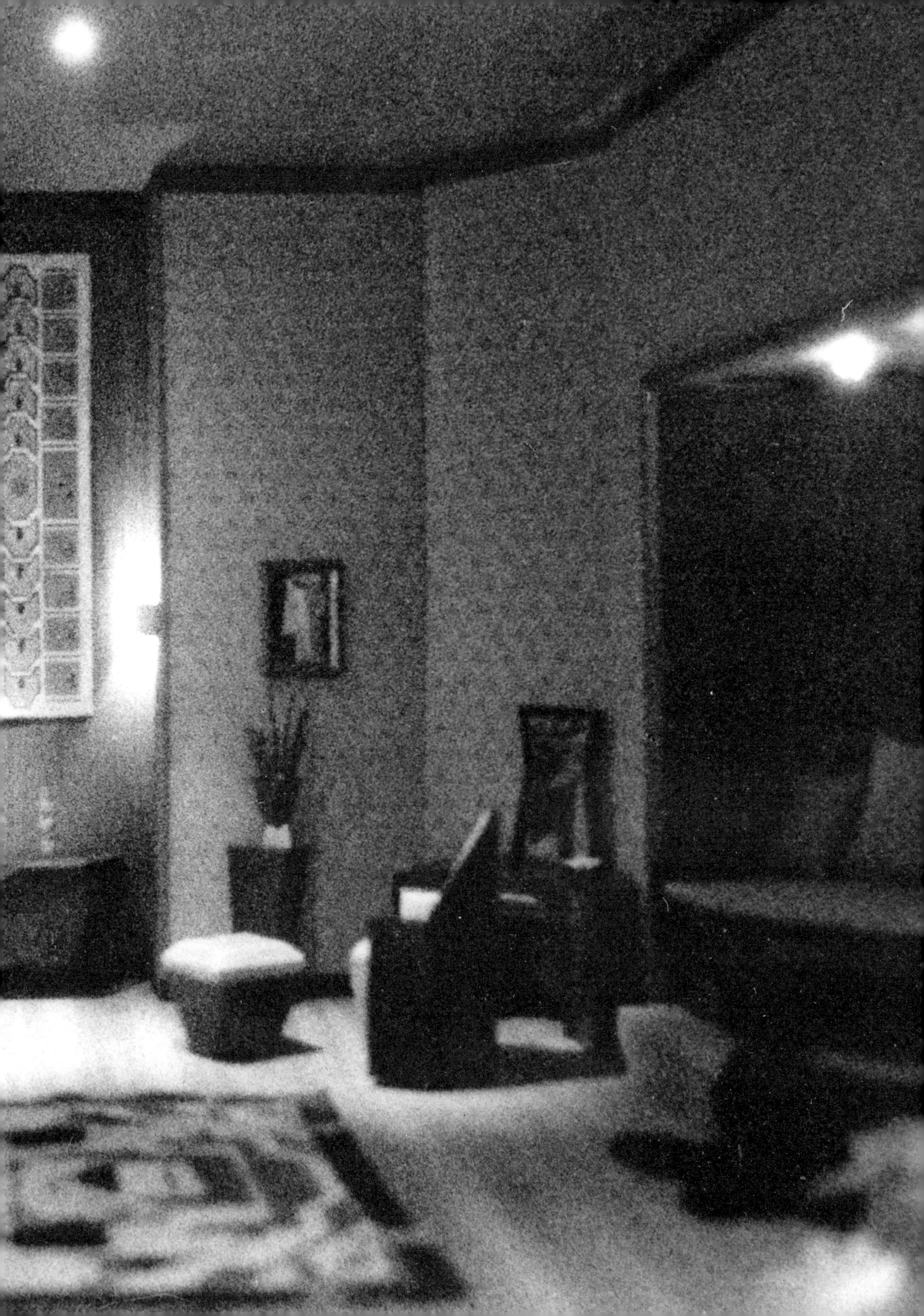

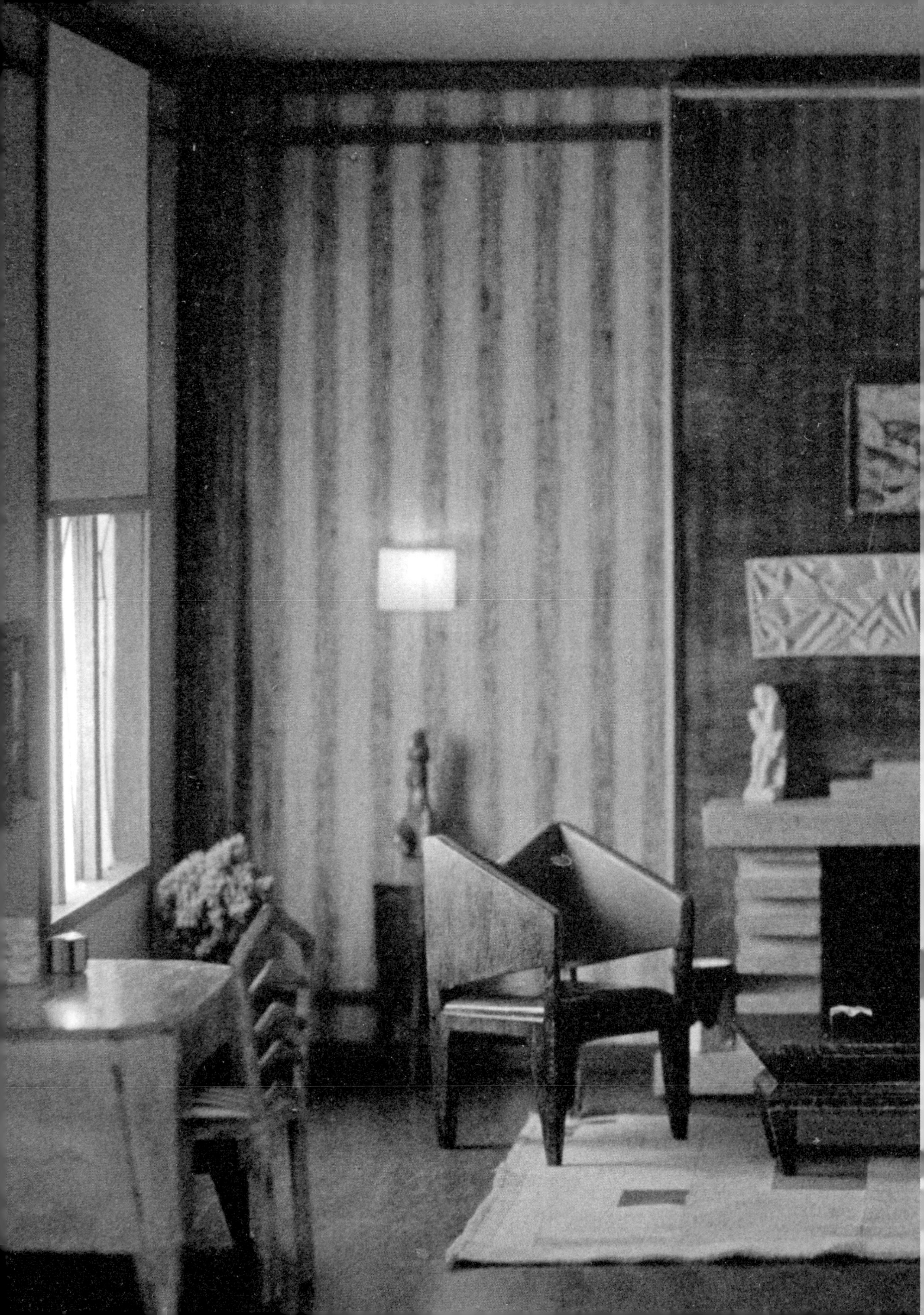

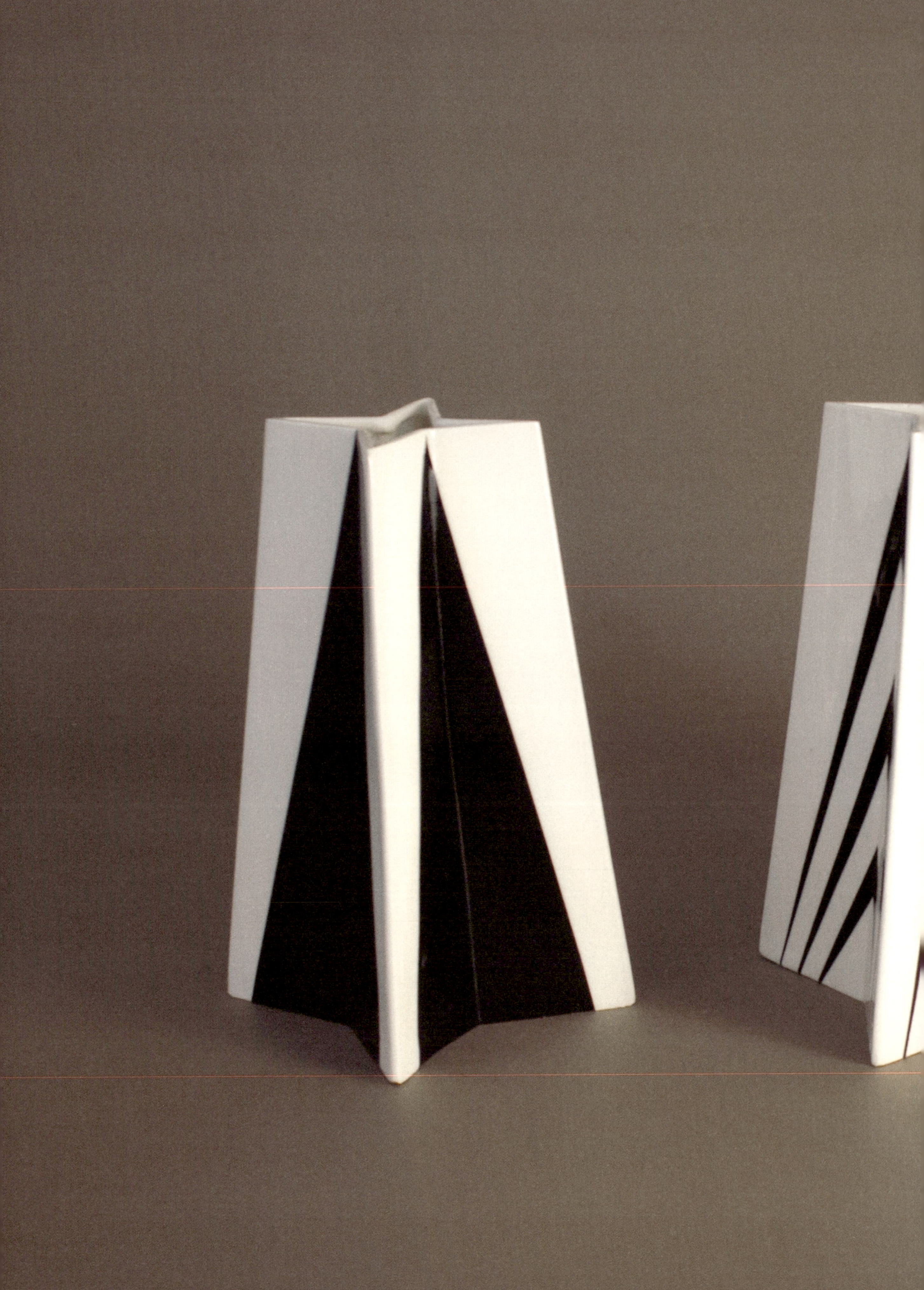

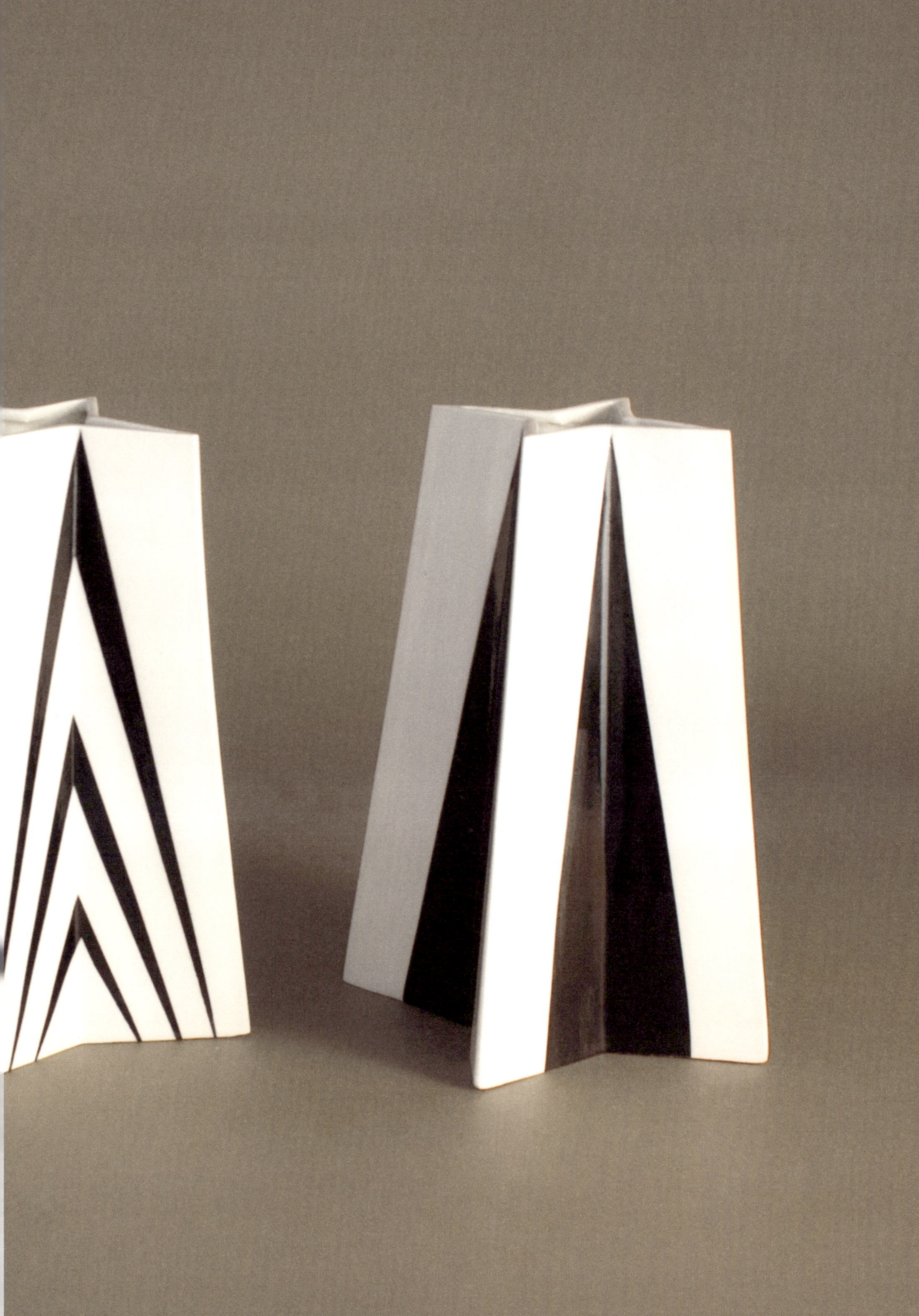

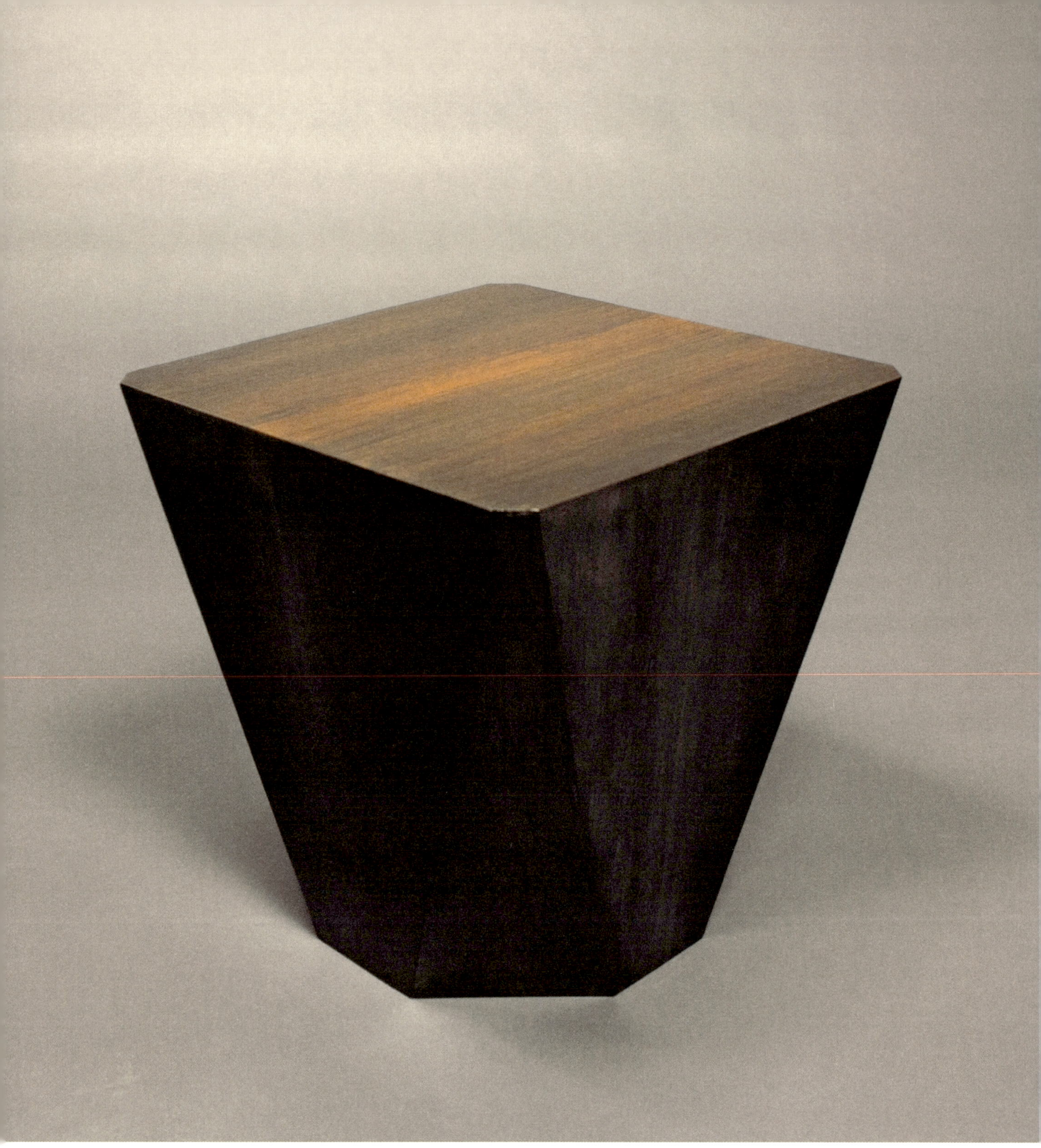

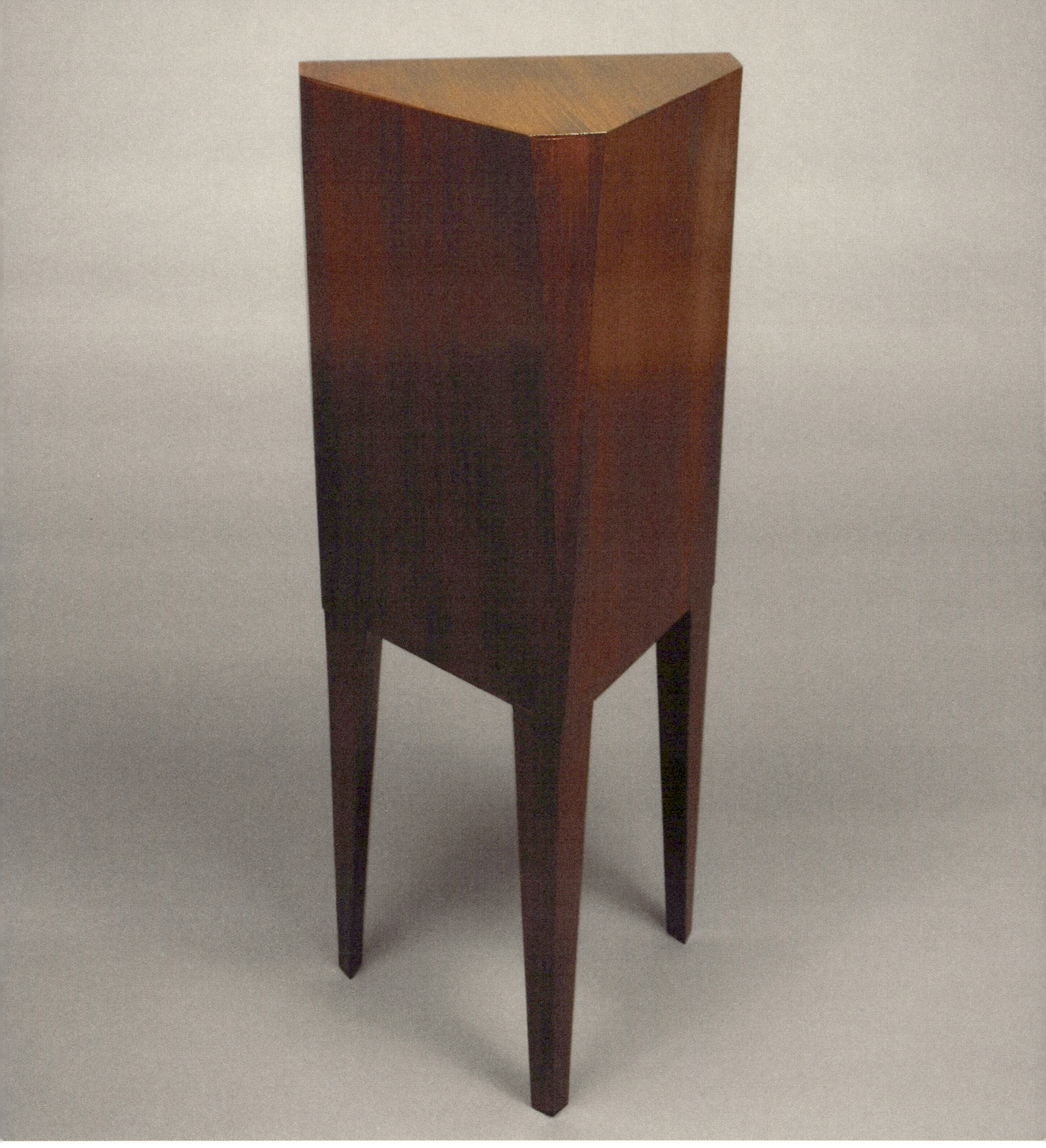

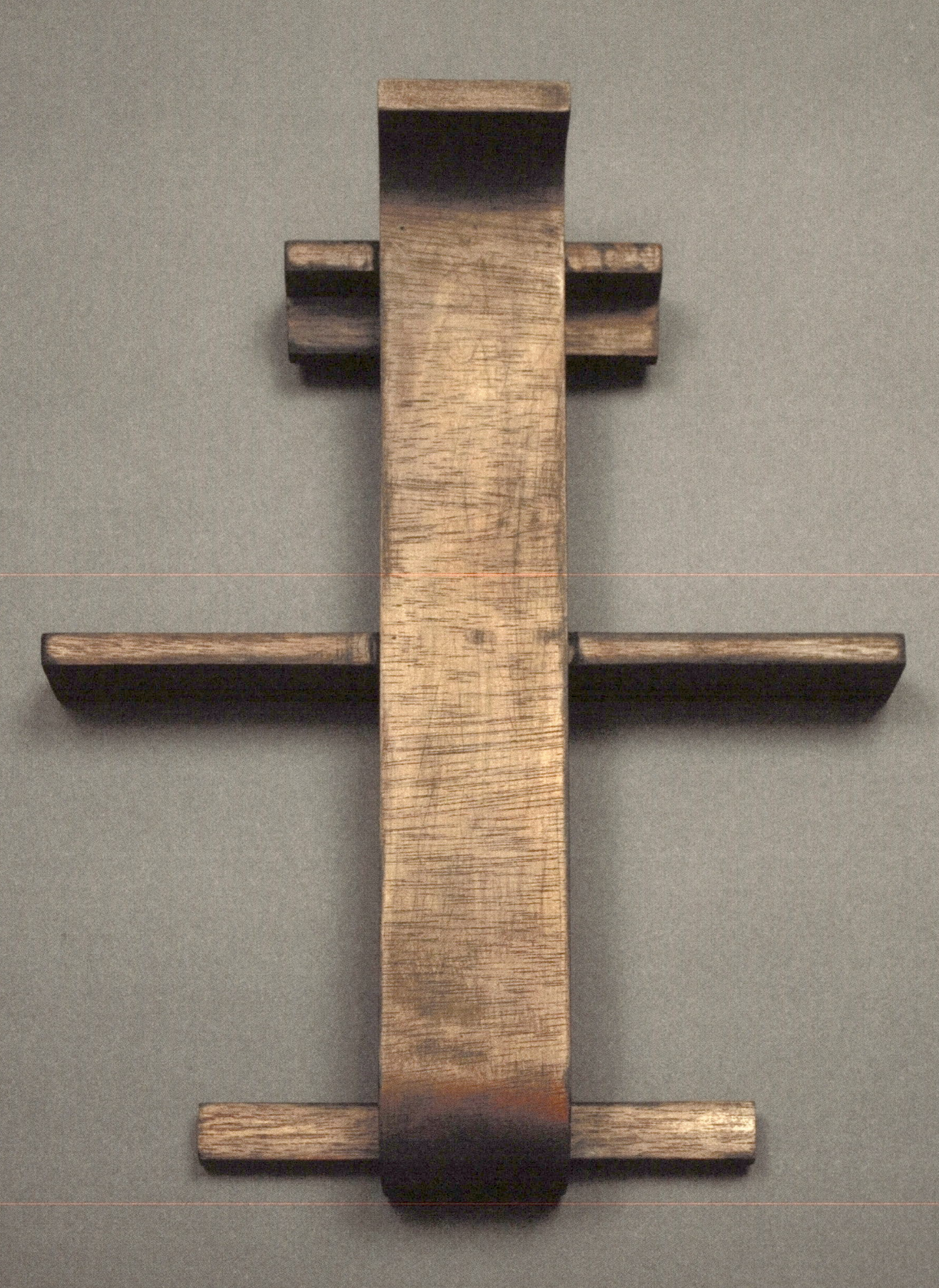

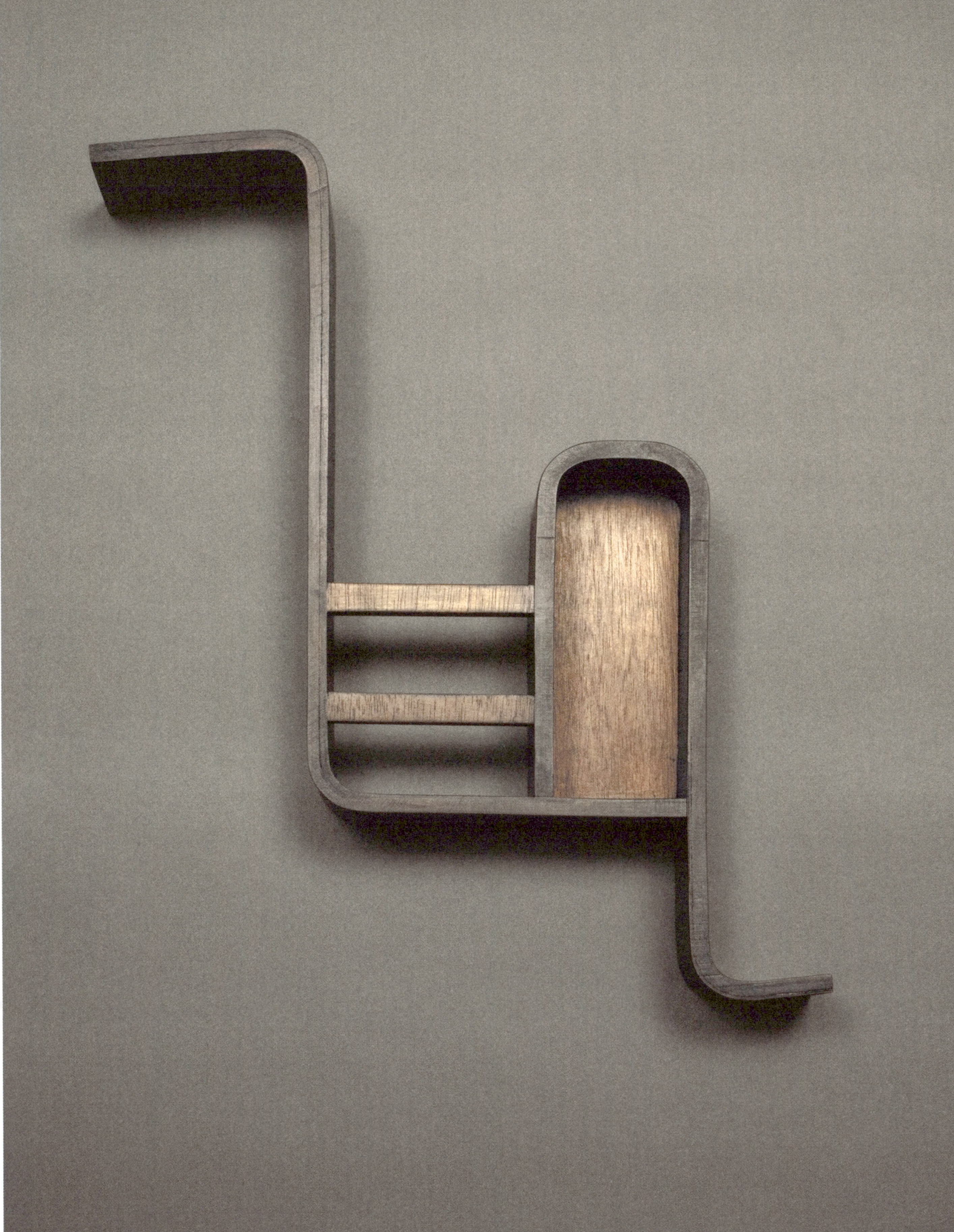

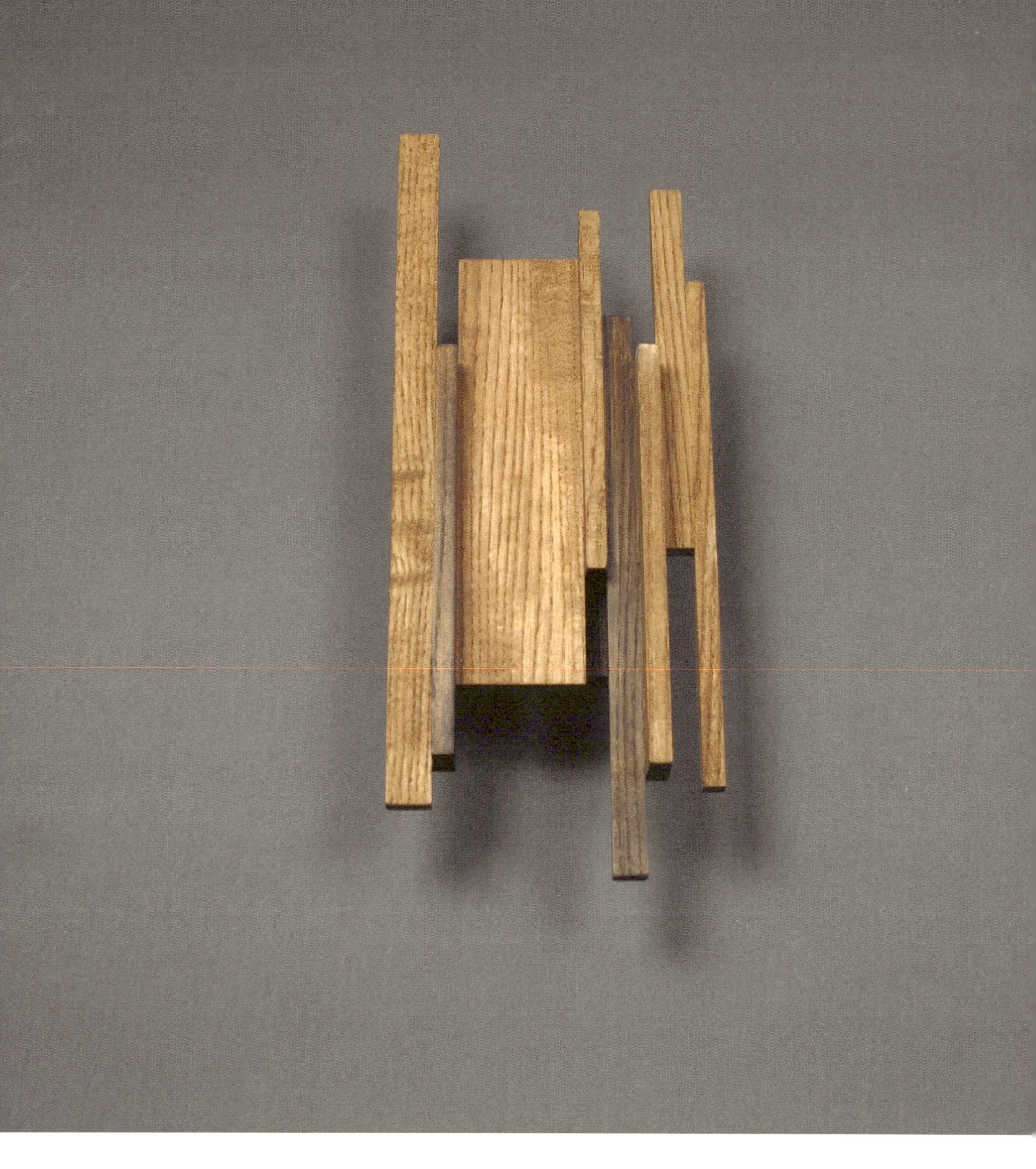

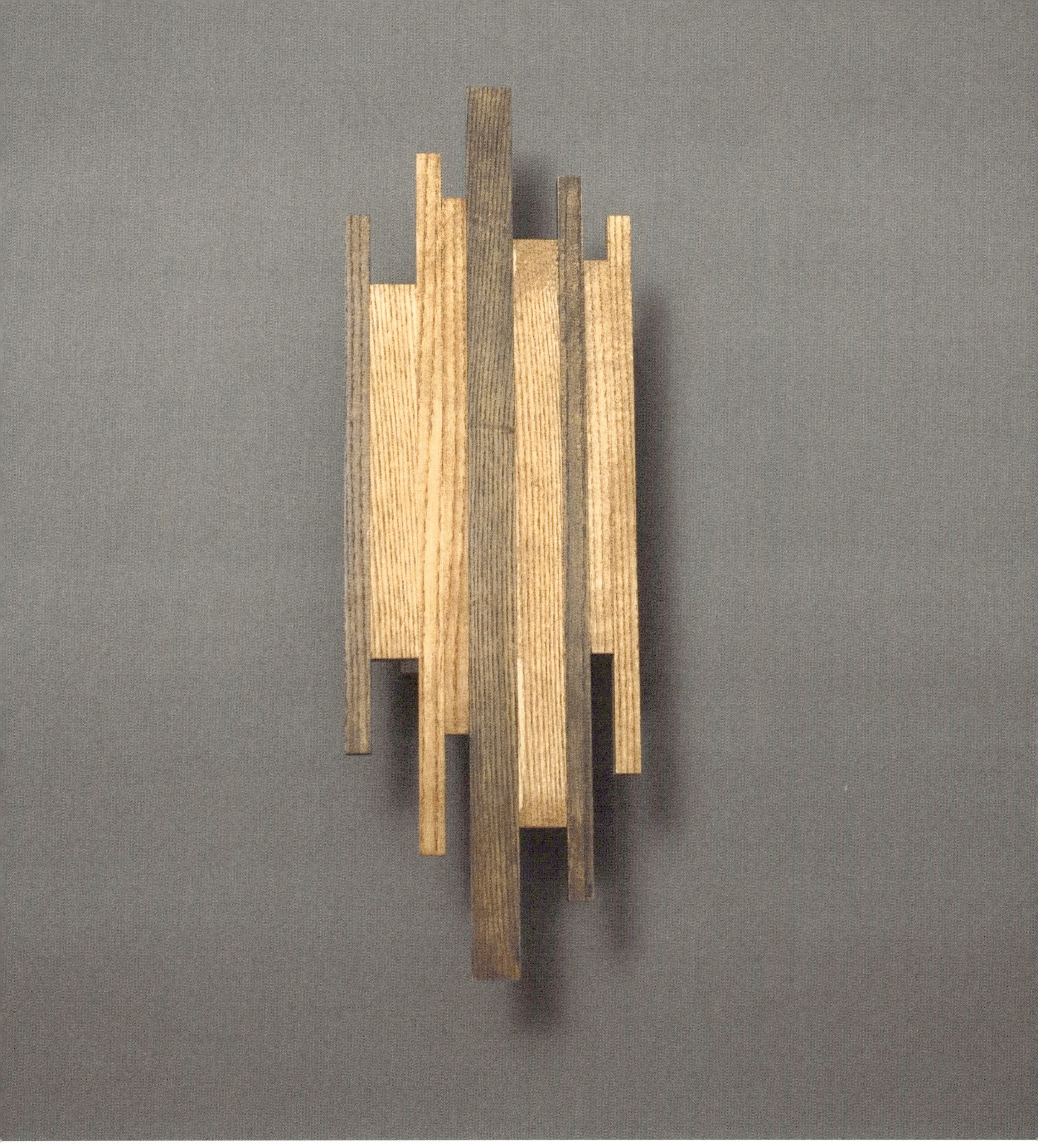

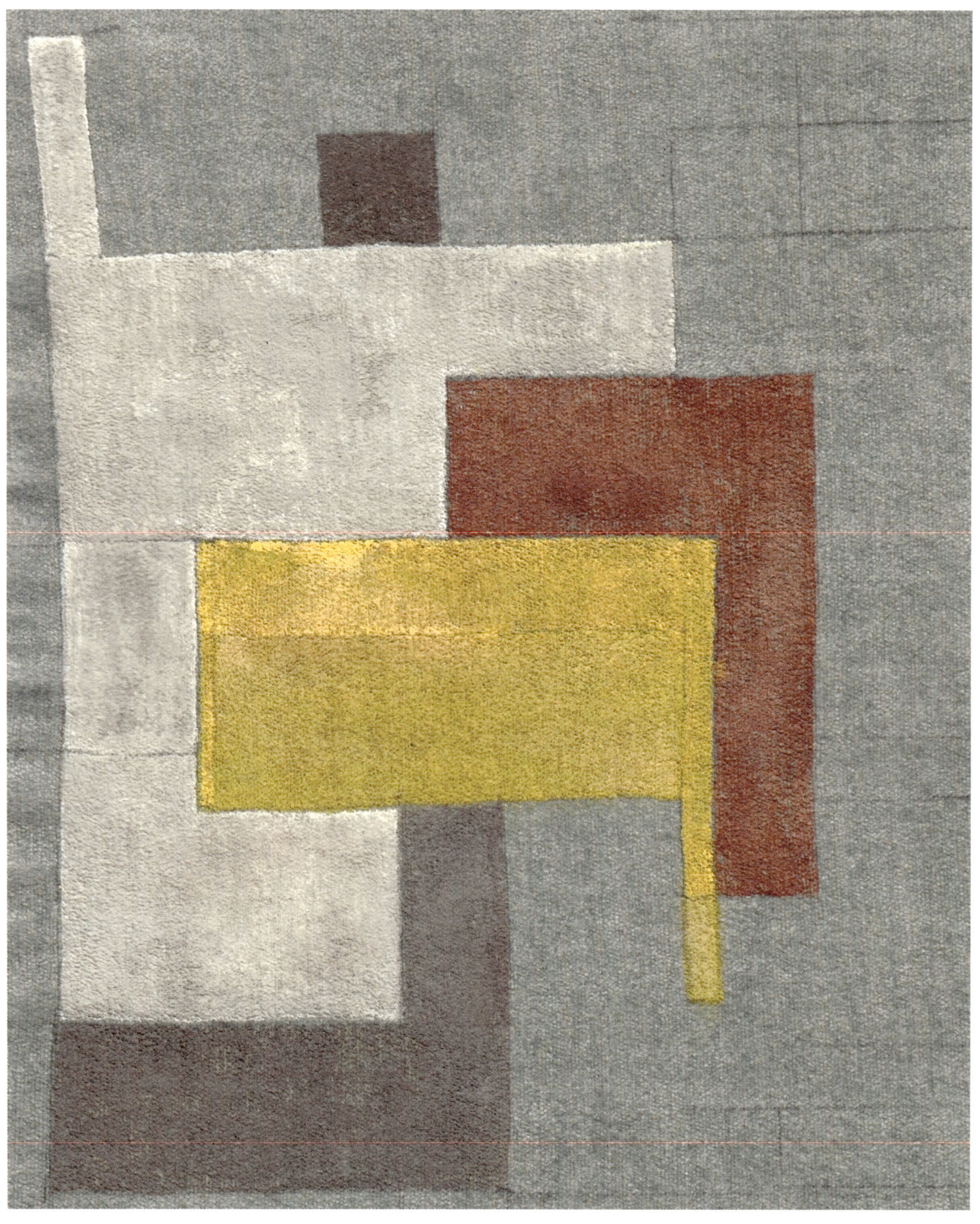

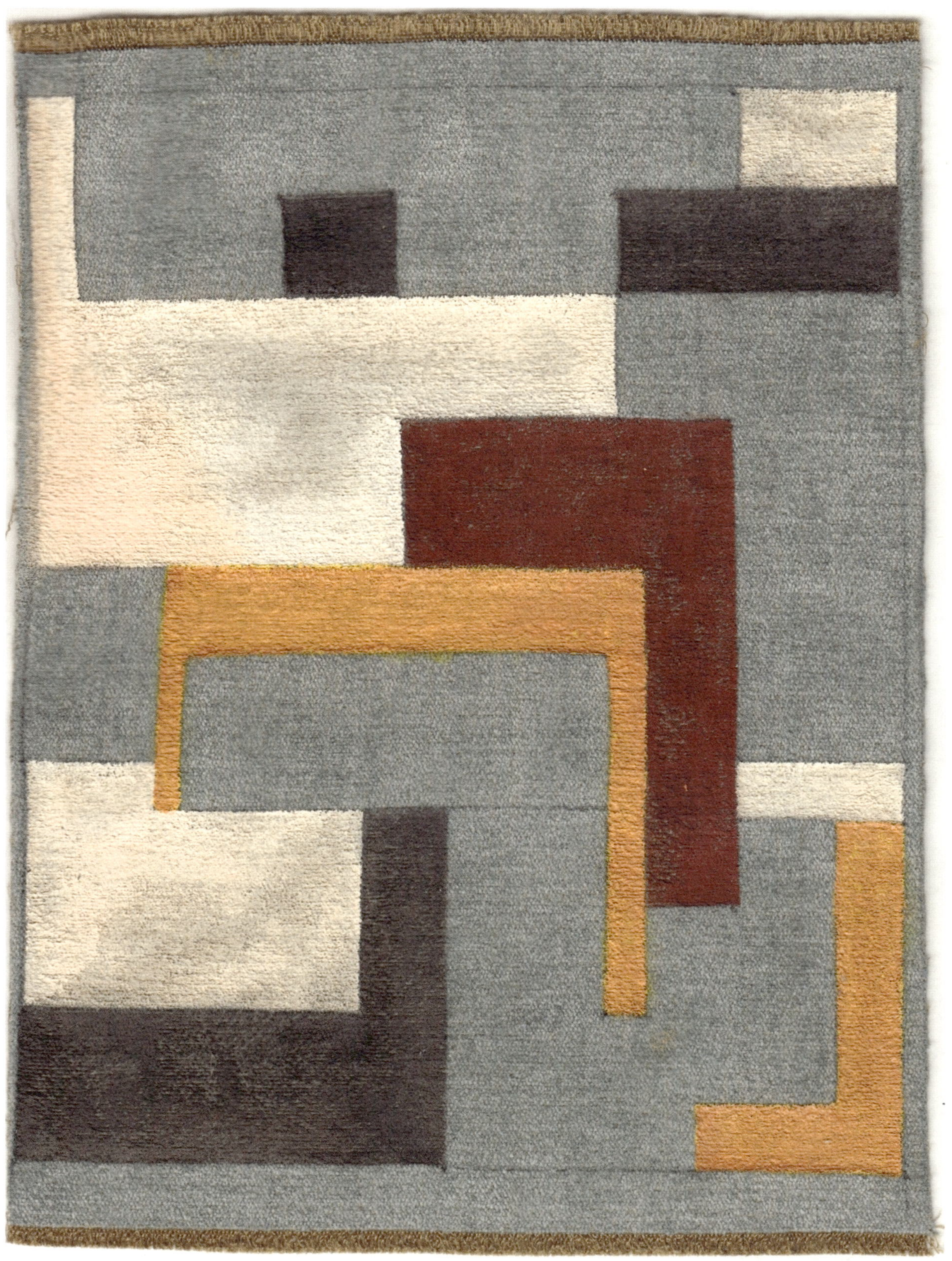

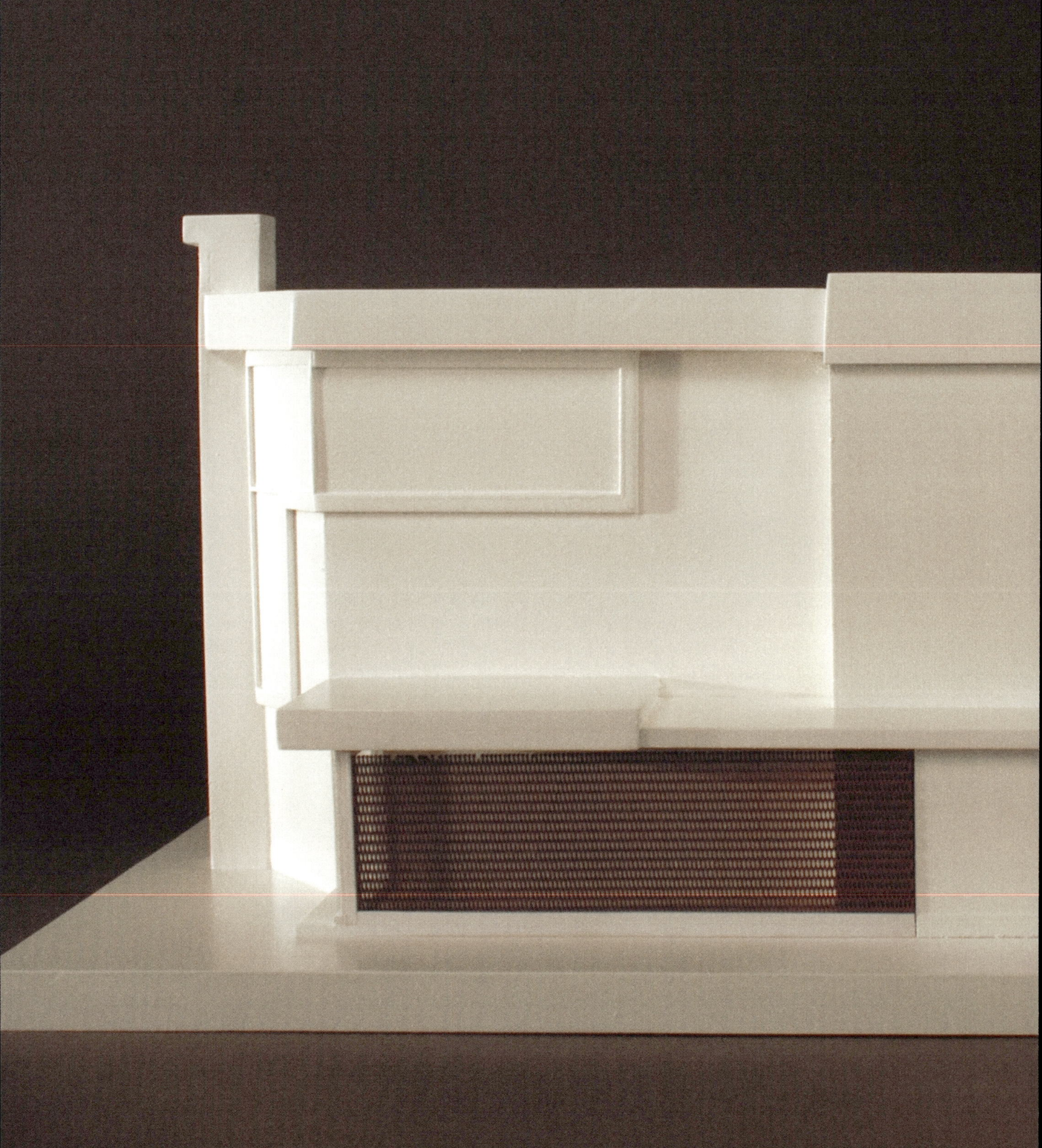

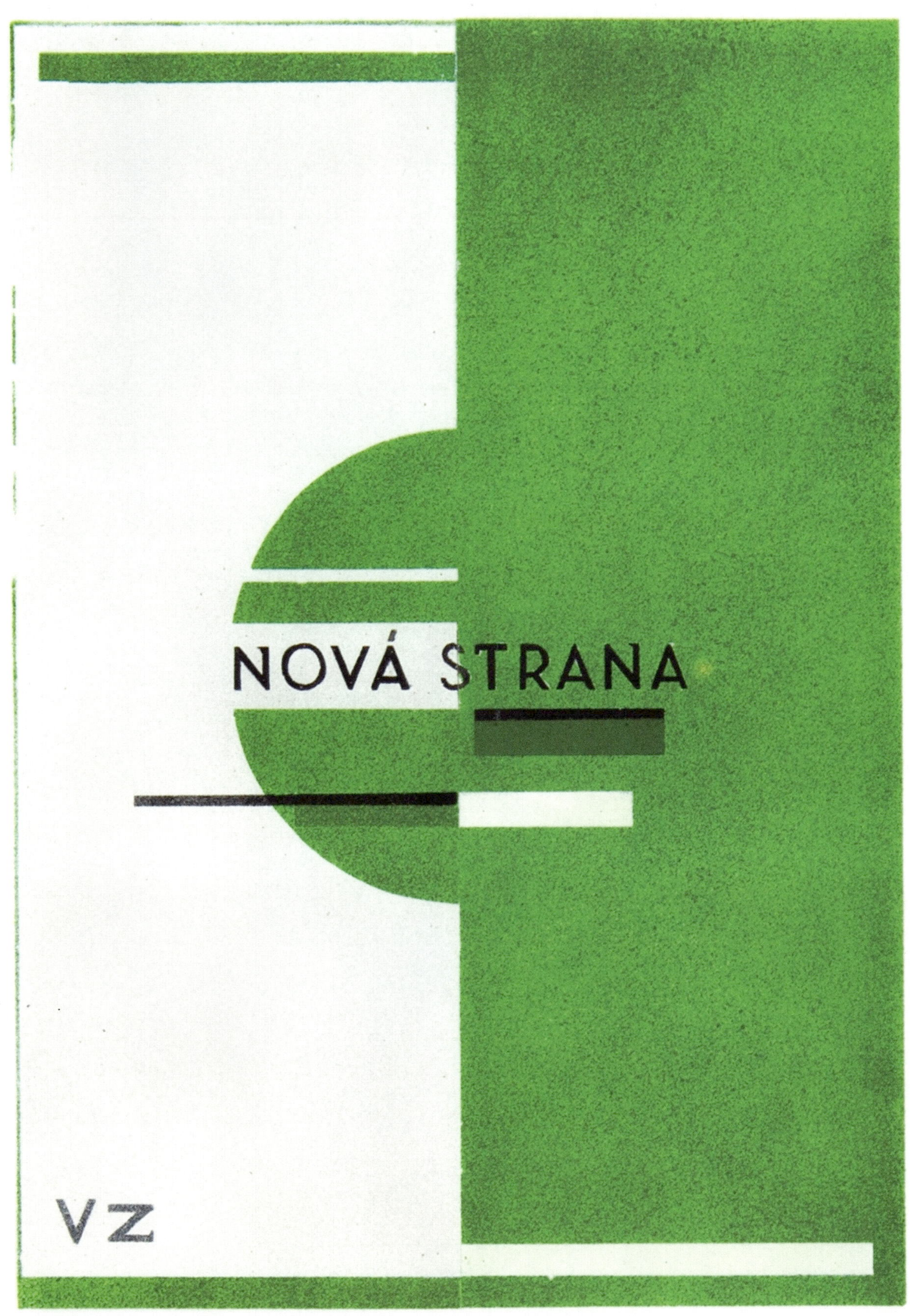
NOVÁ STRANA
VZ

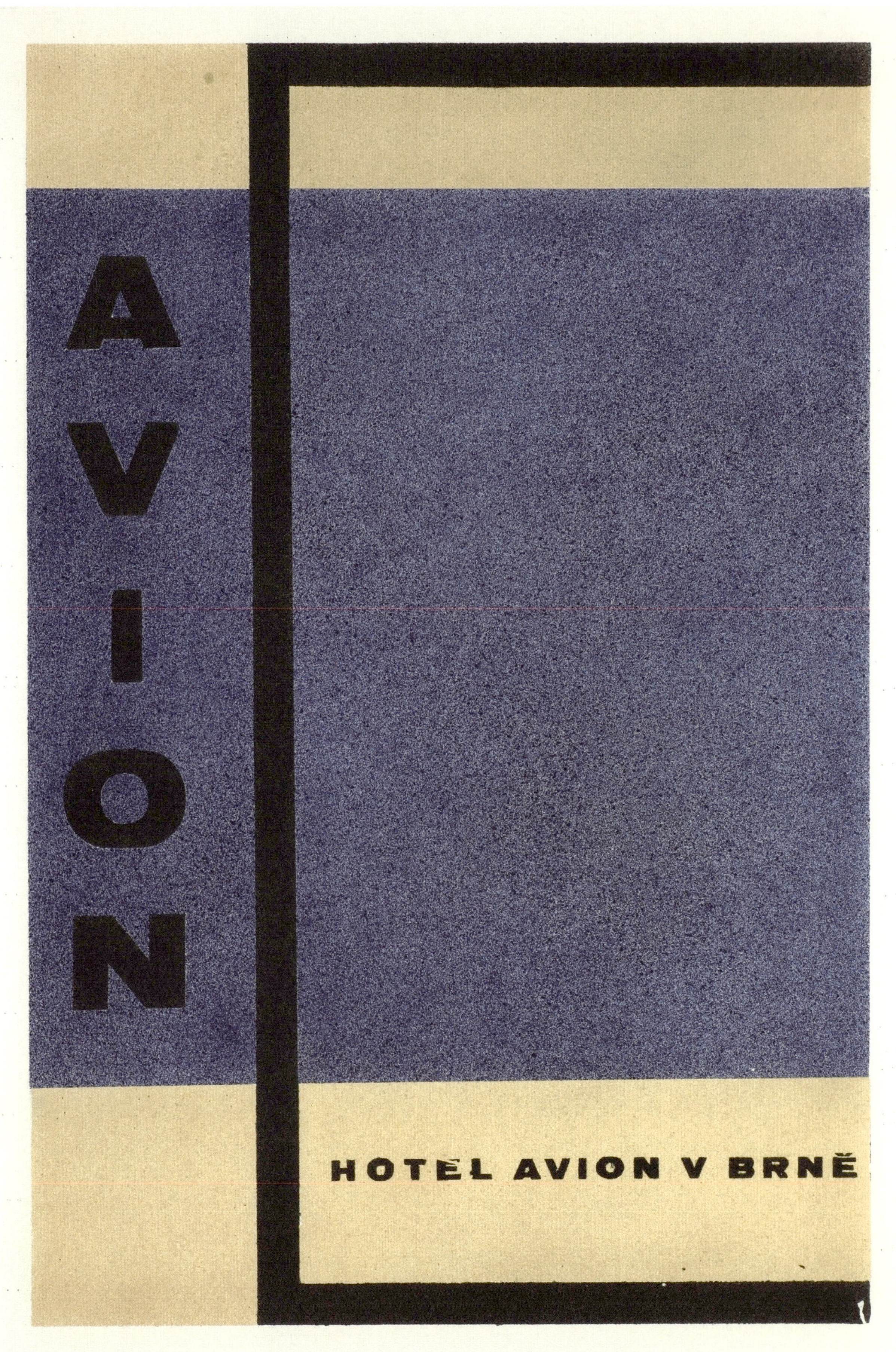

AVION
HOTEL AVION V BRNĚ

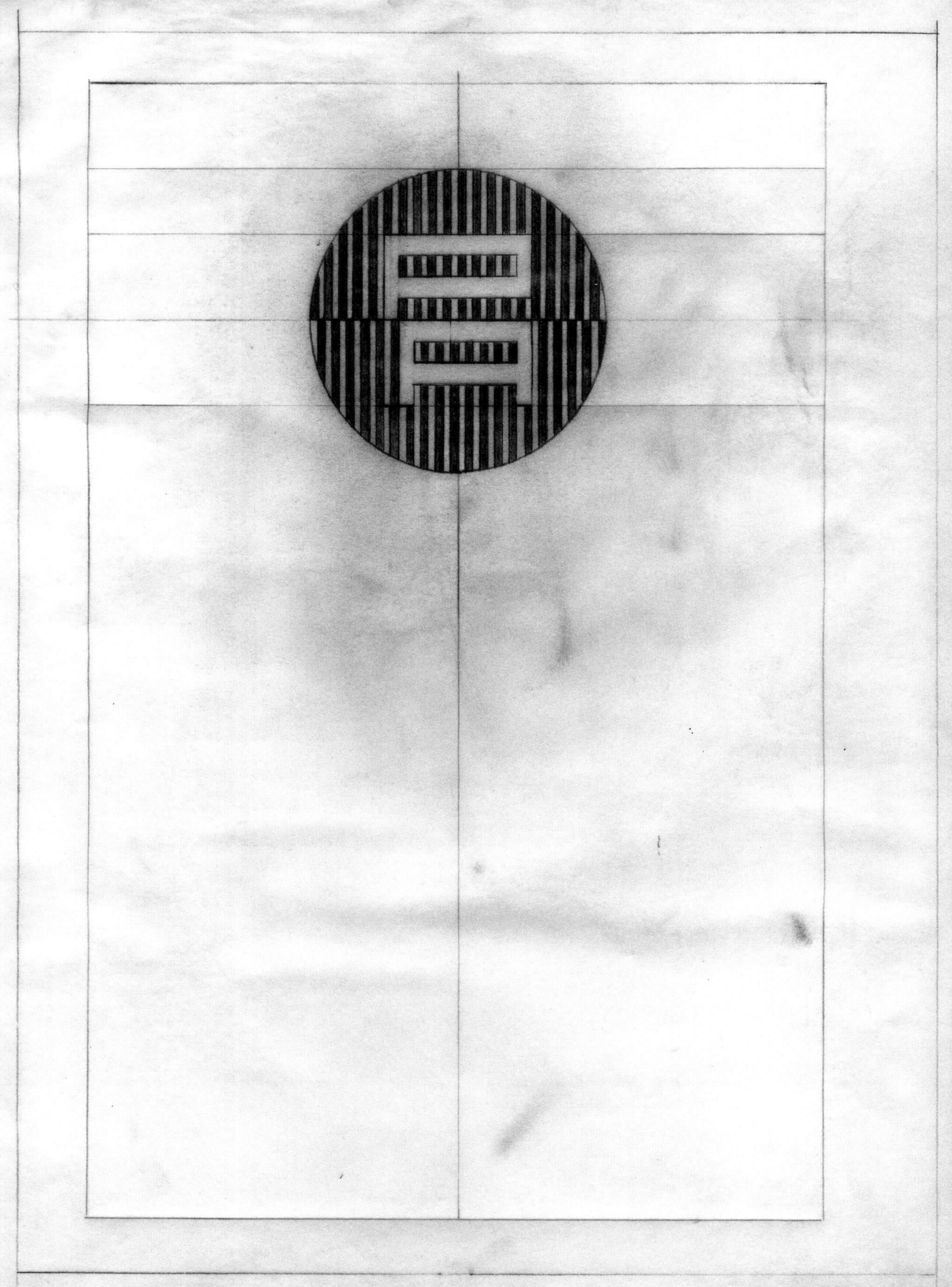

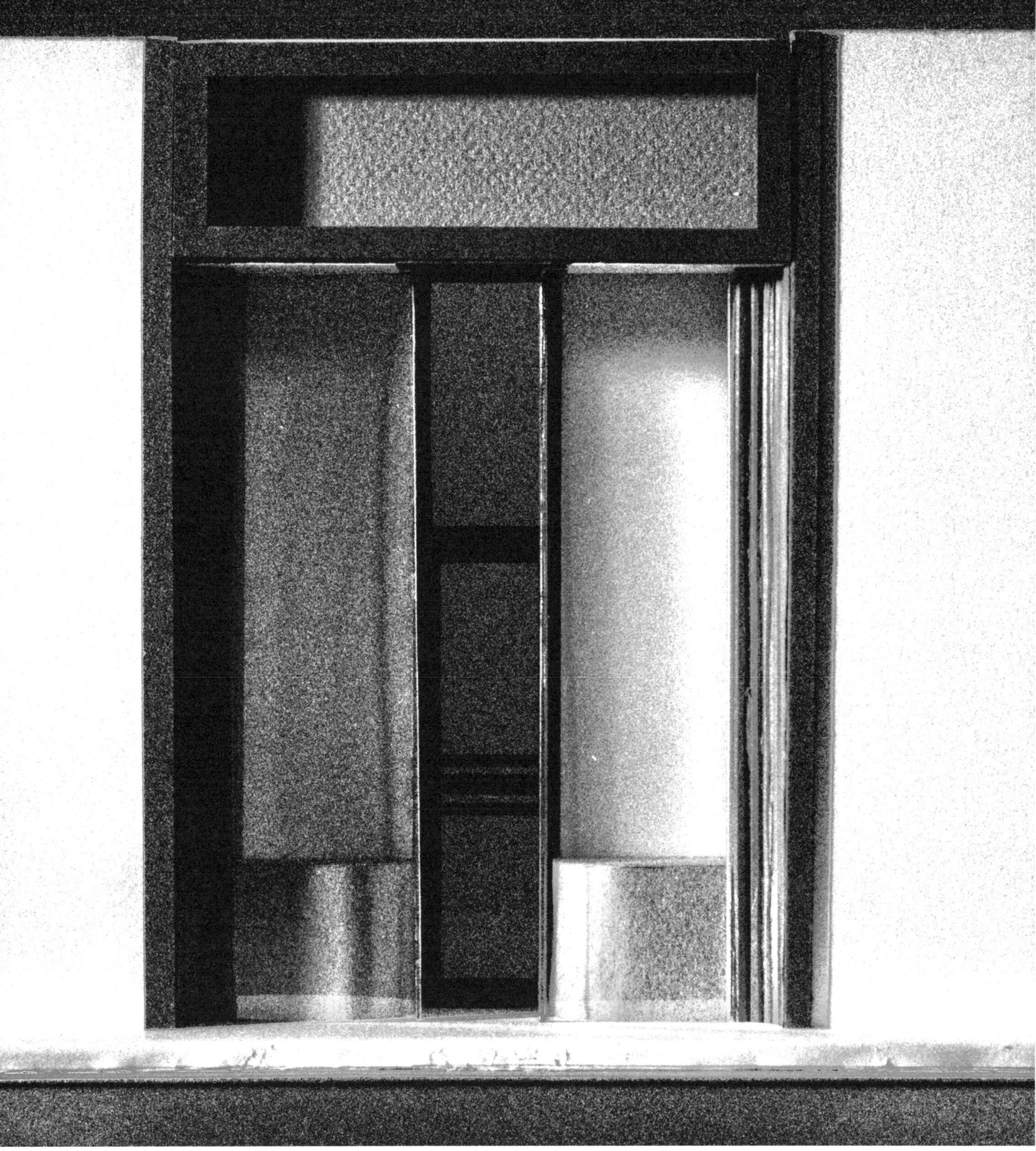

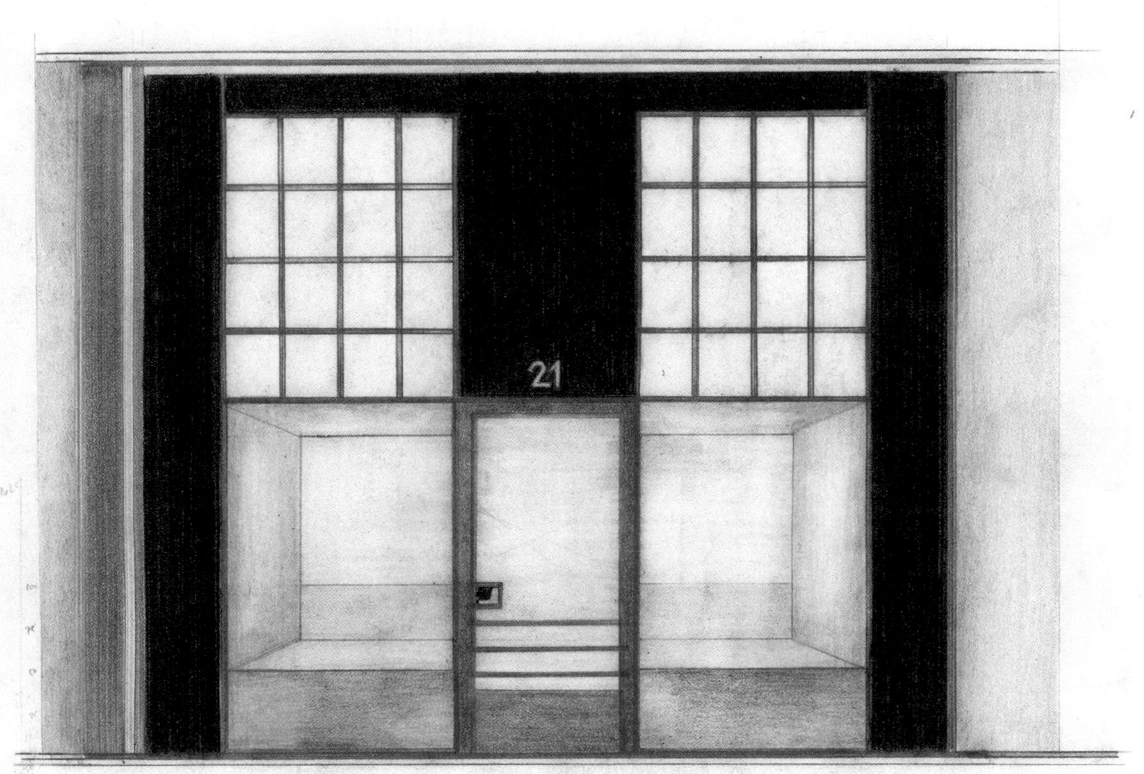

DS ulice lužická

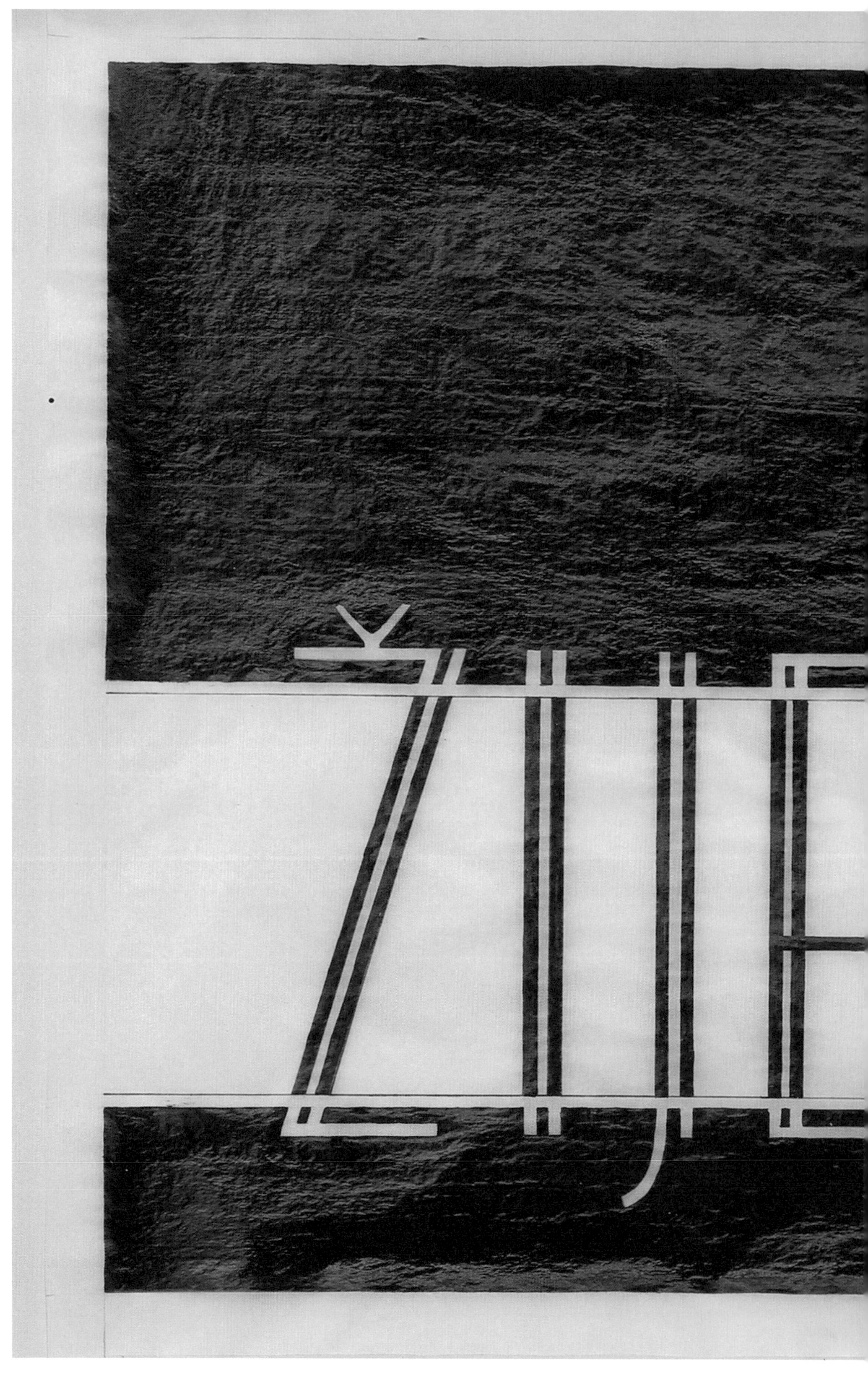

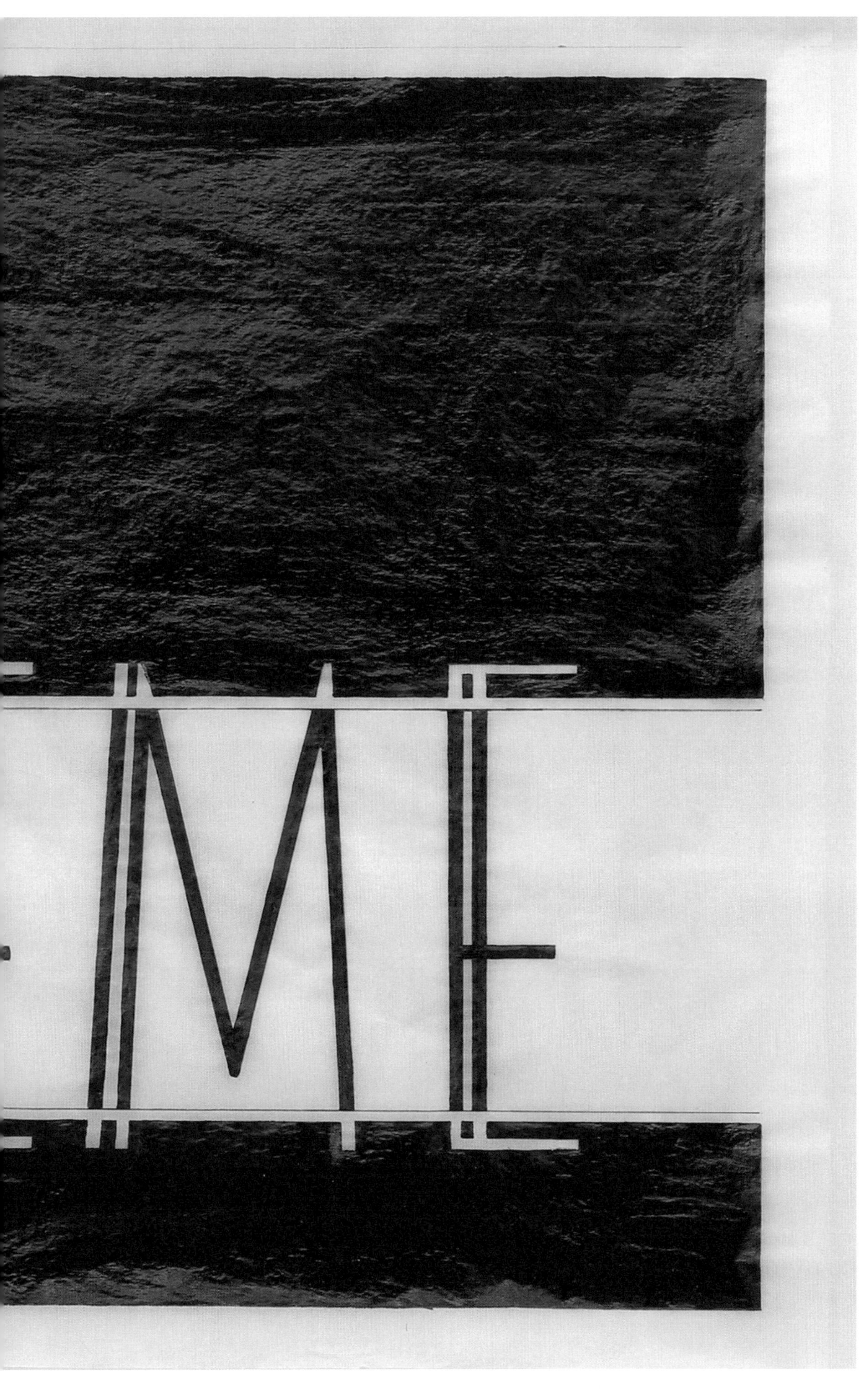

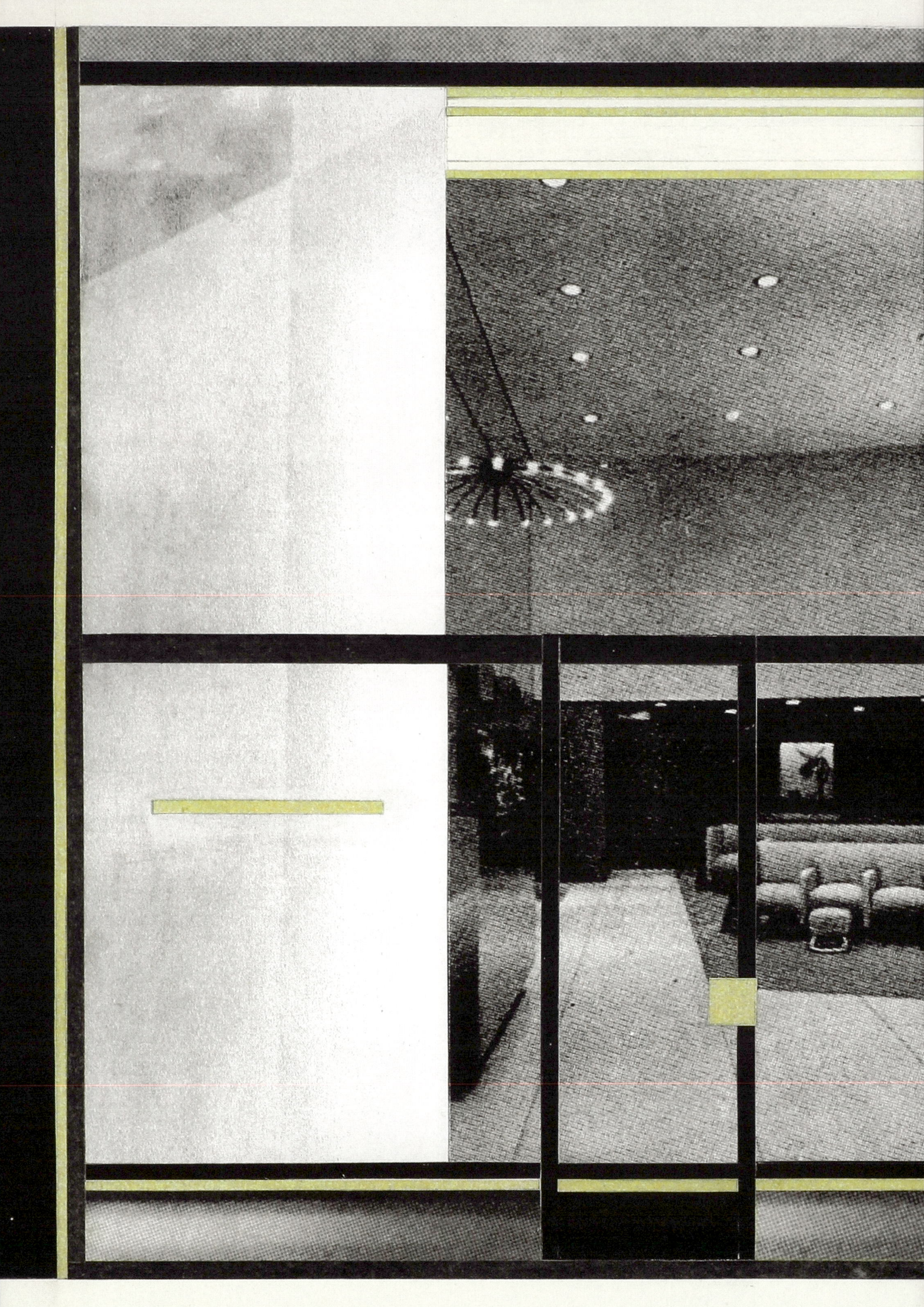

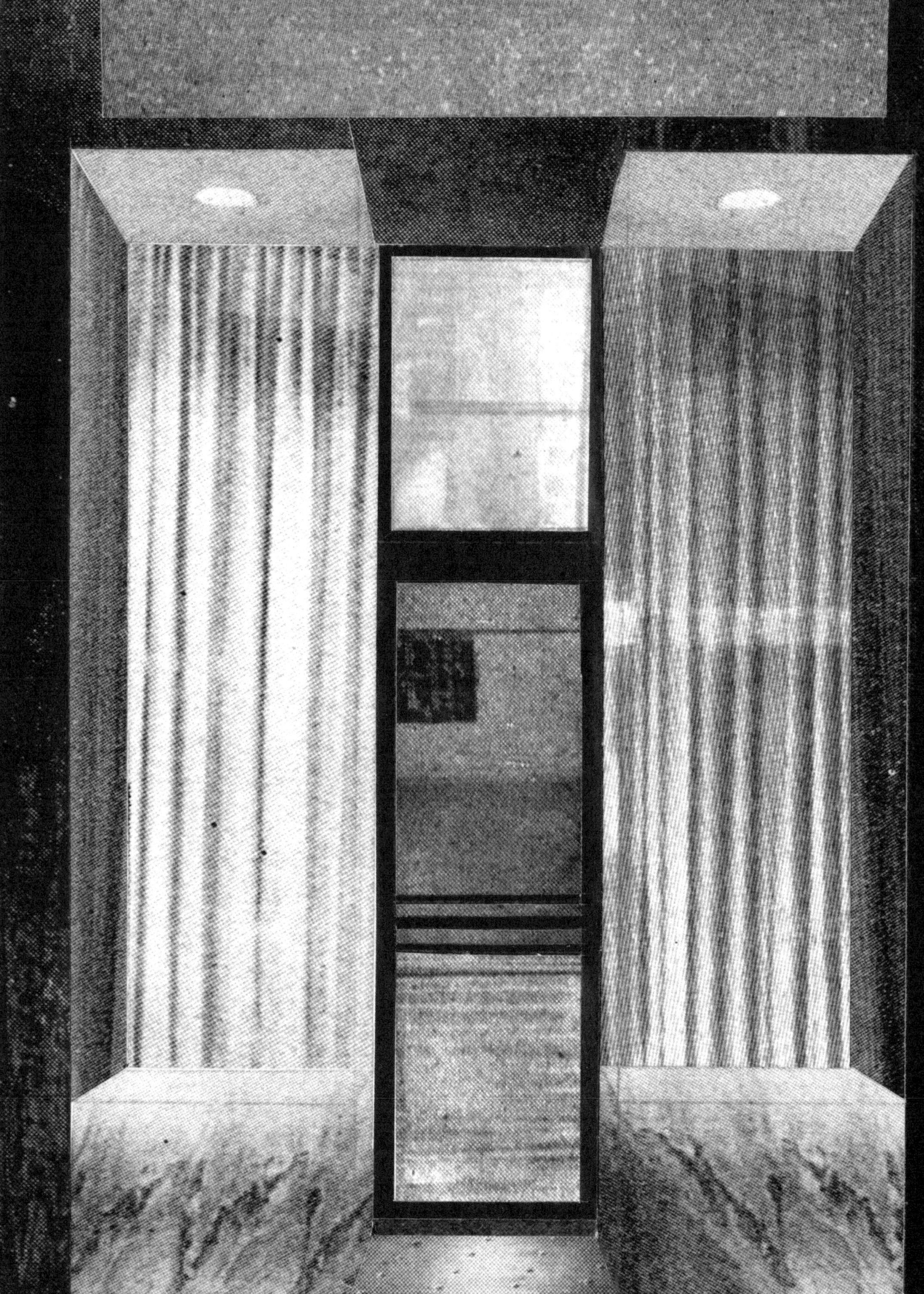

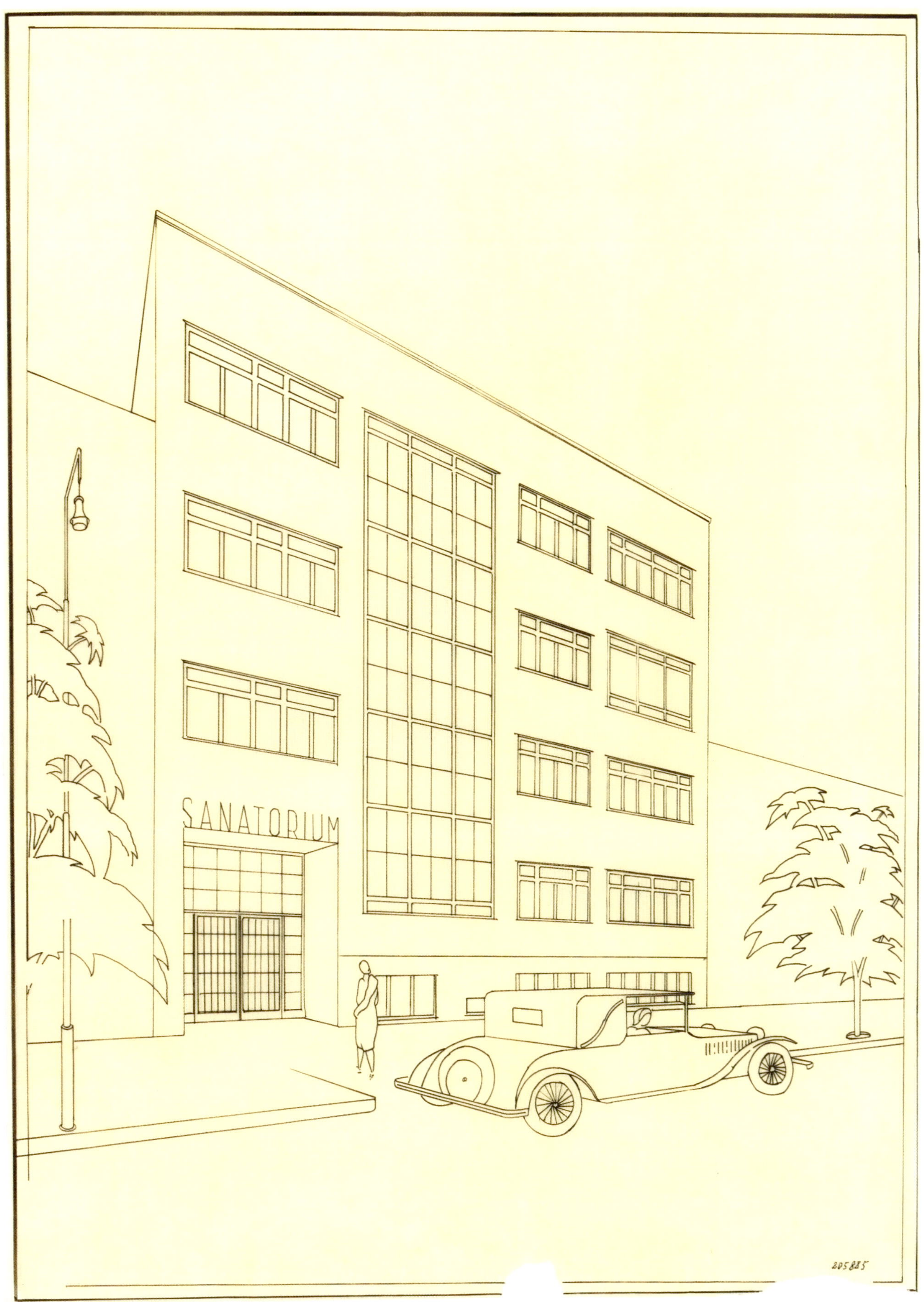
SANATORIUM

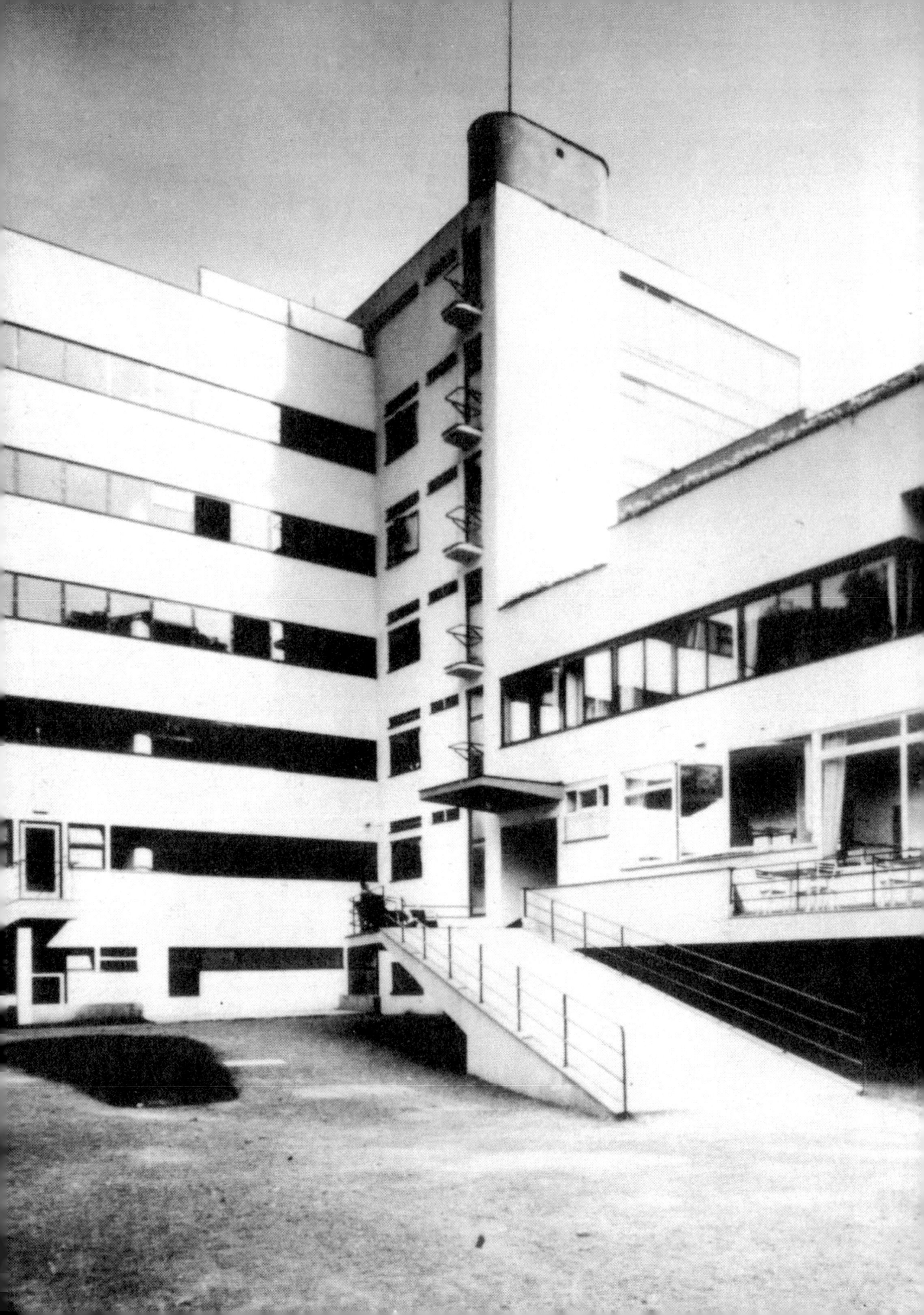

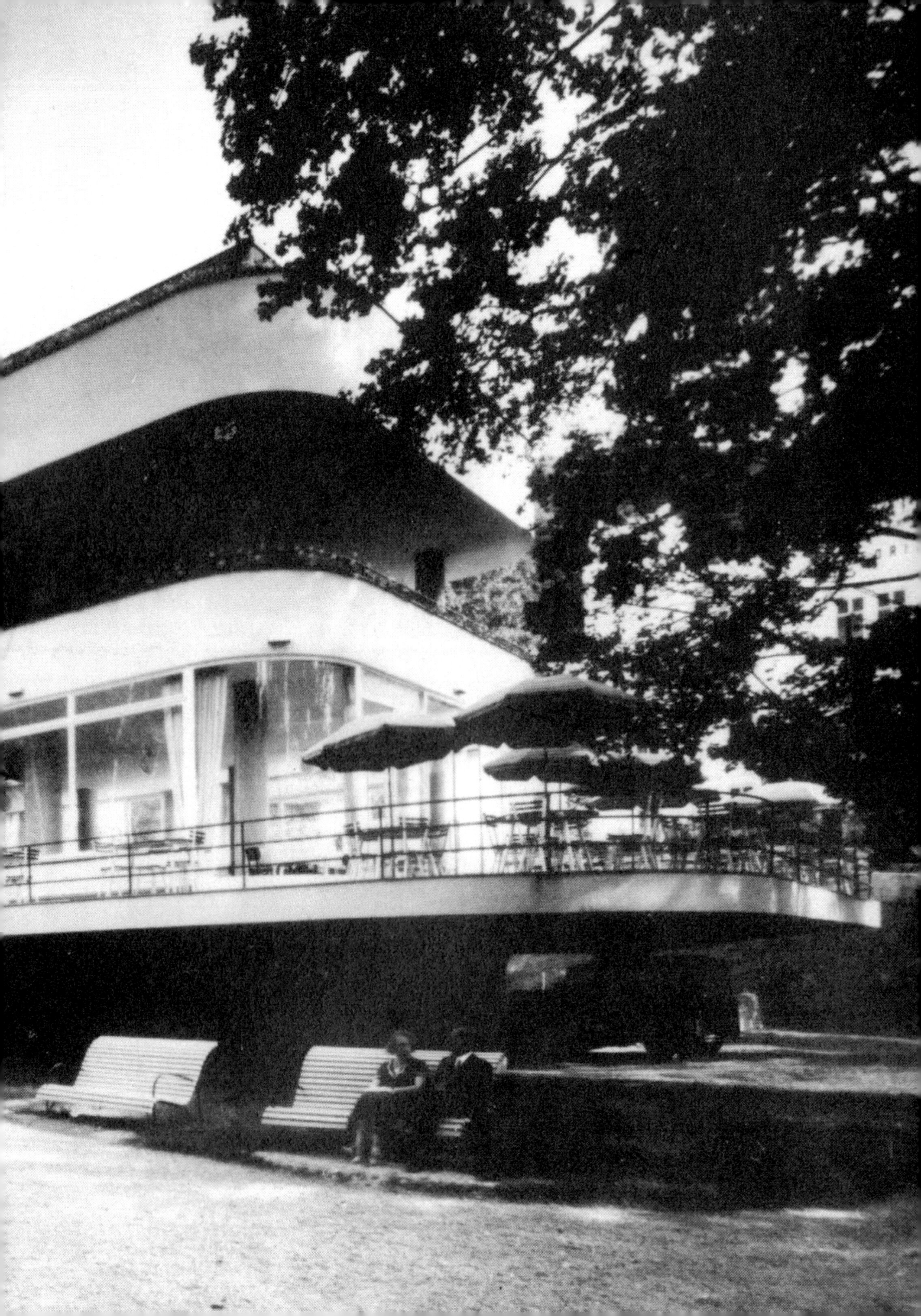

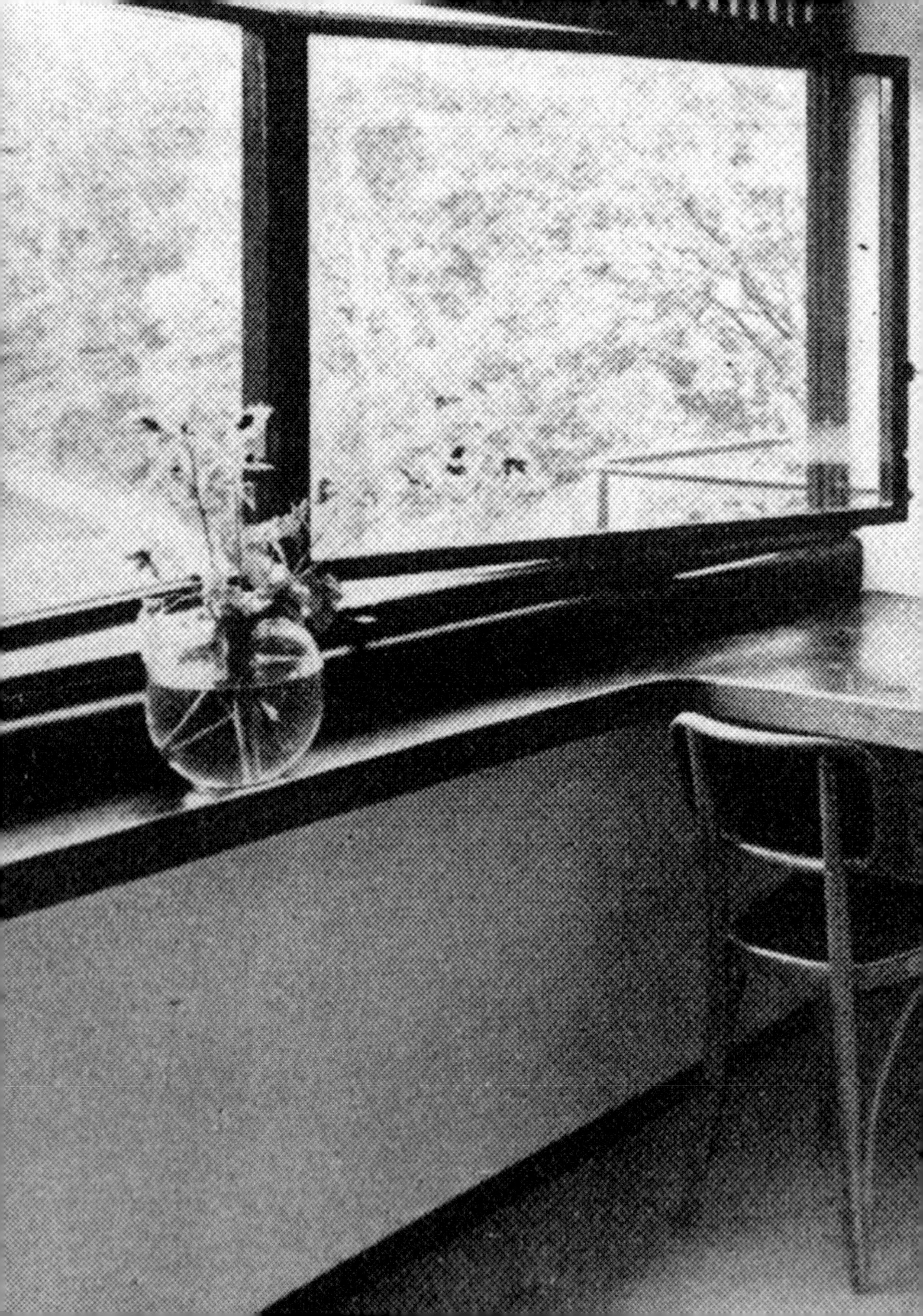

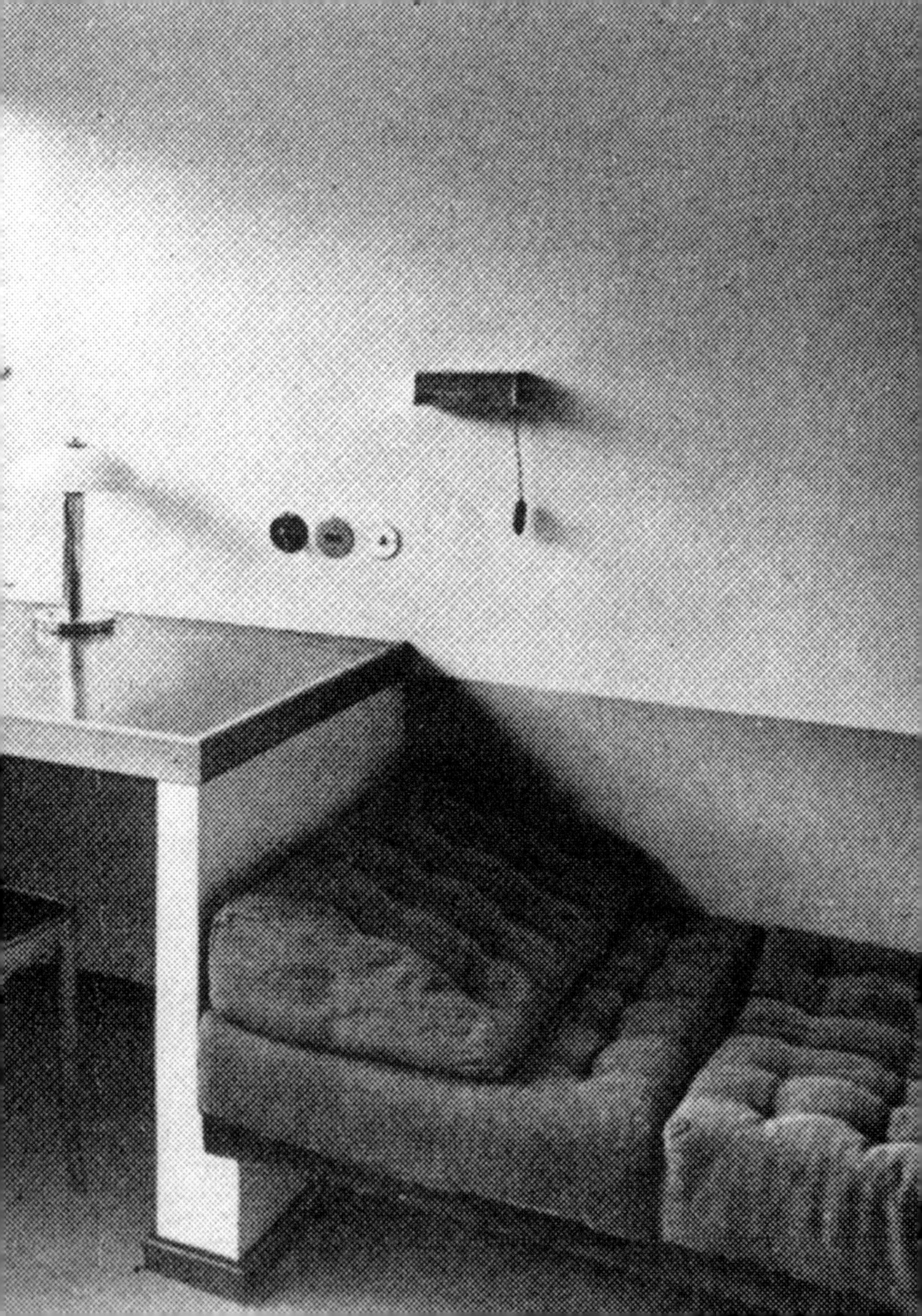

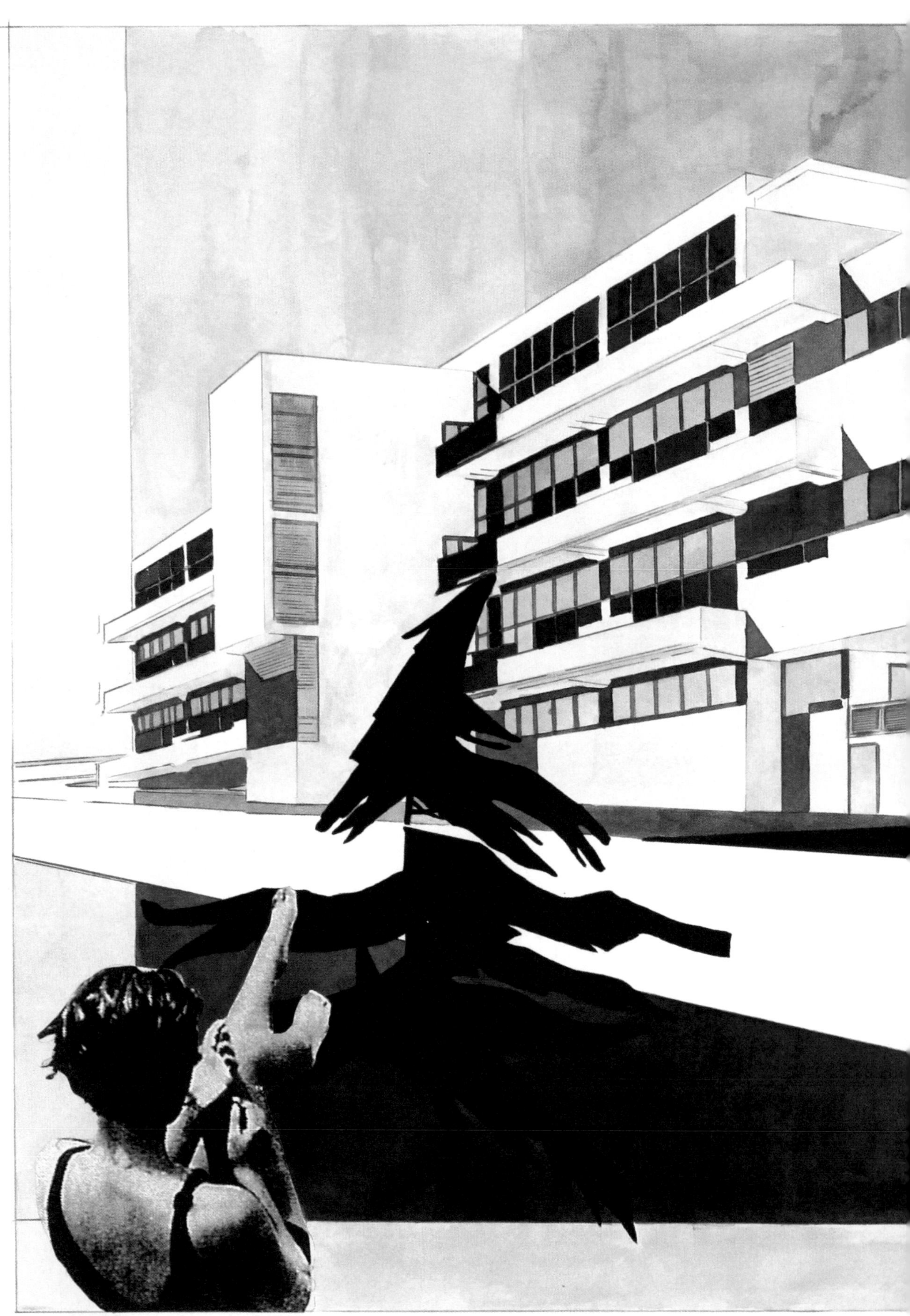

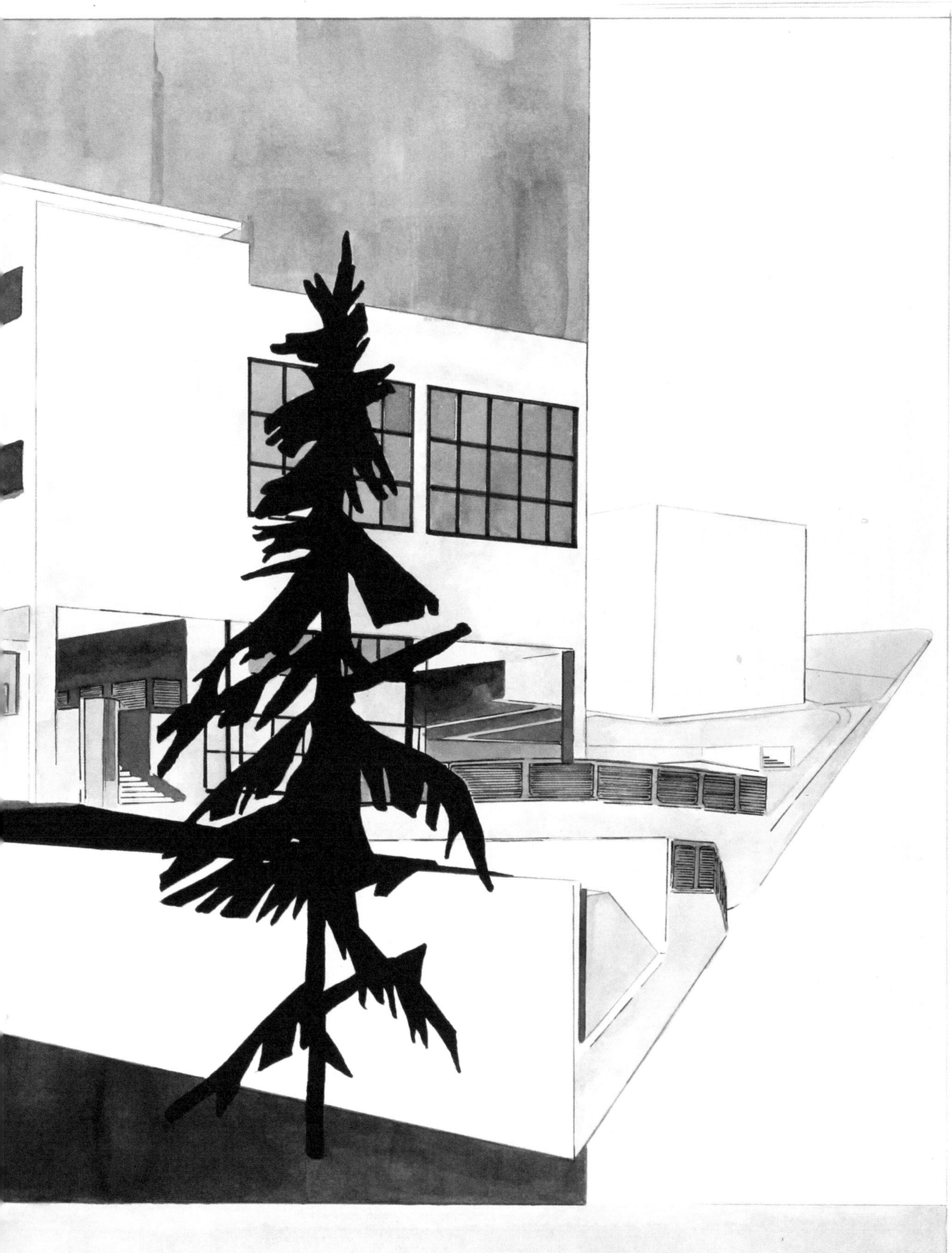

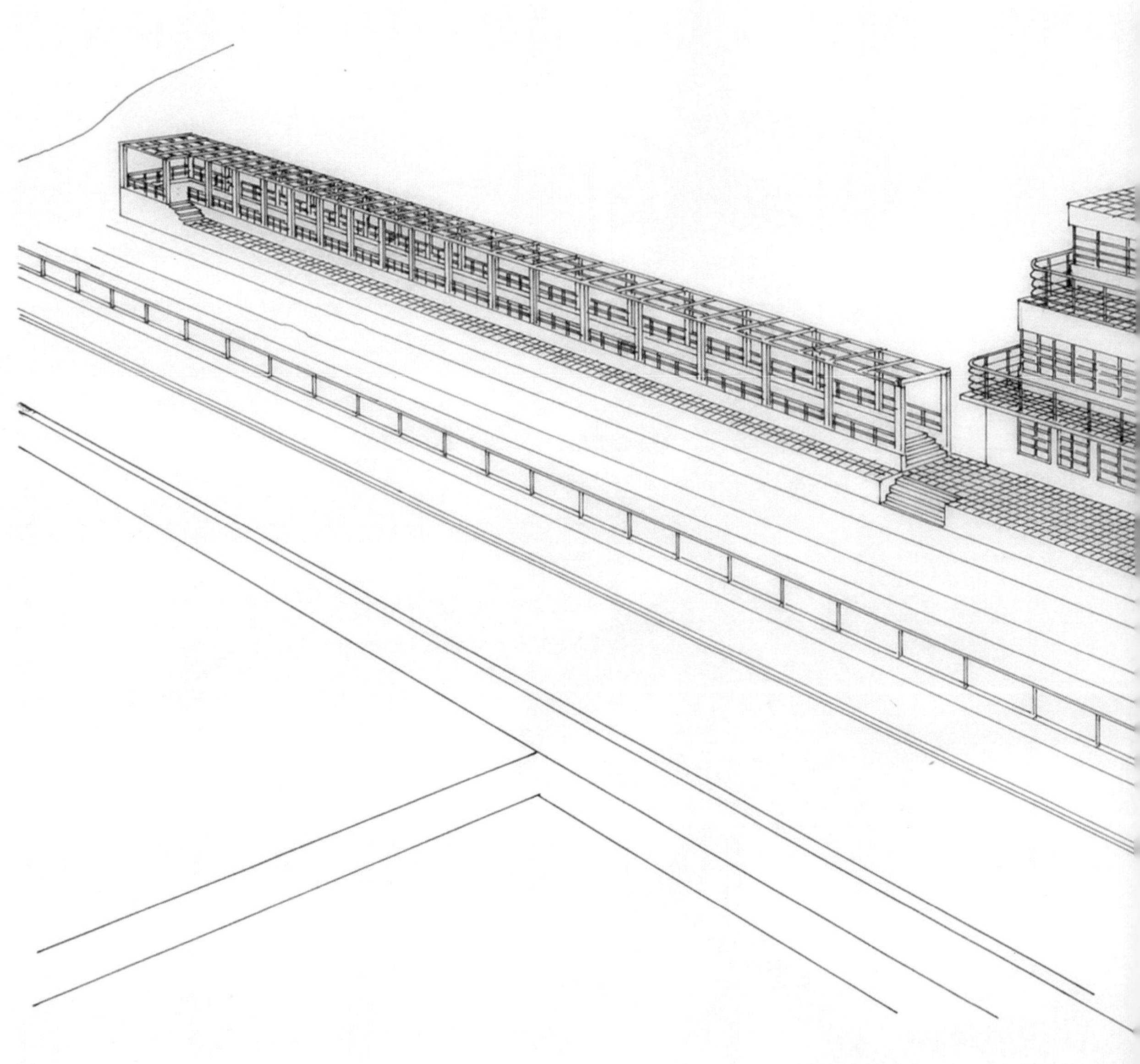

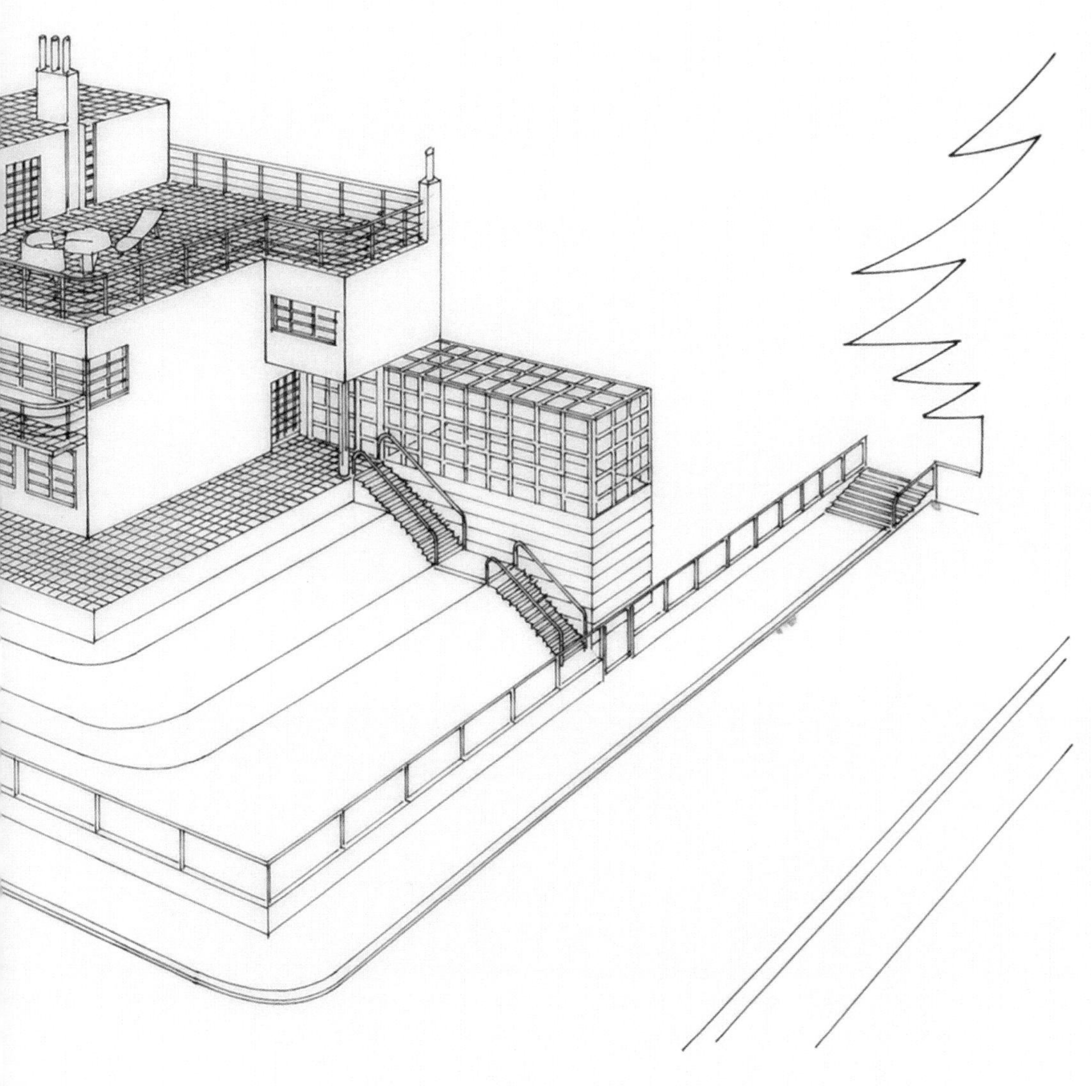

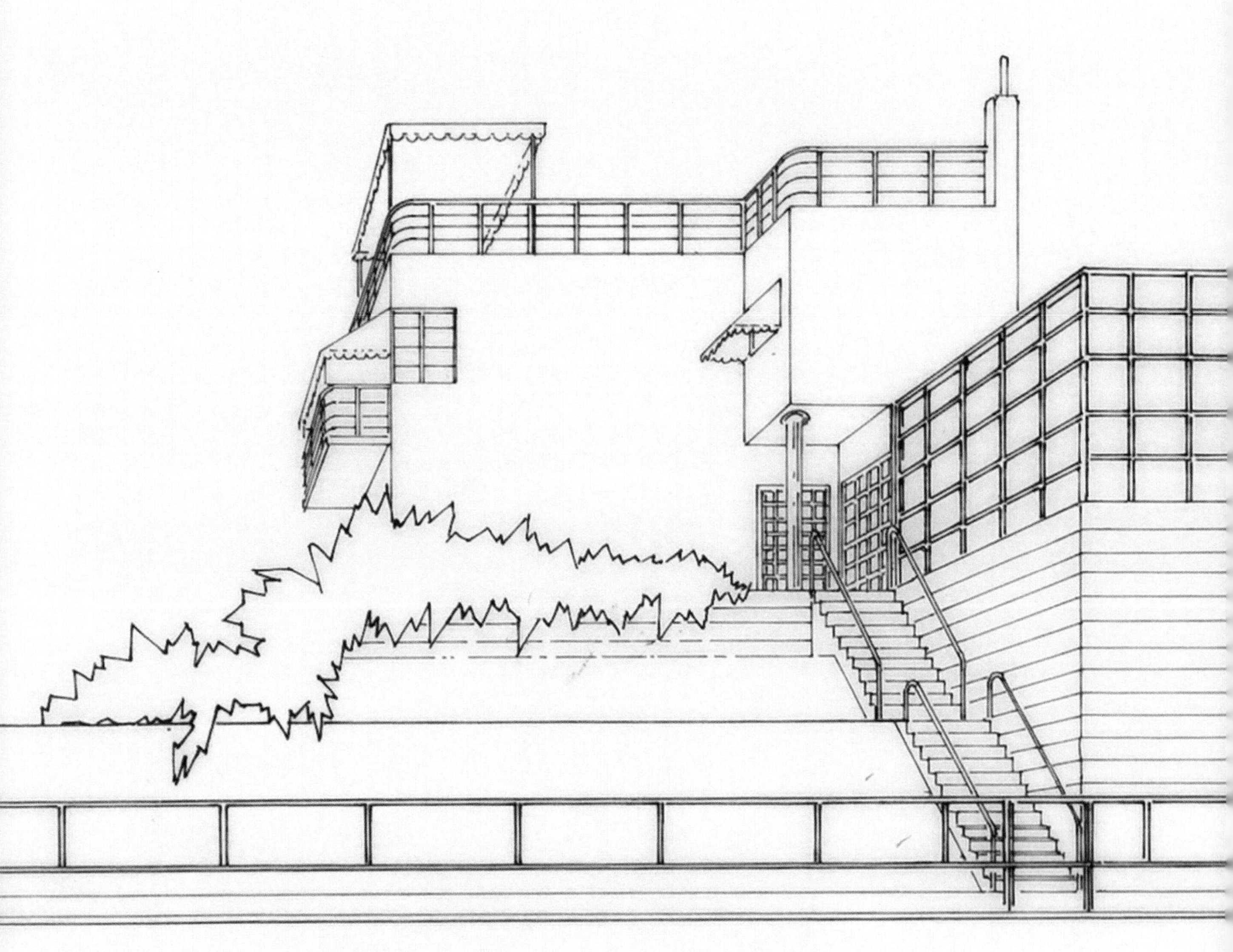

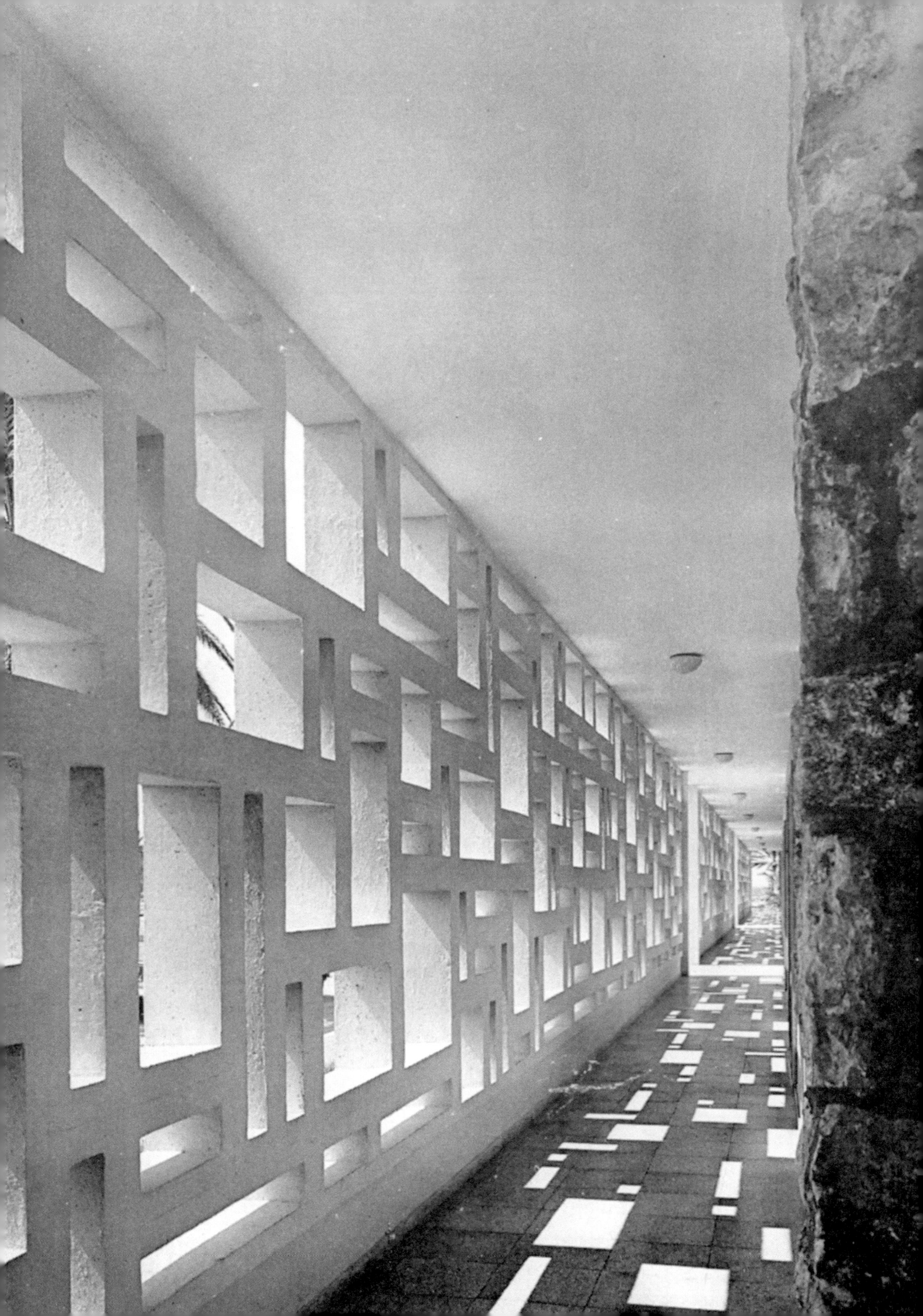

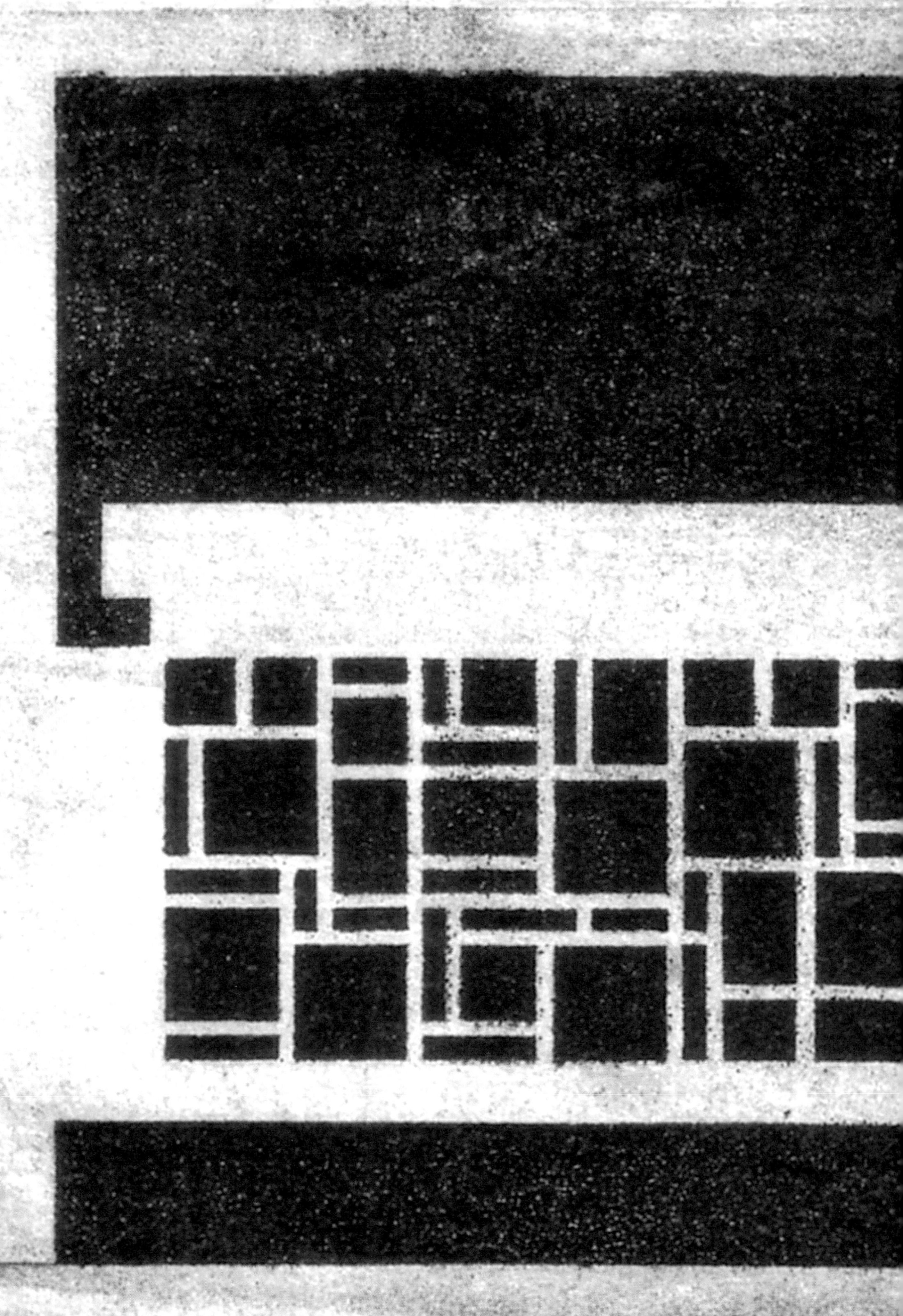

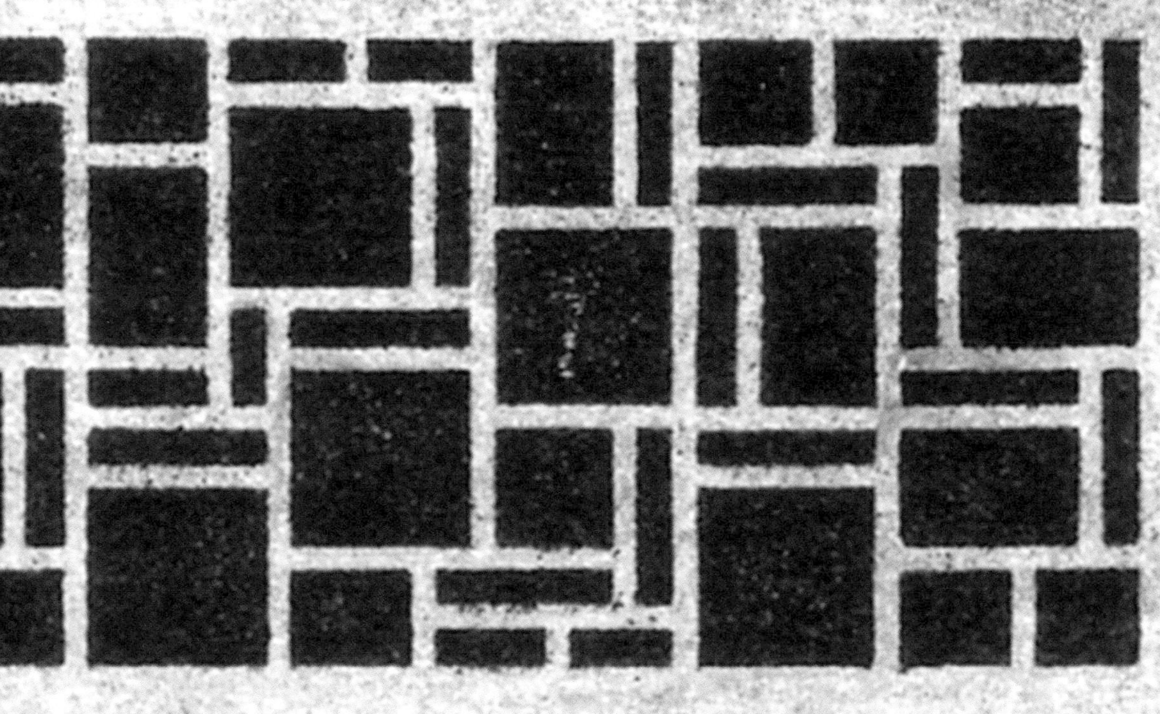

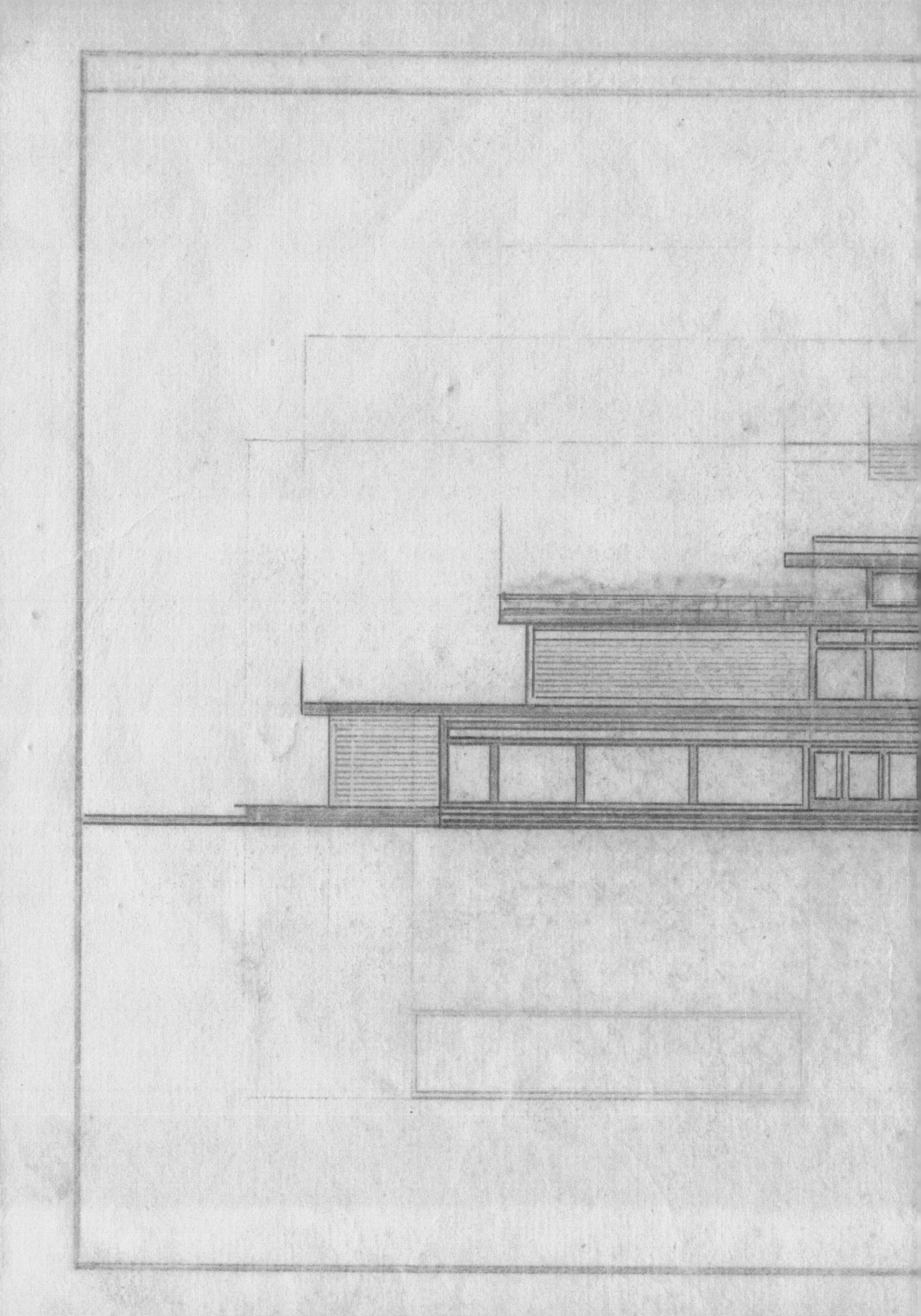

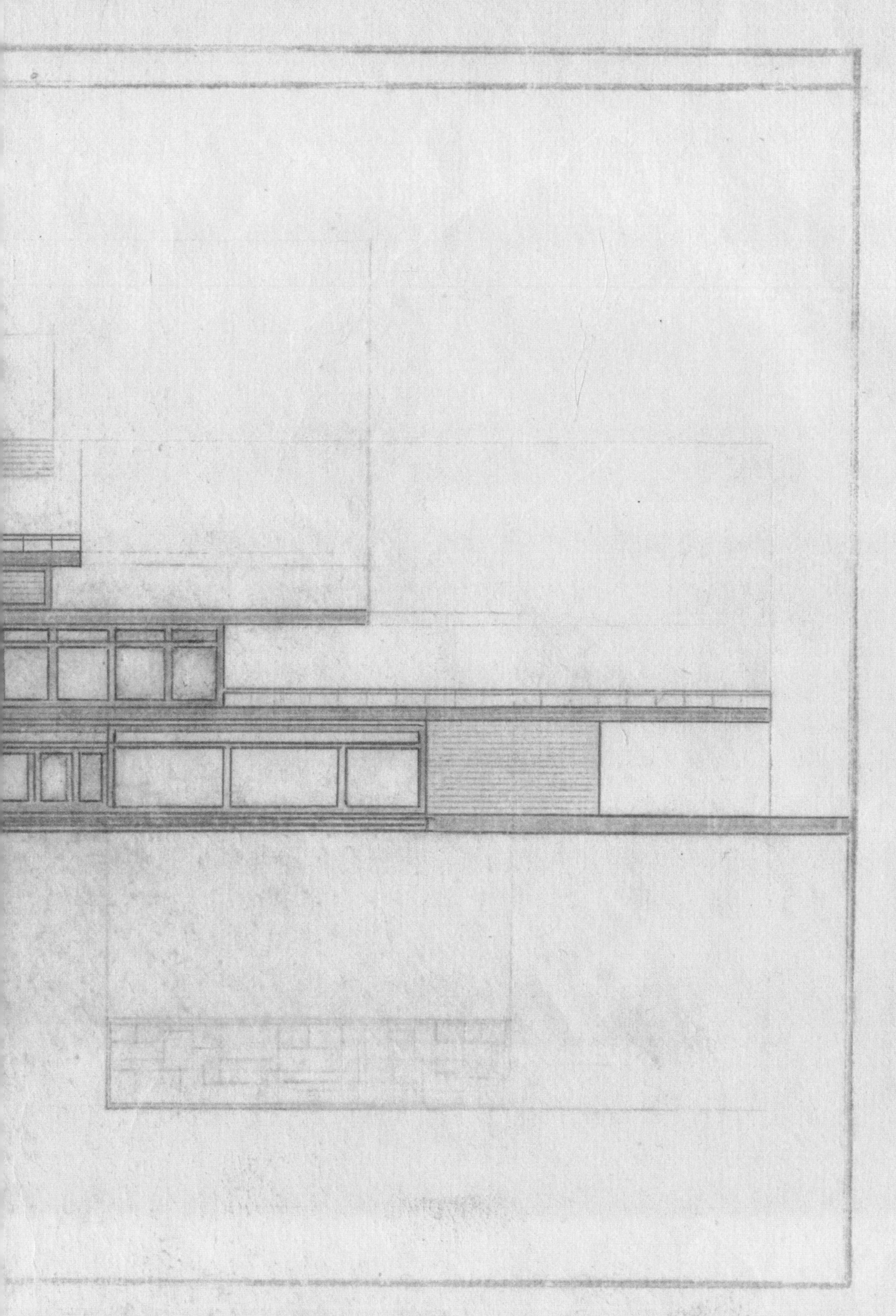

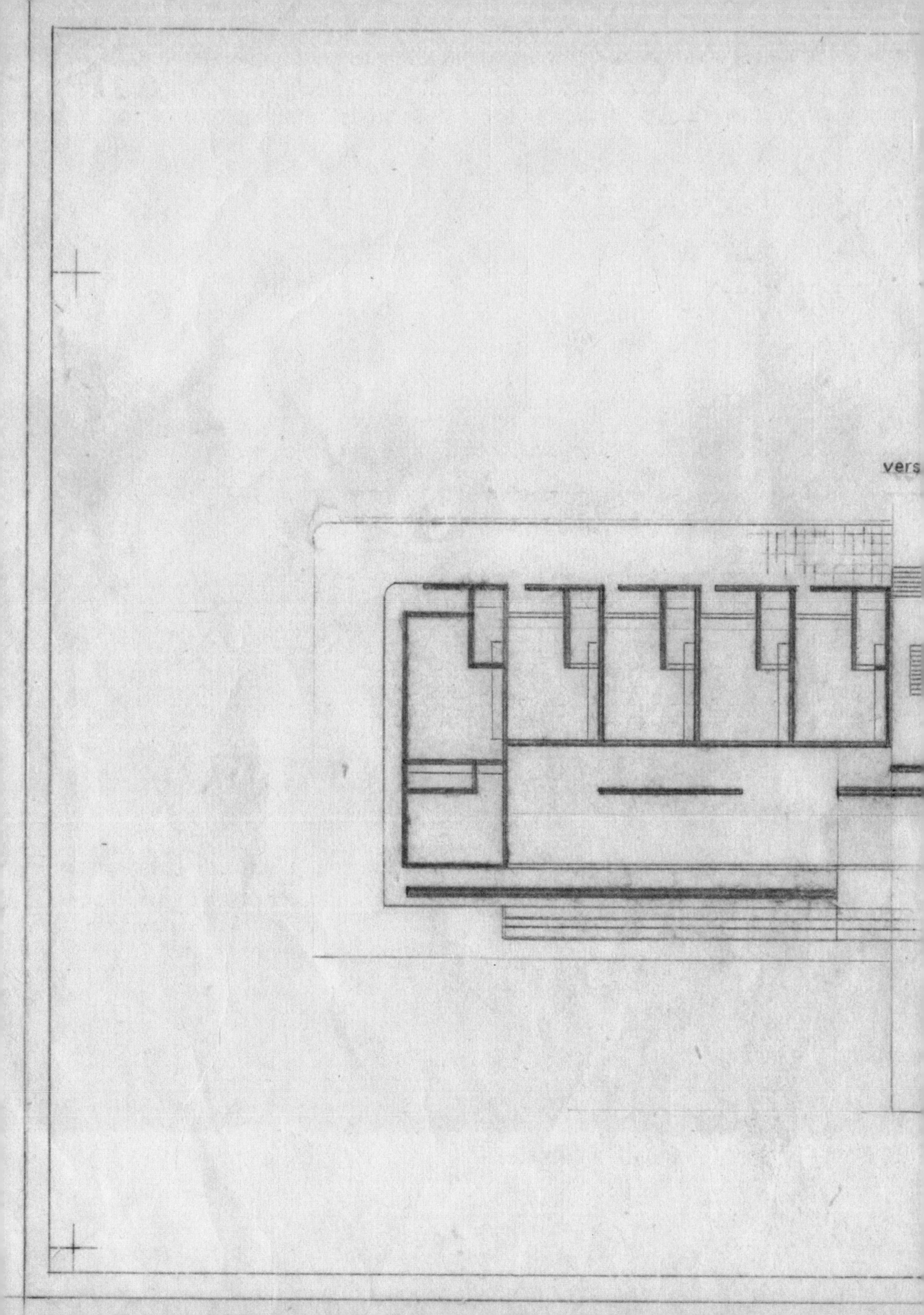
vers

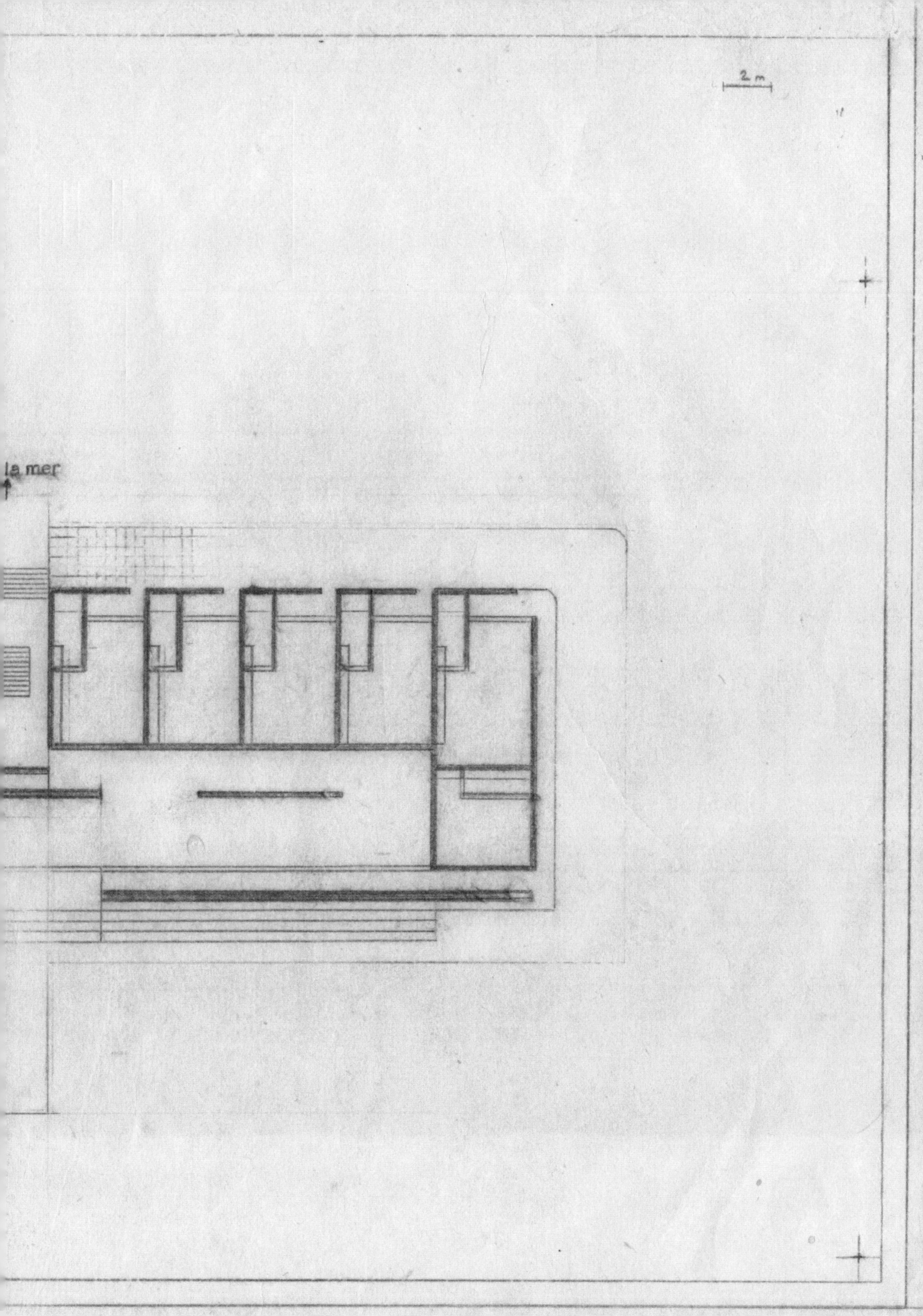
la mer
2 m

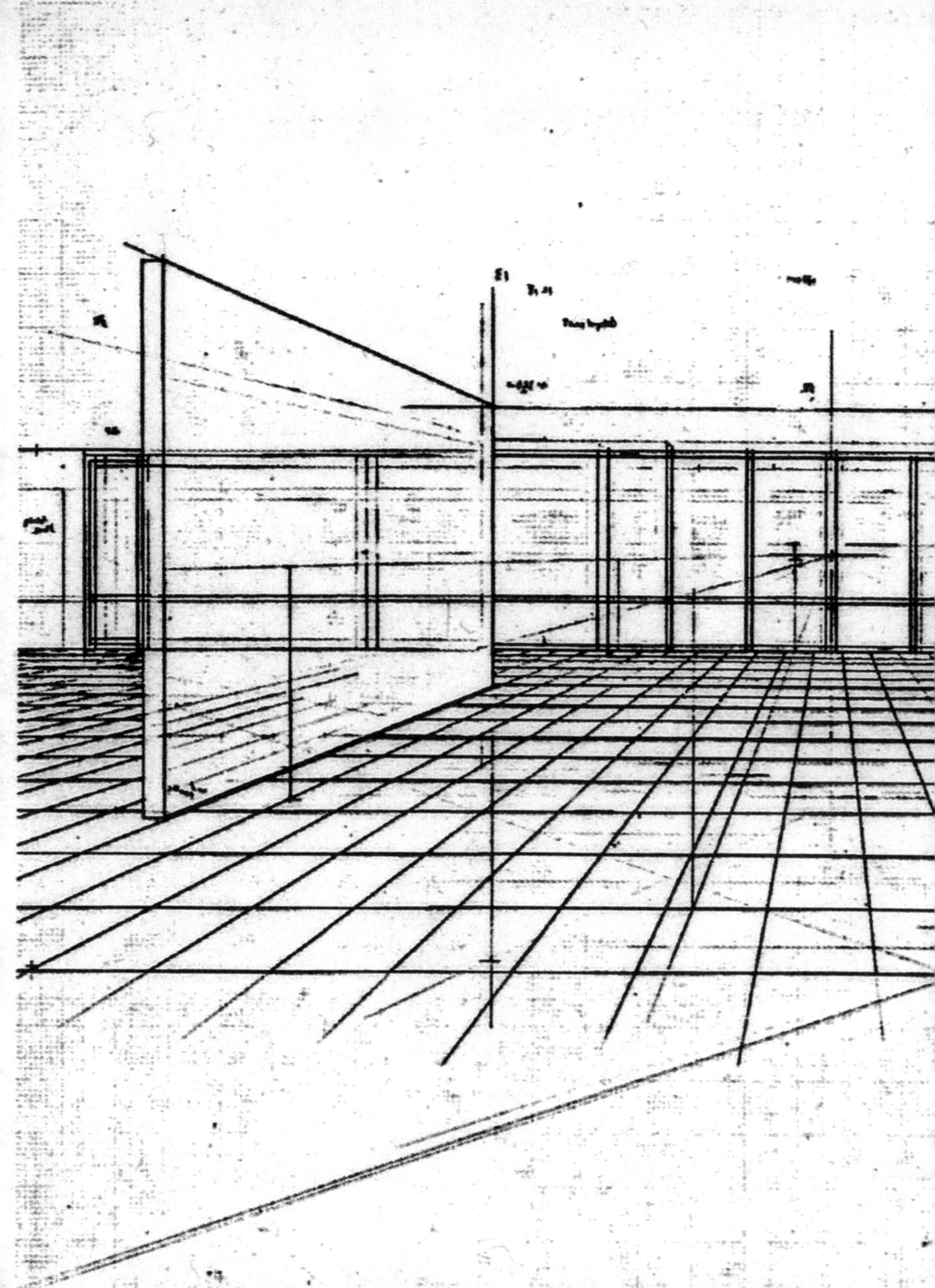

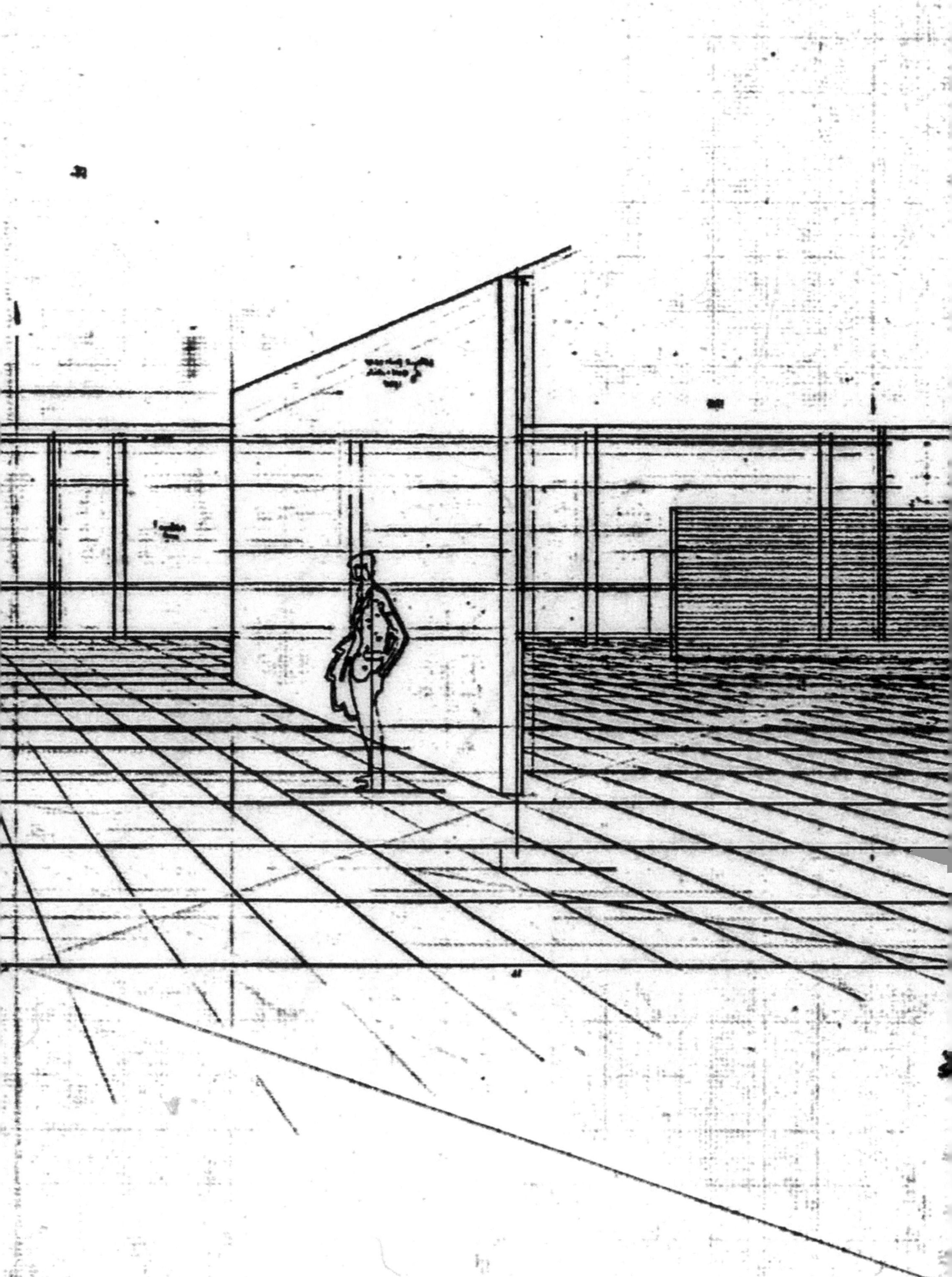

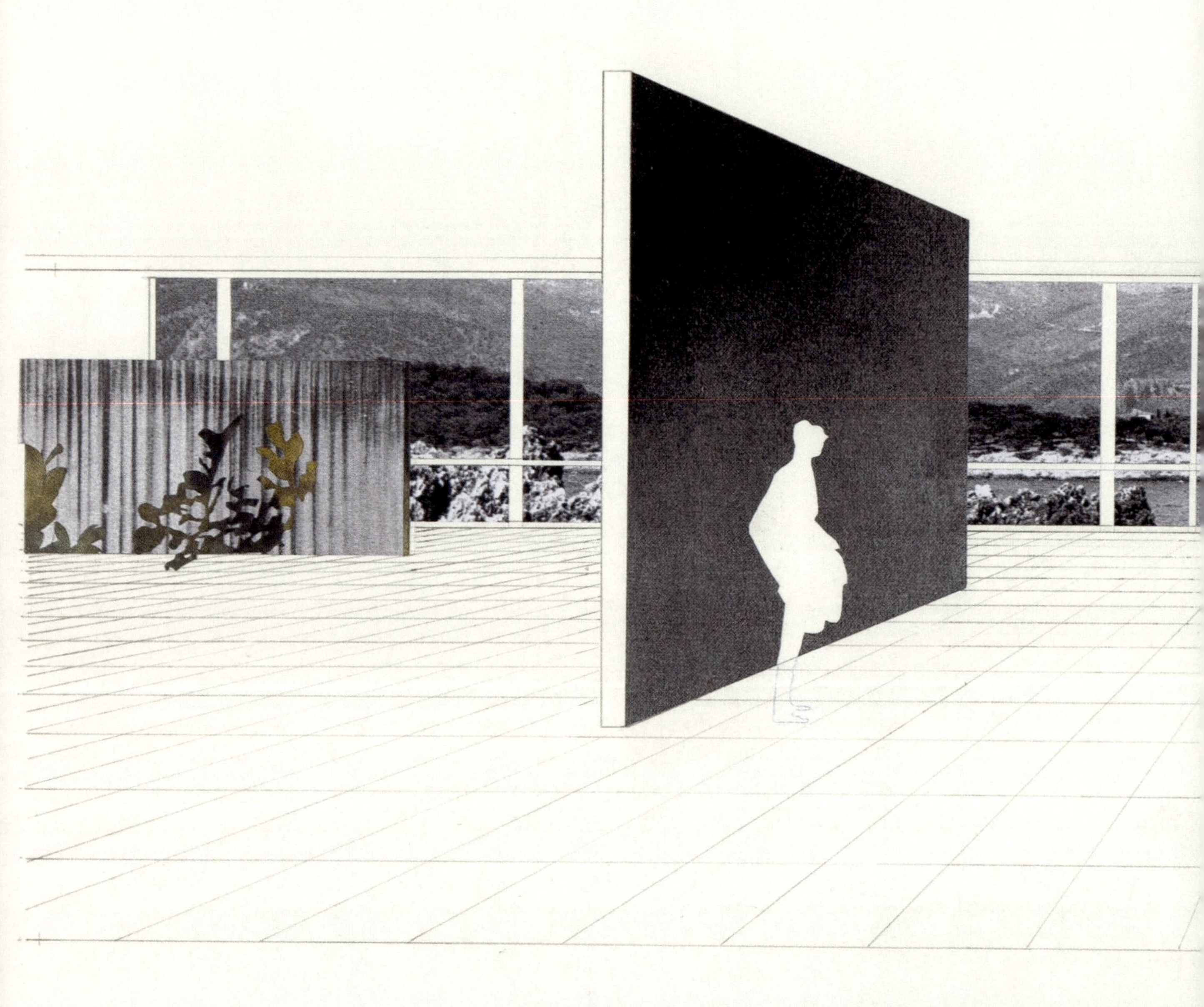

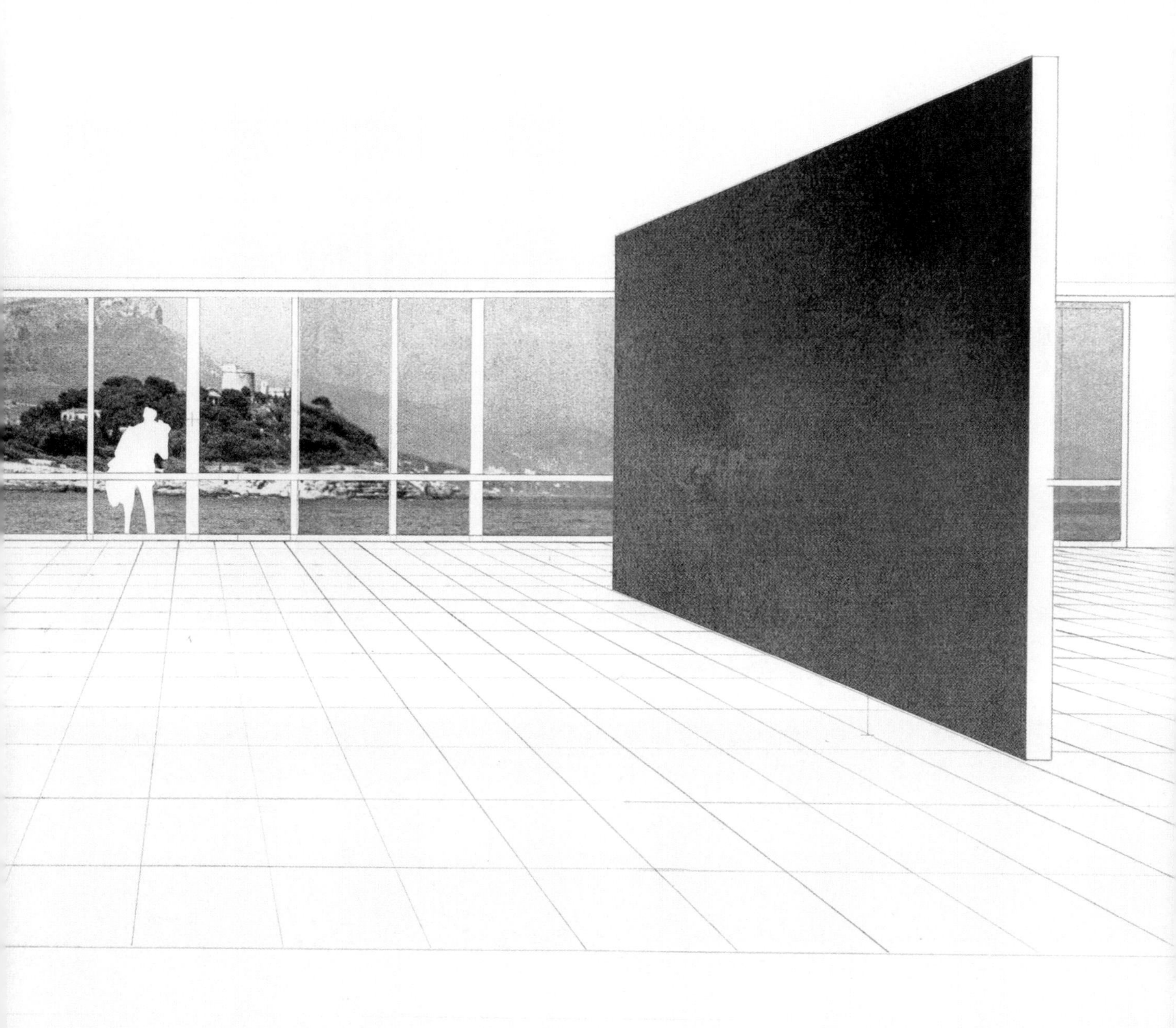

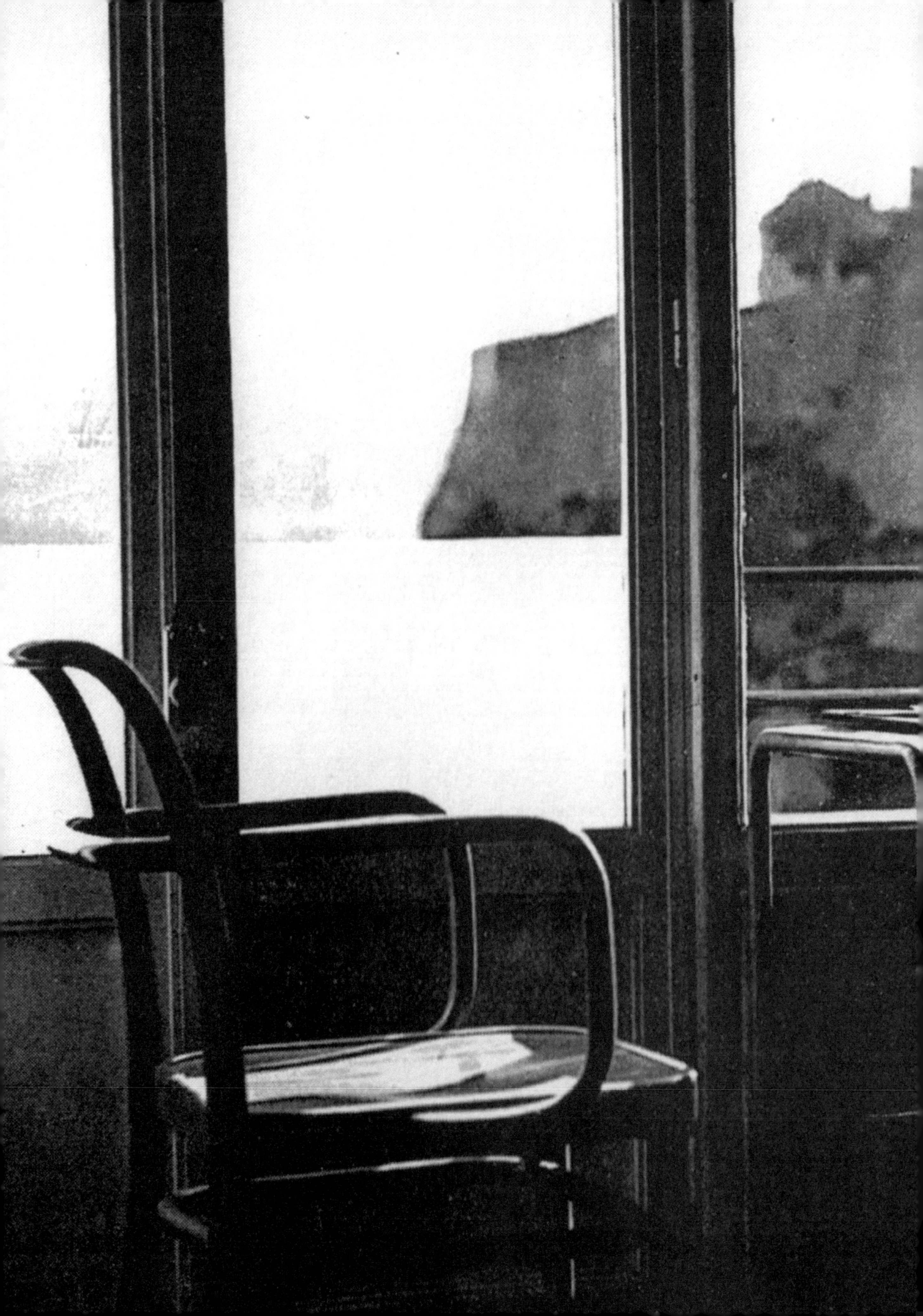

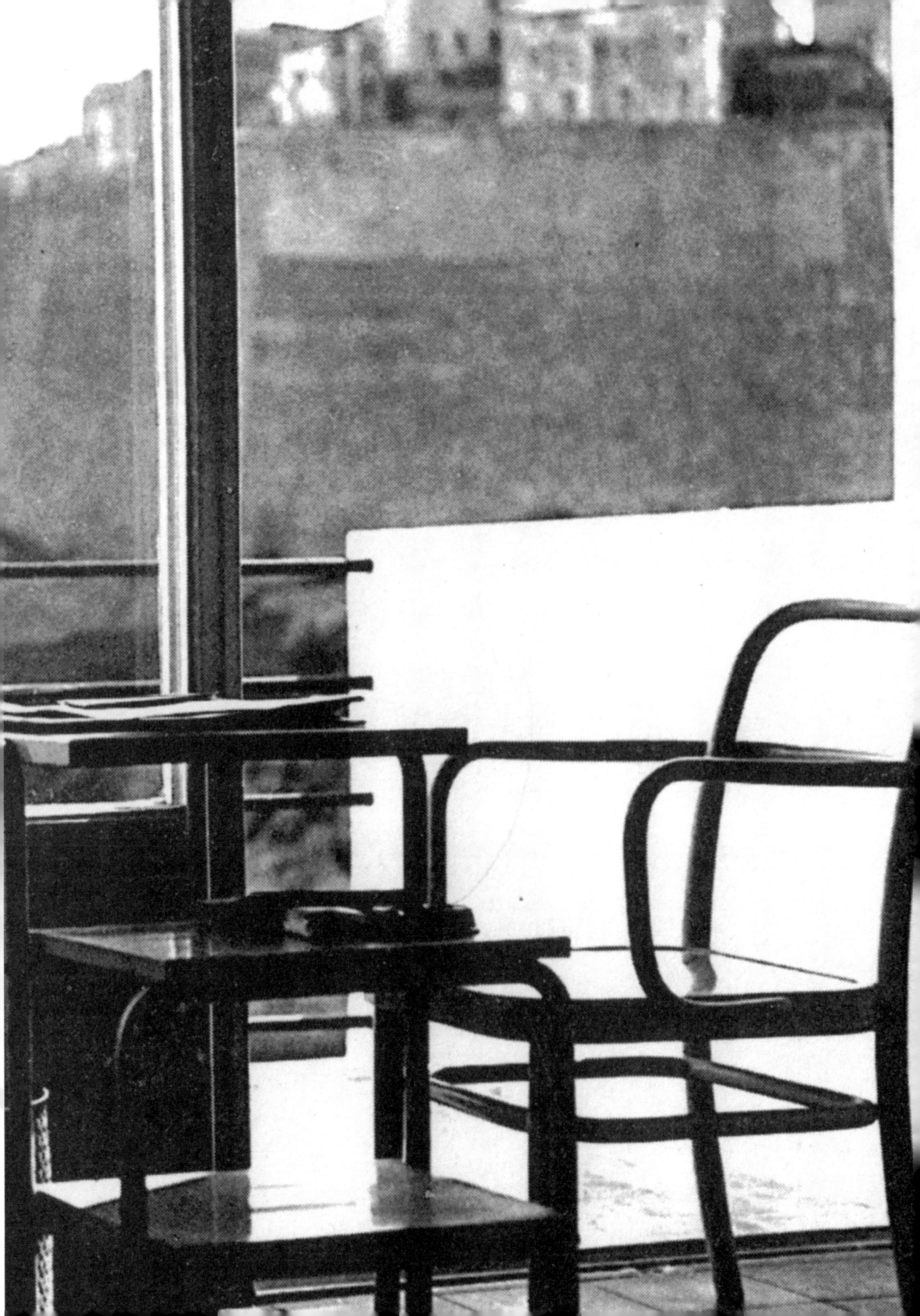

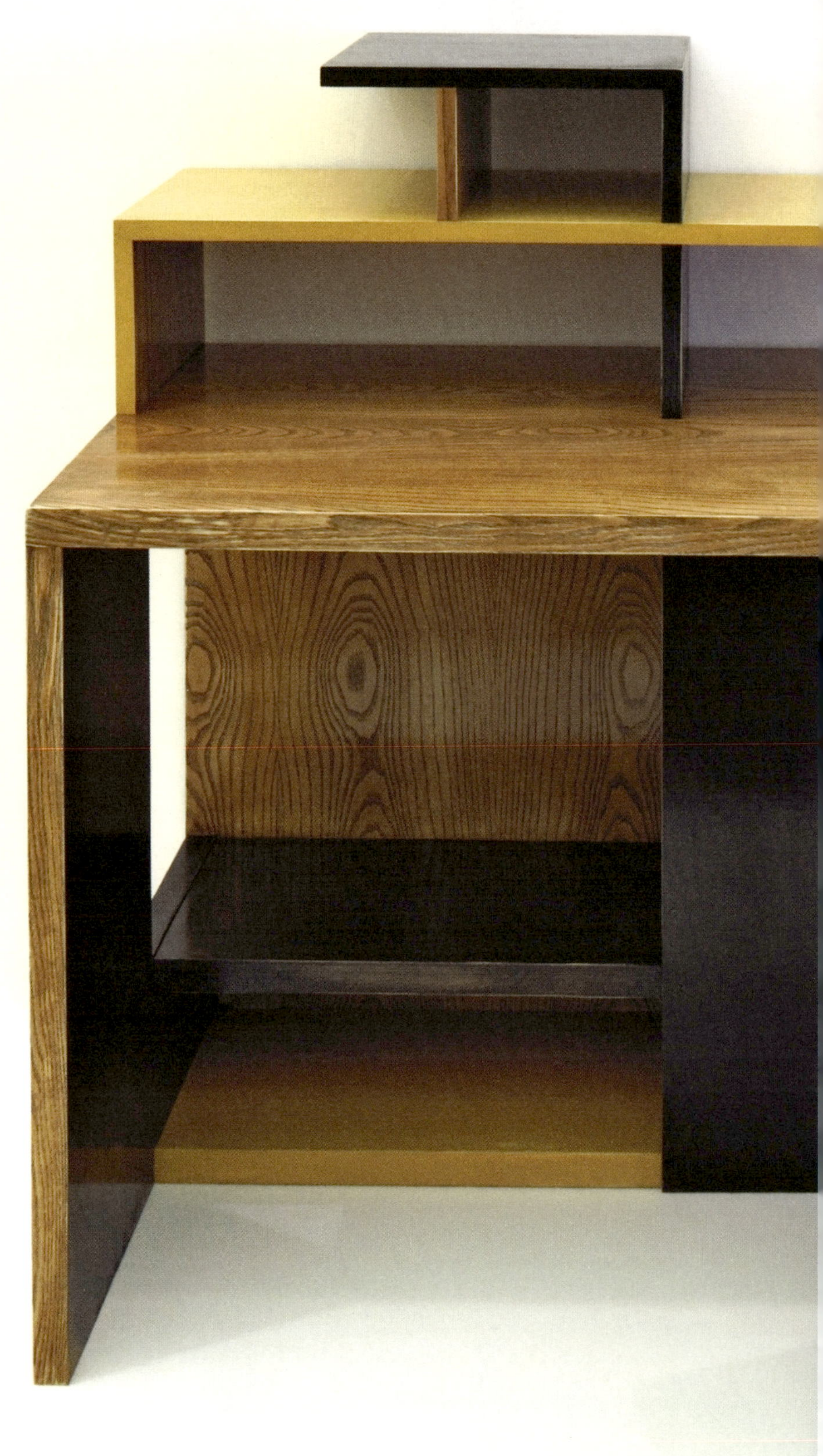

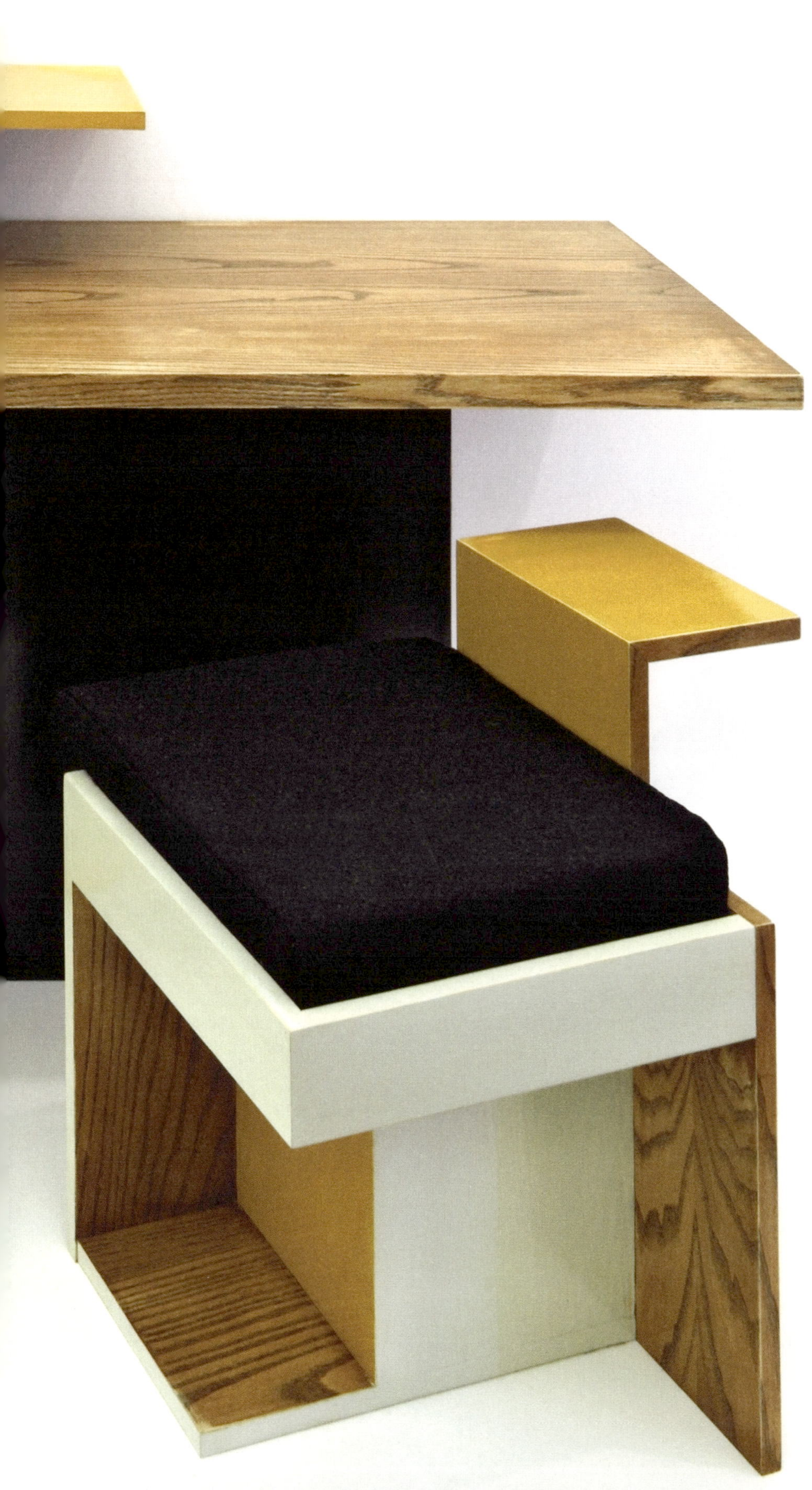

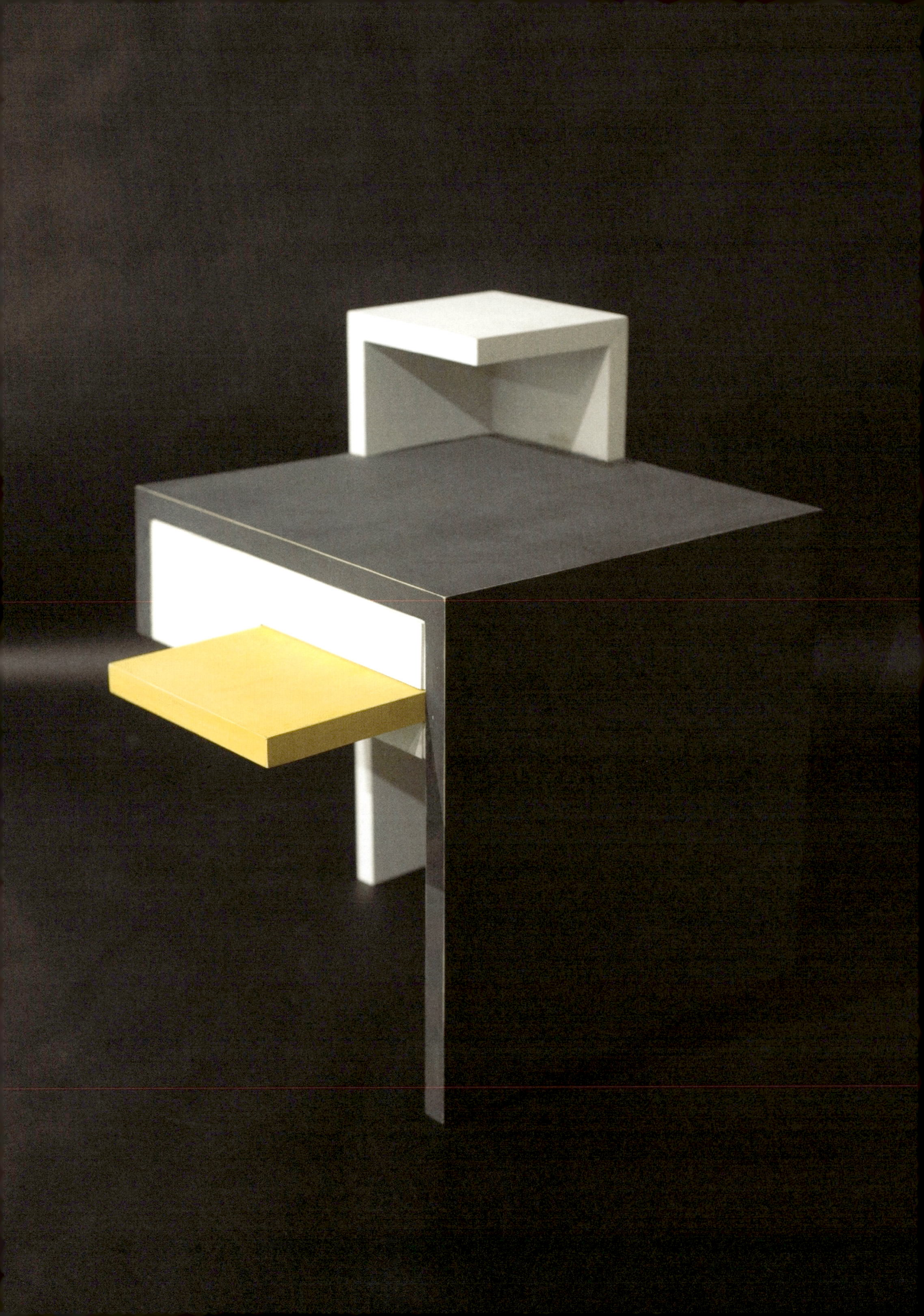

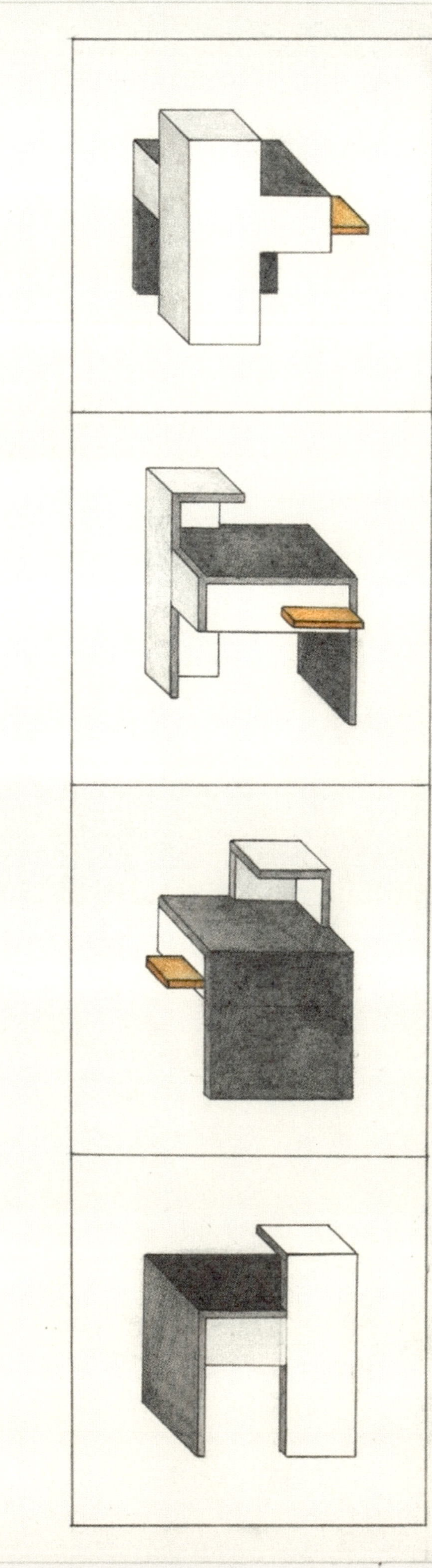

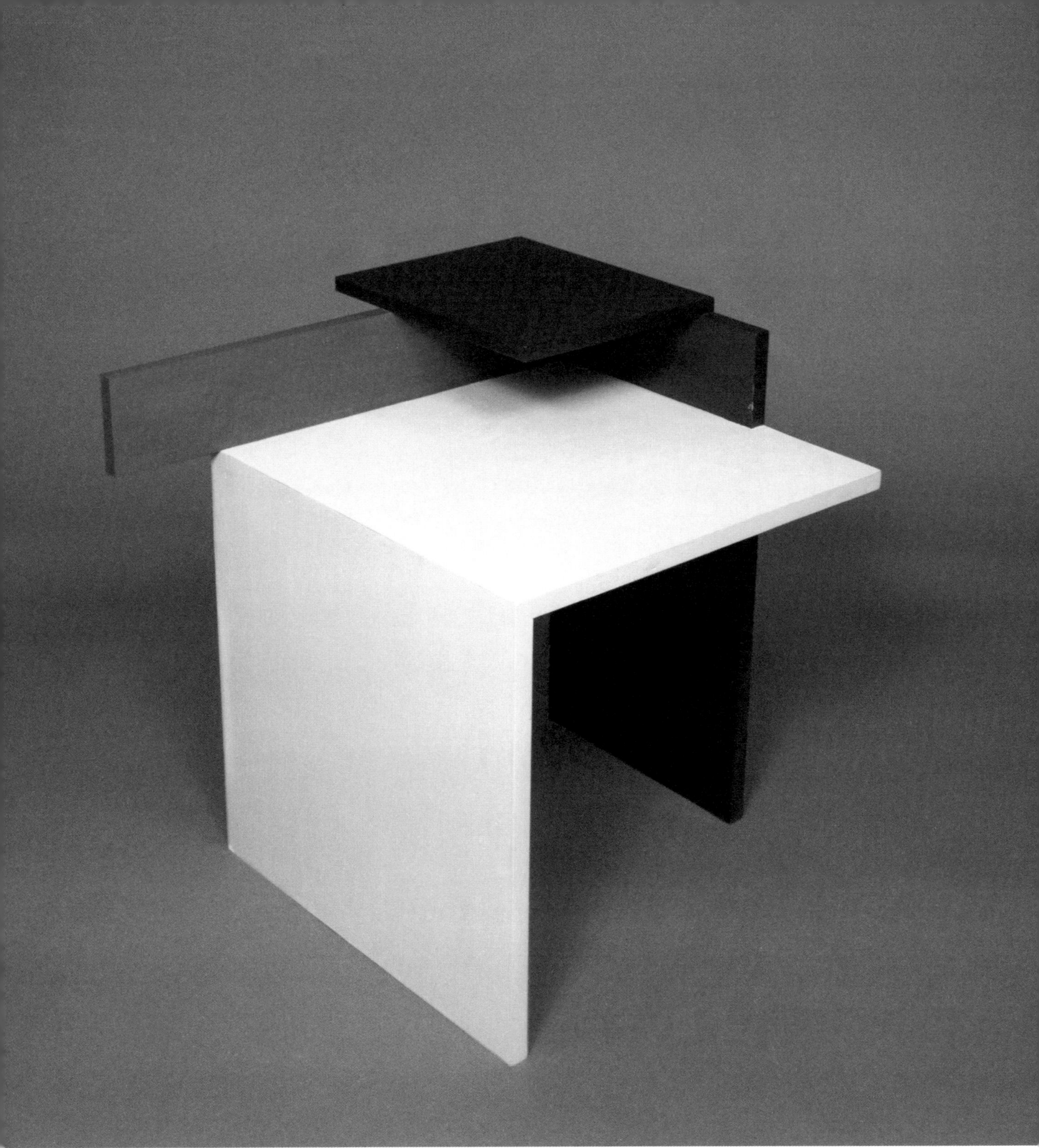

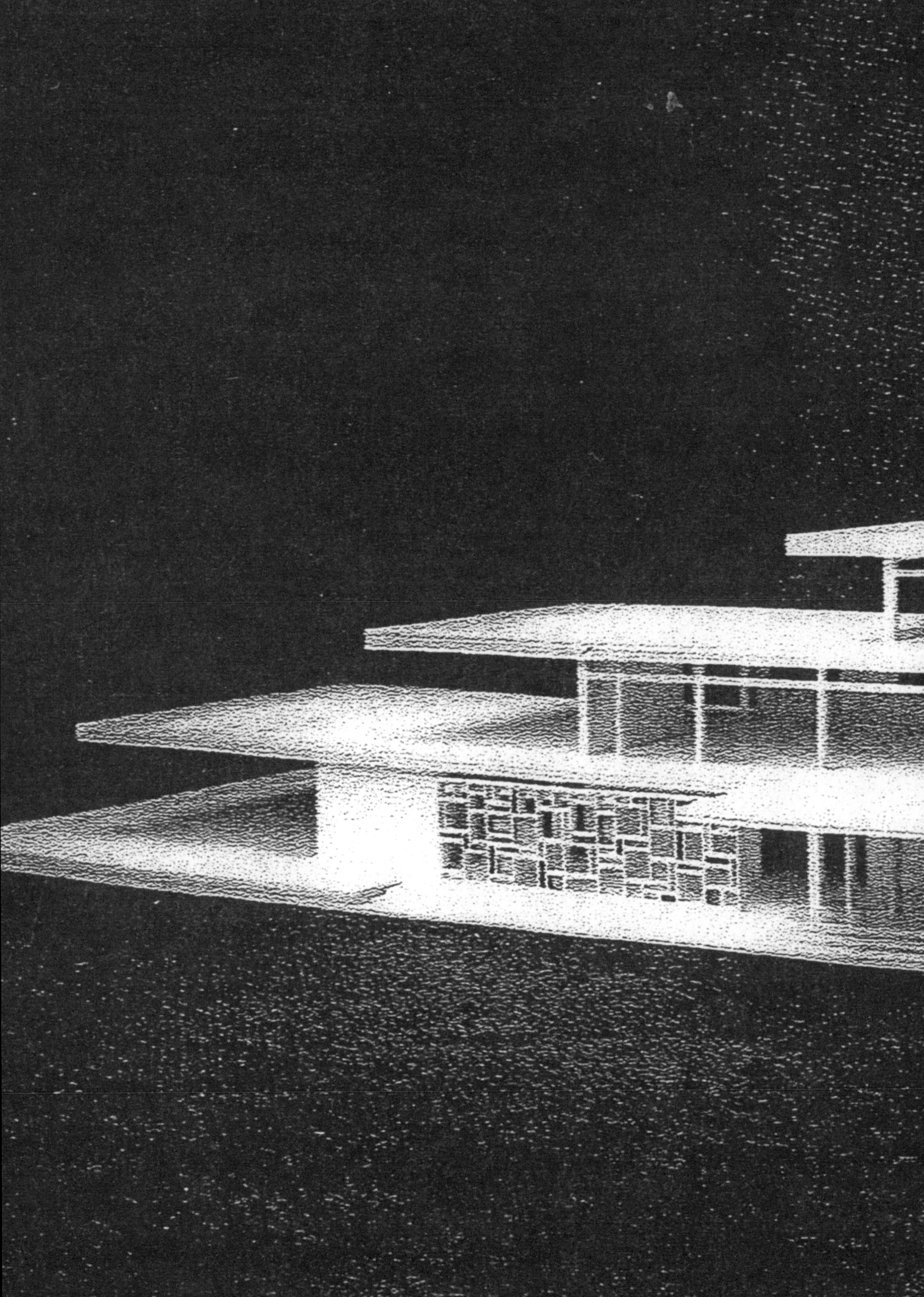

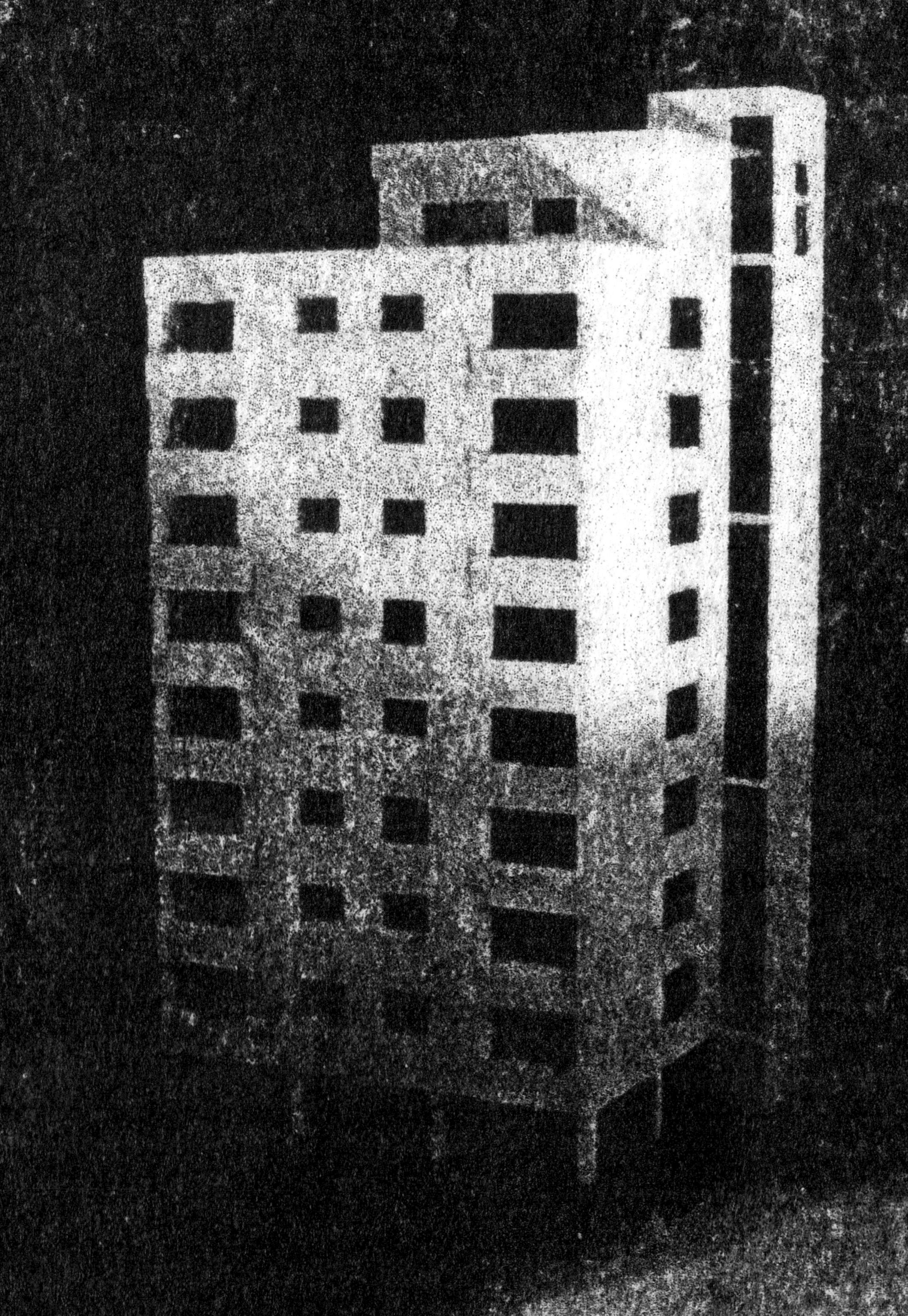

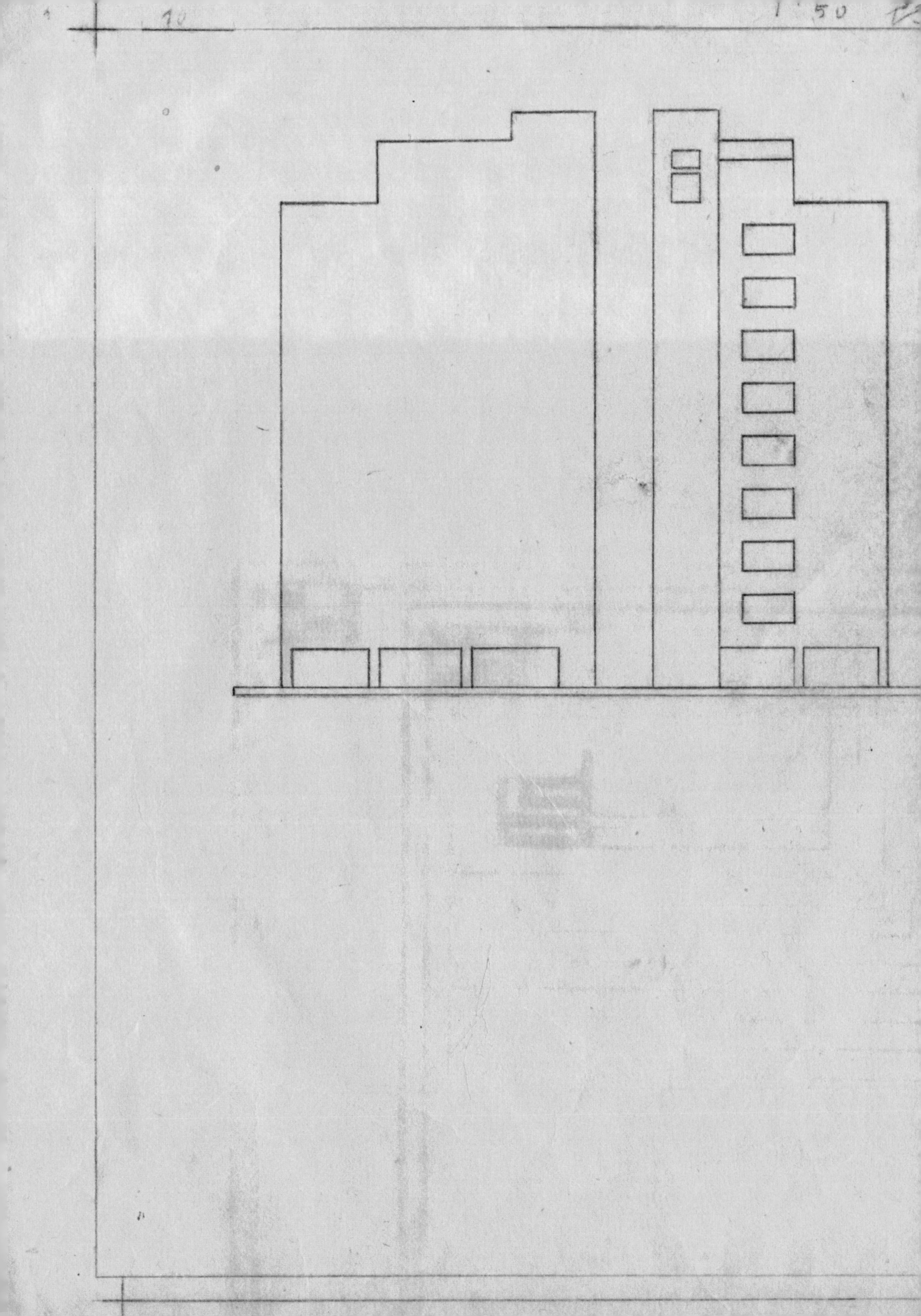

10
1:50

odu forcy

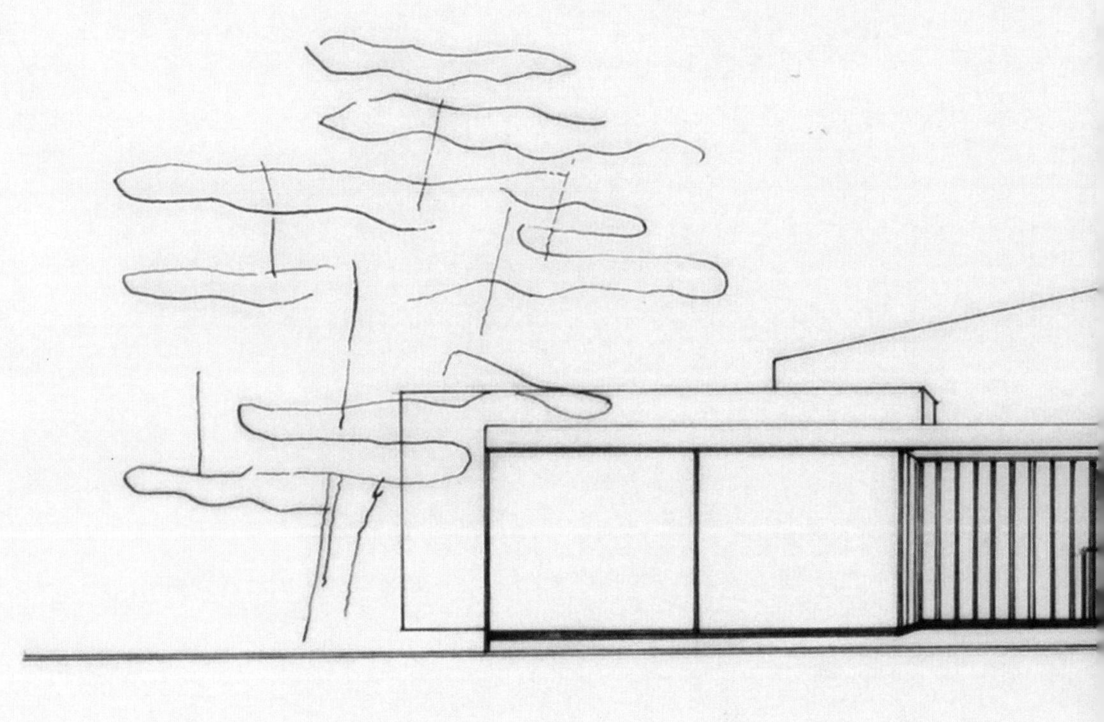

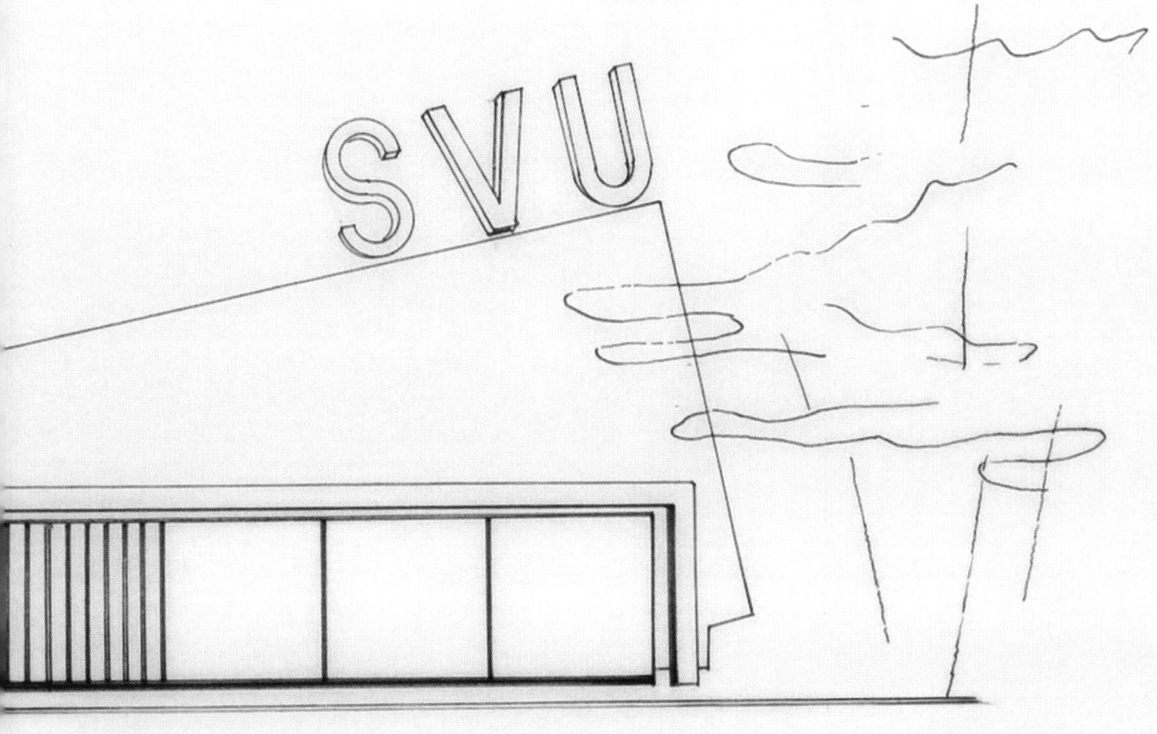
SVU

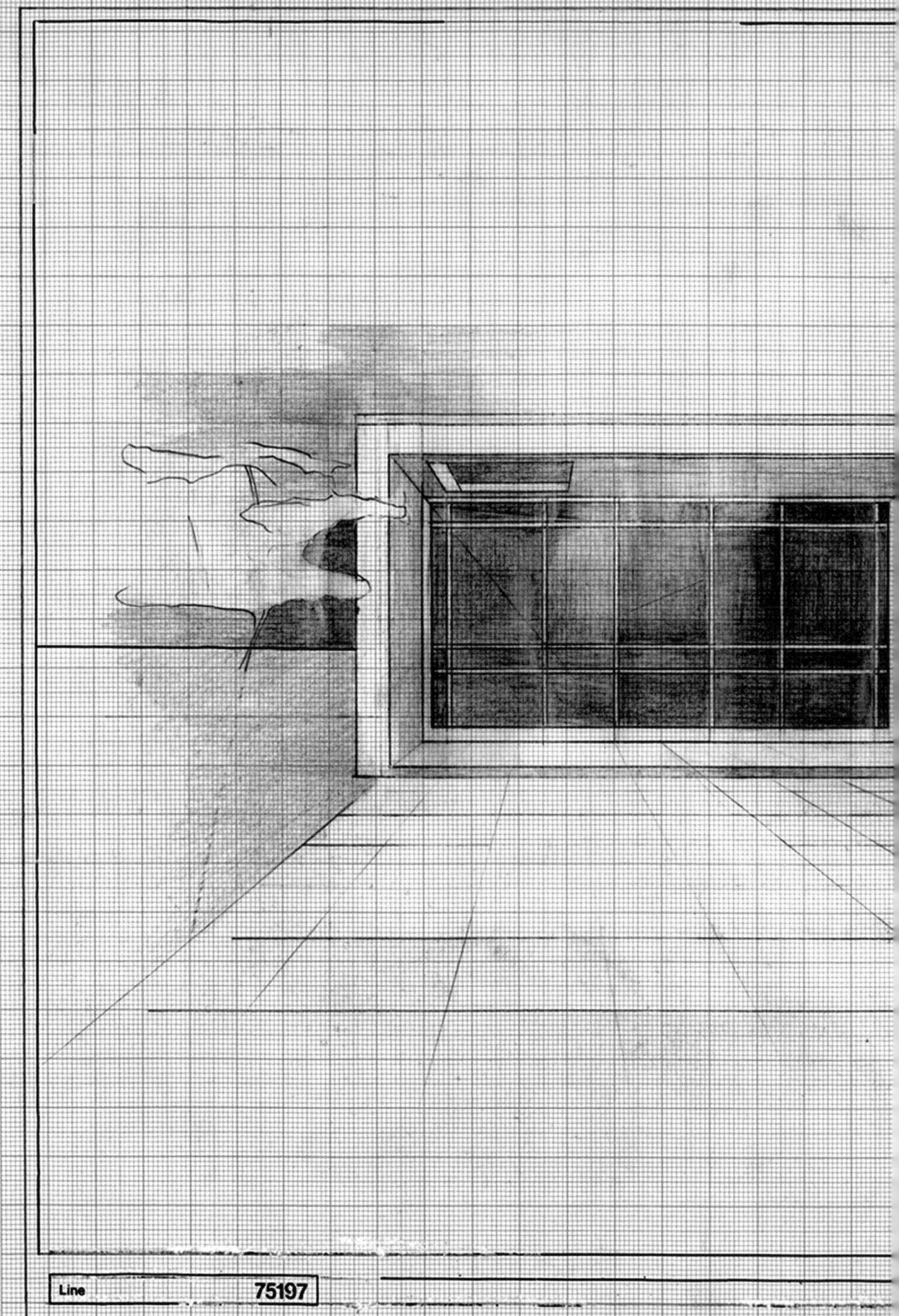

Line
75197

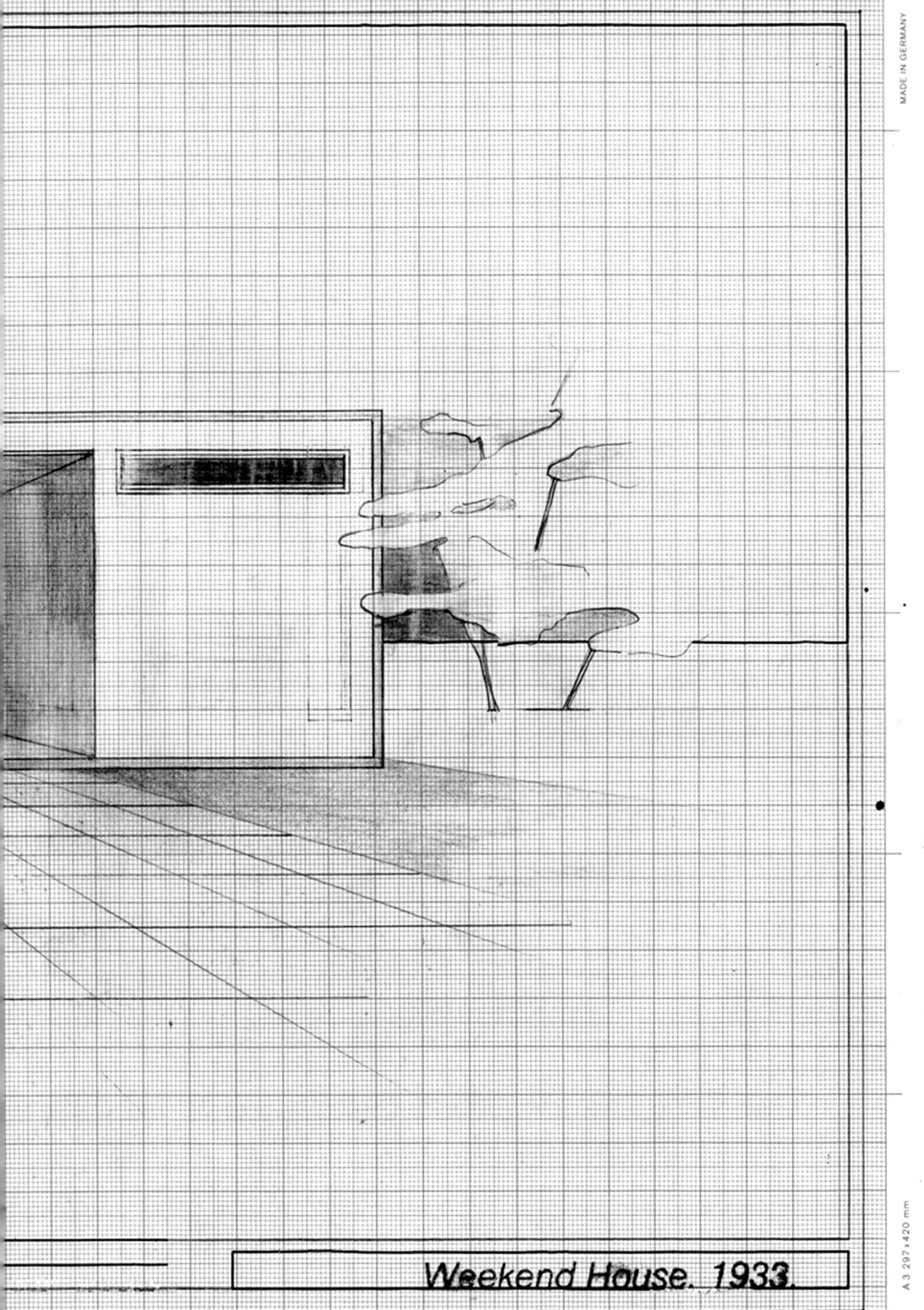
Weekend House. 1933.

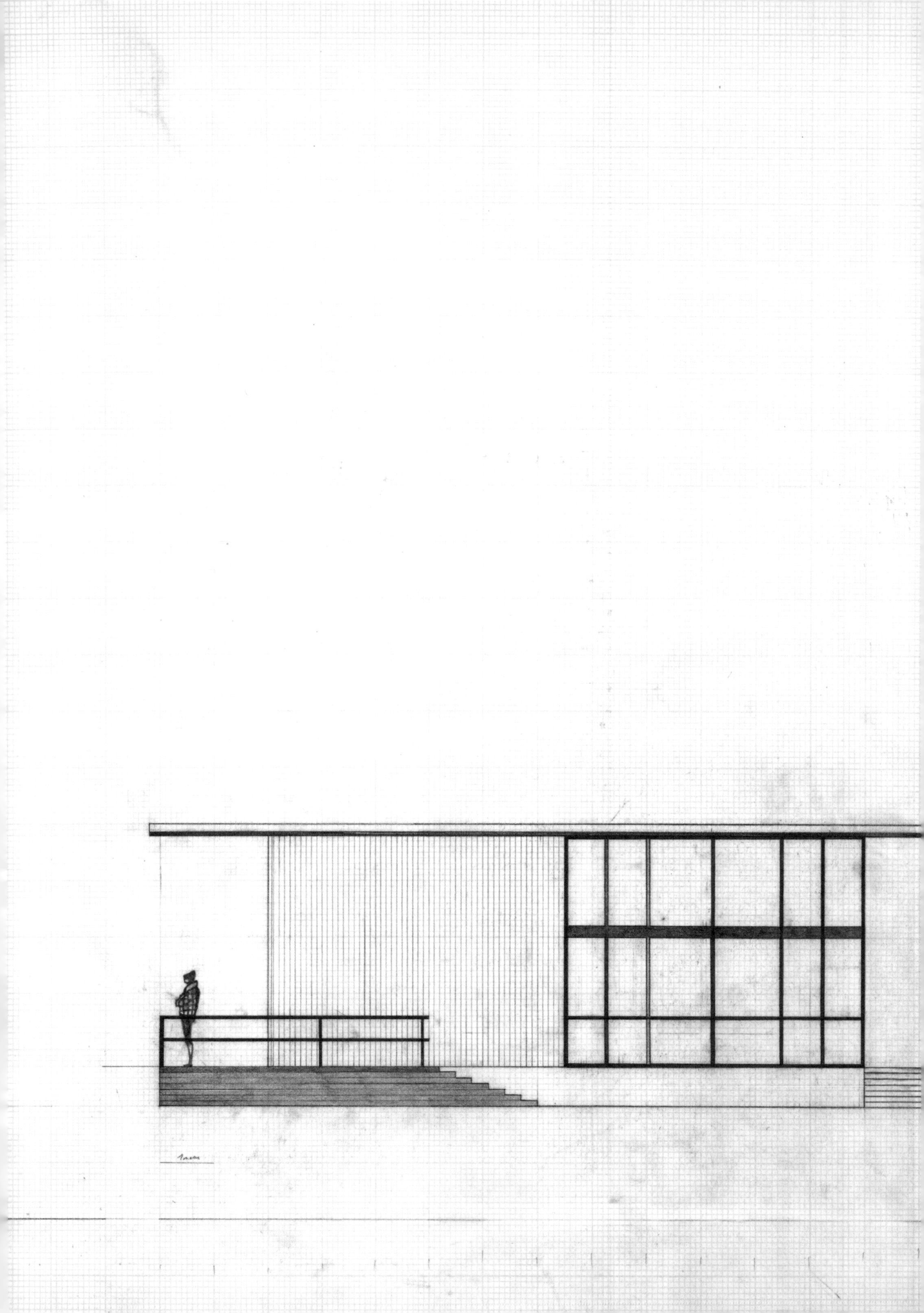

1m

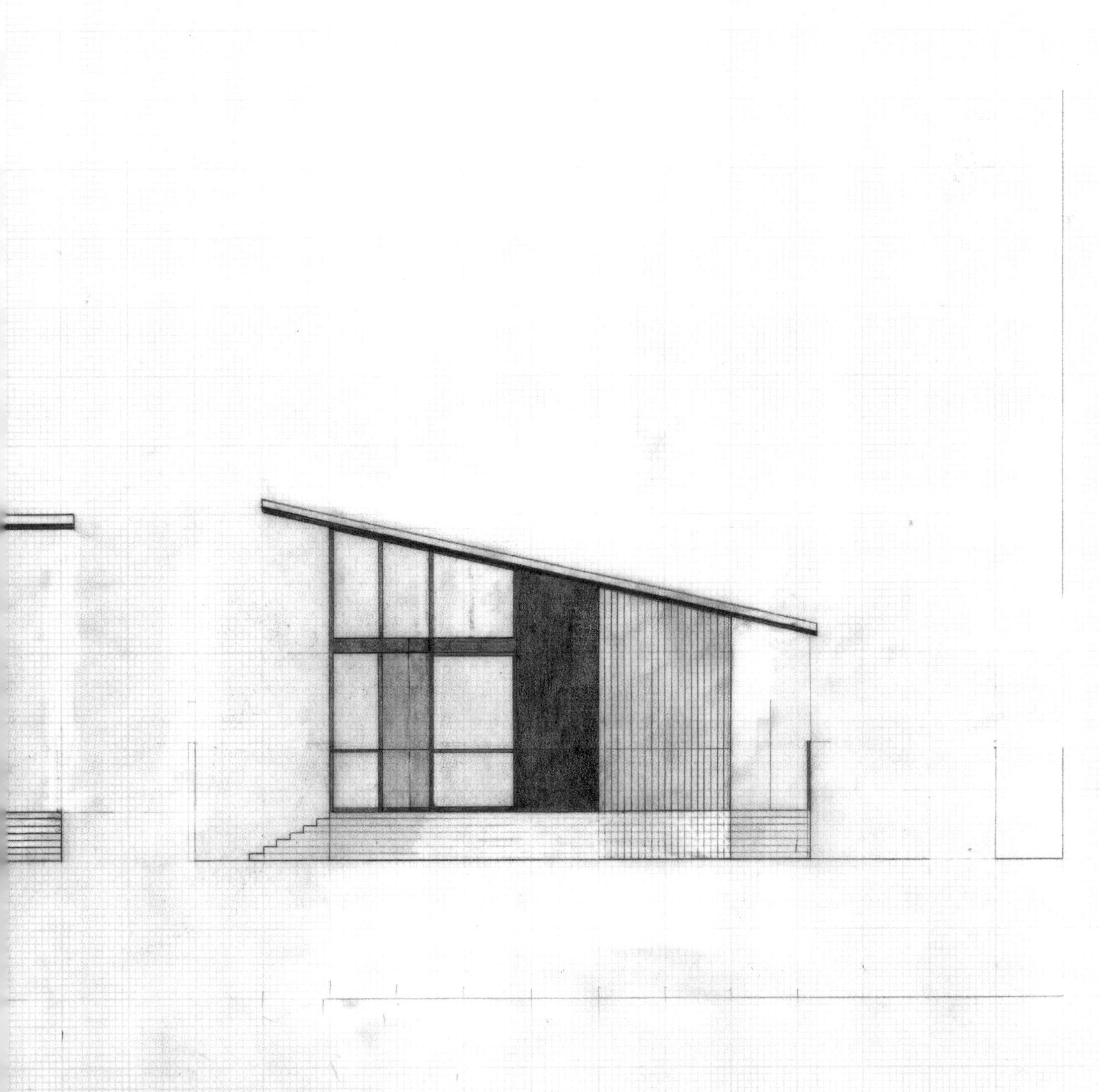

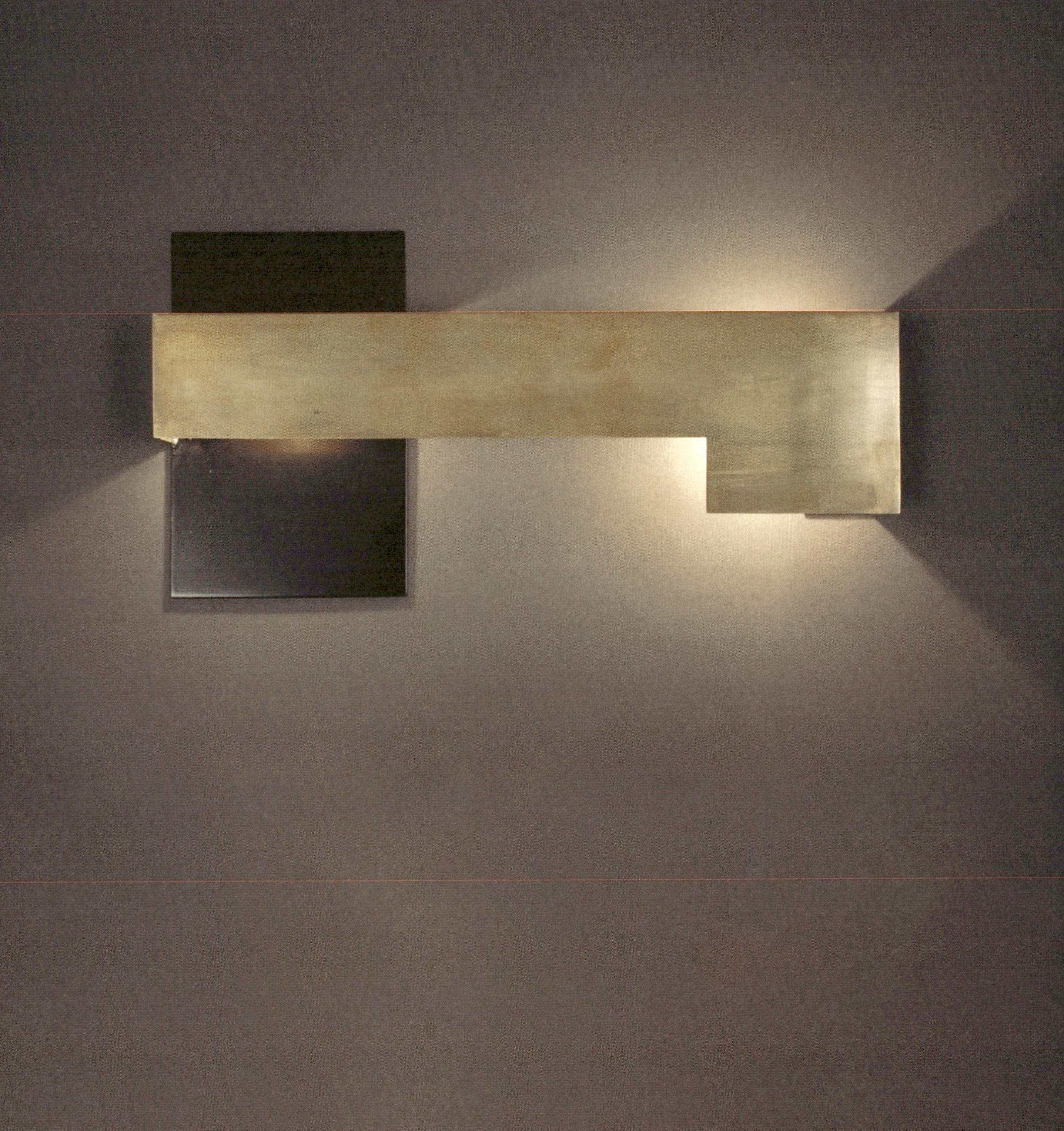

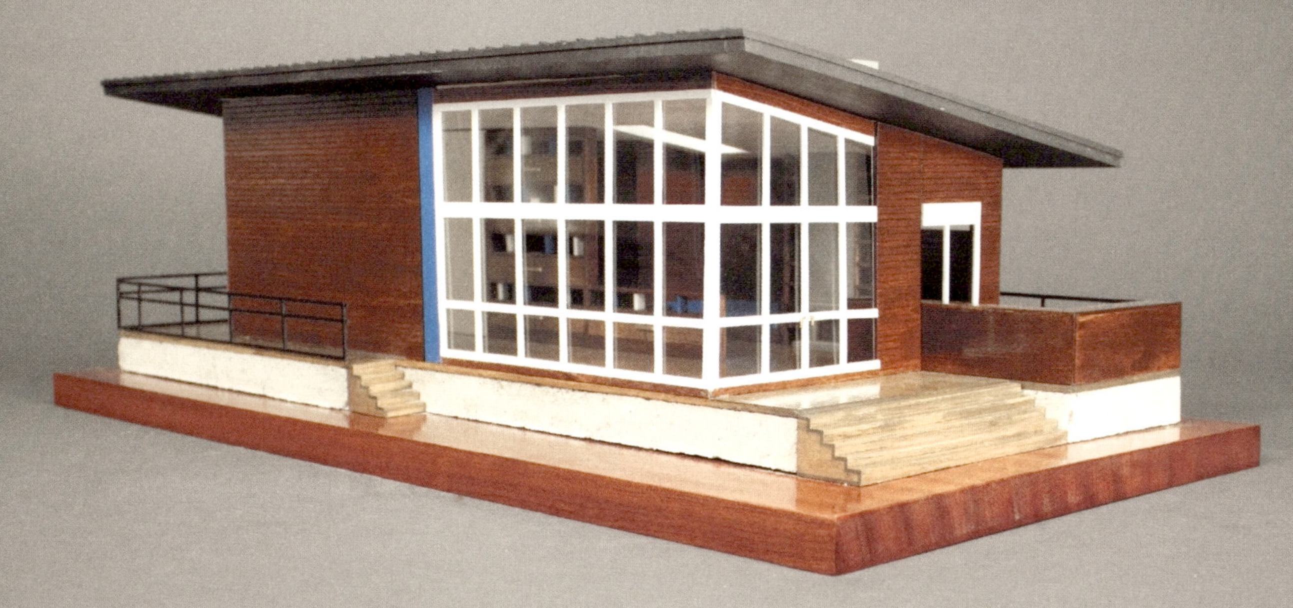

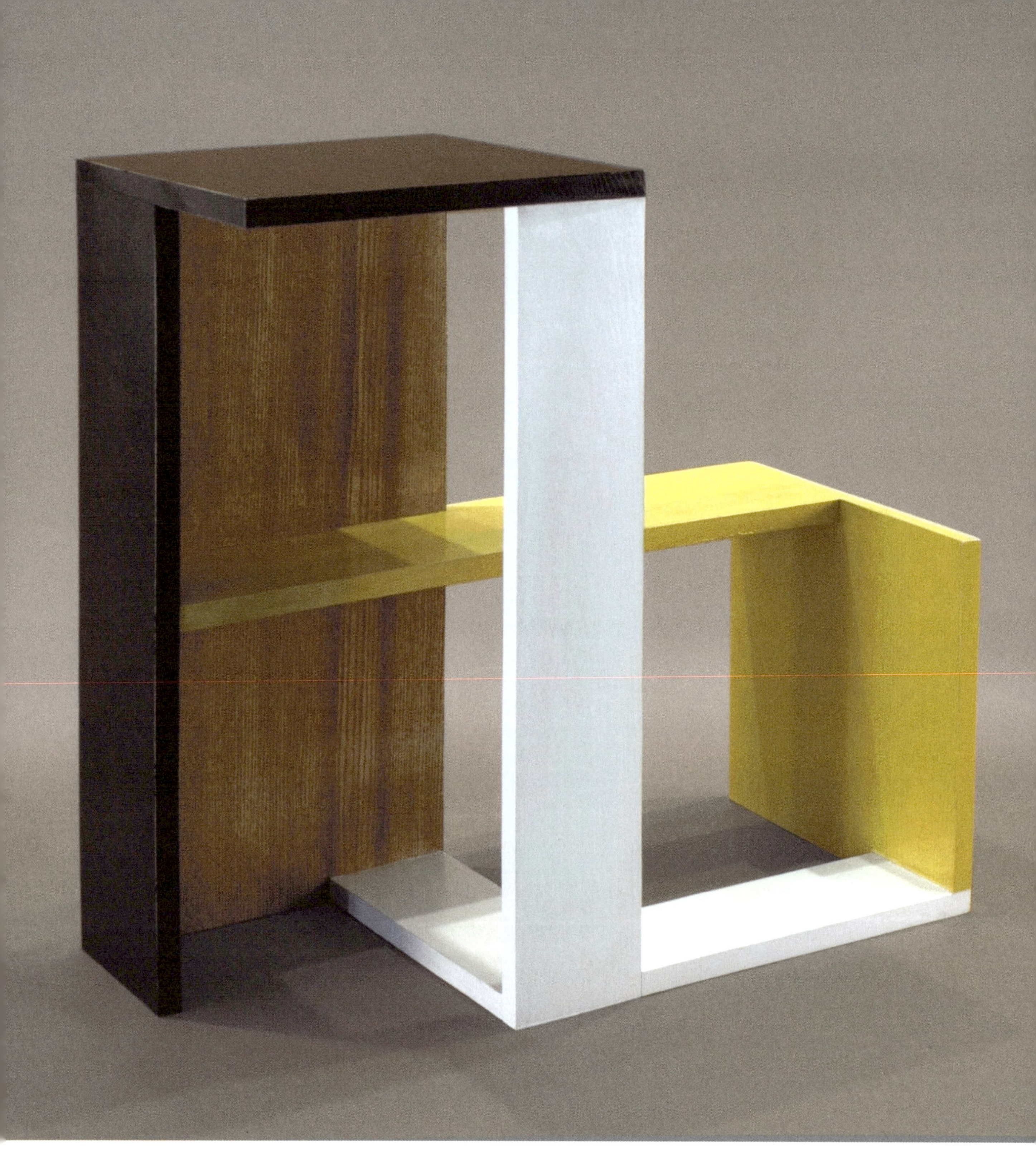

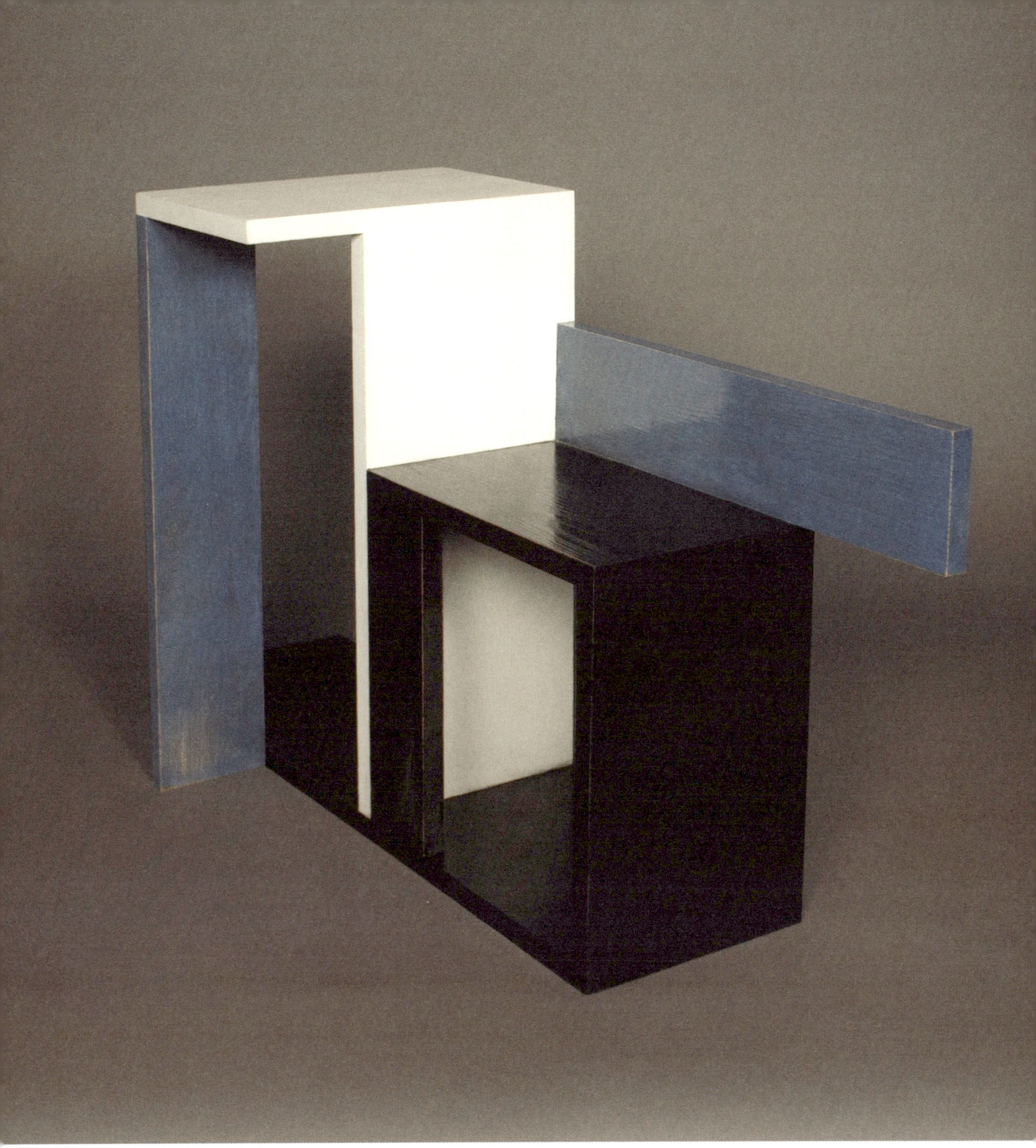

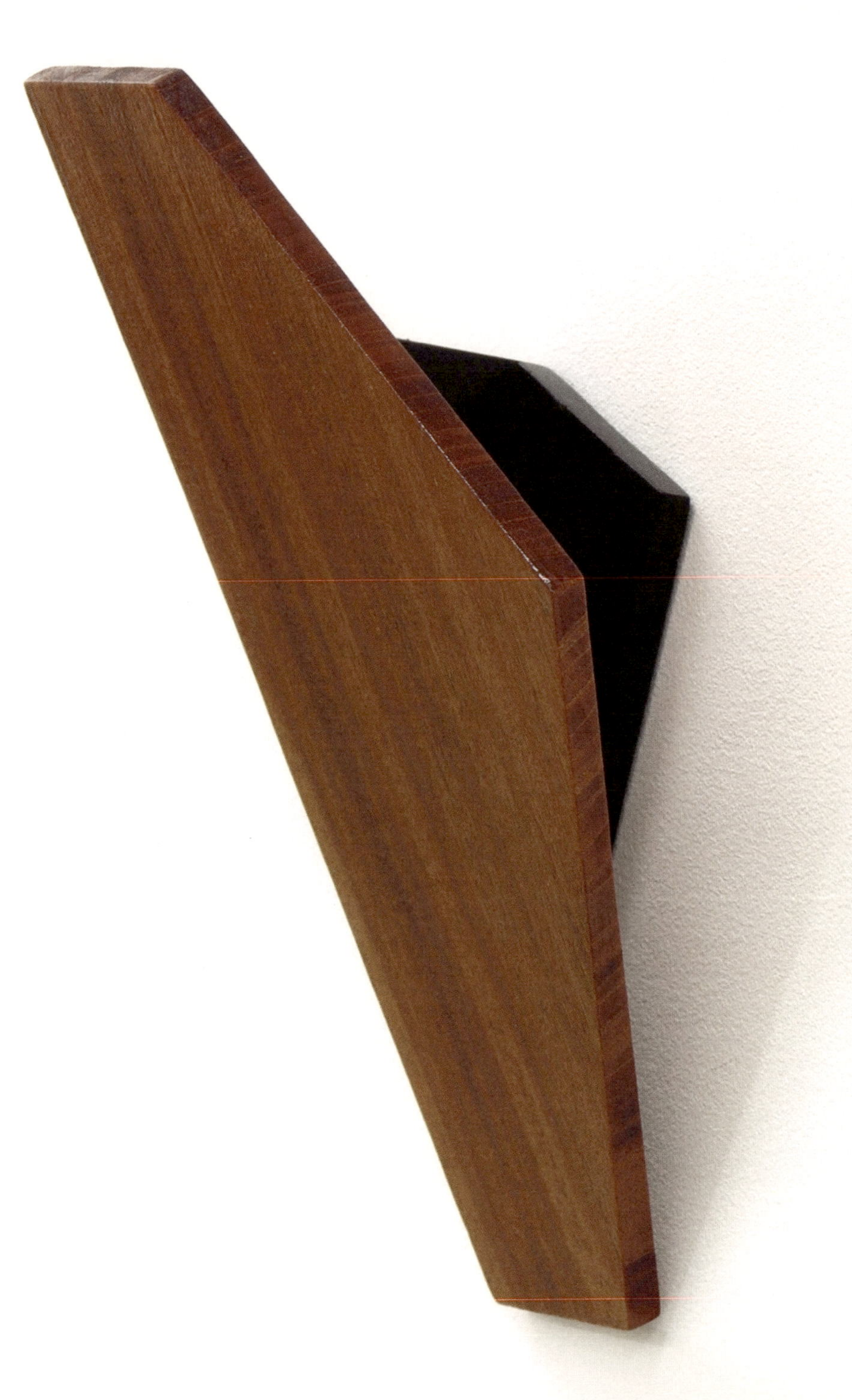

33
Petra Andrejova-Molnár, brise soleil for entrance, prototype design, Czechoslovakian Pavilion, 1925

34–35
Petra Andrejova-Molnár, Josef Gočár, interior for a modern woman, Czechoslovakian Pavilion, 1924–25

36–37
Petra Andrejova-Molnár, Josef Gočár, interior for a modern man, Czechoslovakian Pavilion, 1924–25

38–39
Ceramic Vases, Czechoslovakian Pavilion, 1918–22

40–41
Petra Andrejova-Molnár, pedestals for ceramic display, Czechoslovakian Pavilion, 1925

42–43
Petra Andrejova-Molnár, mahogany mirror brackets for the modern woman's interior, Czechoslovakian Pavilion, 1925

44–45
Petra Andrejova-Molnár, wood wall sconces, prototypes for Pavilion Lobby (vertical strips), 1927

46–47
Petra Andrejova-Molnár, rug designs for modern man's interior, Czechoslovakian Pavilion, 1925

48
Czechoslovakian Pavilion Model, Paris Arts Decoratifs, 1925/2015

51
Petra Andrejova-Molnár, cover design, Nová Strana, Vol. 2, 1928

52–53
Josef Zamazal, *Hotel Avion* in Brno, special reprint from Výtvarné snahy X, 1928–29

Petra Andrejova-Molnár, monogram design, ca. 1922

54–55
Petra Andrejova-Molnár, model for second project for storefront design, Žijeme, Brno, 1925–29

First project for storefront design, Žijeme, Ulica Lužická, Brno, 1929

56–57
Petra Andrejova-Molnár, drawing for Žijeme, storefront signage, Brno, 1925–29

58–59
Petra Andrejova-Molnár, project for storefront design, Brno 1937–39

60
Petra Andrejova-Molnár, second project for storefront design, Žijeme, Brno, 1925–29

63
Jan Víšek, project for Silhan Sanatorium, perspective view, Brno-Veveří, 1929–35

64–65
Jaromír Krejcar, Sanatorium Machnač, Trečianské Teplice, 1930–32

66–67
Jaromír Krejcar, Sanatorium Machnač interior room, Trečianské Teplice, 1930–32

68–69
Bohuslav Fuchs, alternative project for the Vesna Women's Vocational School, Brno-Stránice, 1929

70–71
Jaromír Krejcar, villa for a doctor, Zbraslav, near Prague, 1923

72
Jaromír Krejcar, villa for a doctor, Zbraslav, near Prague, 1923

75
Hotel Nord-Sud, north shade wall, view of corridor

76–77
Petra Andrejova–Molnár, drawing for north shade wall, Hotel Nord-Sud, 1932–34

78–79
North and south elevation drawings, Hotel Nord-Sud, 1932–34

80–81
Plan of ground floor showing hotel lobby and rooms, Hotel Nord-Sud, 1932–34

82–83
Hotel Nord-Sud, view from room interior, ca. 1938

84–85
Petra Andrejova-Molnár, Hotel Nord-Sud lobby interior perspective view, 1932–34

86–87
Hotel Nord-Sud, view from room interior, ca. 1938

88–89
Hotel Nord-Sud, writing desk and chair with cushion, 1930

90–91
Petra Andrejova-Molnár, square night table with drawer, Hotel Nord-Sud, 1930

Drawing for square night table with drawer, Hotel Nord- Sud 1930

92–93
Petra Andrejova-Molnár, hotel wall sconce design, ca. 1930

Petra Andrejova-Molnár, night table with blue, Hotel Nord- Sud, 1930

94
Petra Andrejova-Molnár, model, north view, Hotel Nord-Sud, 1932–34

97
Project for modern apartment for Czechoslovak Werkbund model, 1927

98–99
Project for modern apartment for Czechoslovak Werkbund drawing, 1927

100–101
Petra Andrejova-Molnár, competitive project for the Pavilion of the Group of Creative Artists in Brno, 1937

102–103
Petra Andrejova-Molnár, Weekend House, Felsogöd, perspective 1932

104–105
Petra Andrejova-Molnár, second project for Studio Efficiency for countryside, 1938–39

106–107
Petra Andrejova-Molnár, brass wall sconce for Studio Efficiency, 1948

Petra Andrejova-Molnár, model of Studio Efficiency for the Countryside, 1938–1956/2015

108–109
Petra Andrejova-Molnár, occasional table #1, with yellow, 1930

Occasional Table #2, with blue, 1930

110
Mahogany wall sconce with black, ca. 1934

NOM DE PLUME

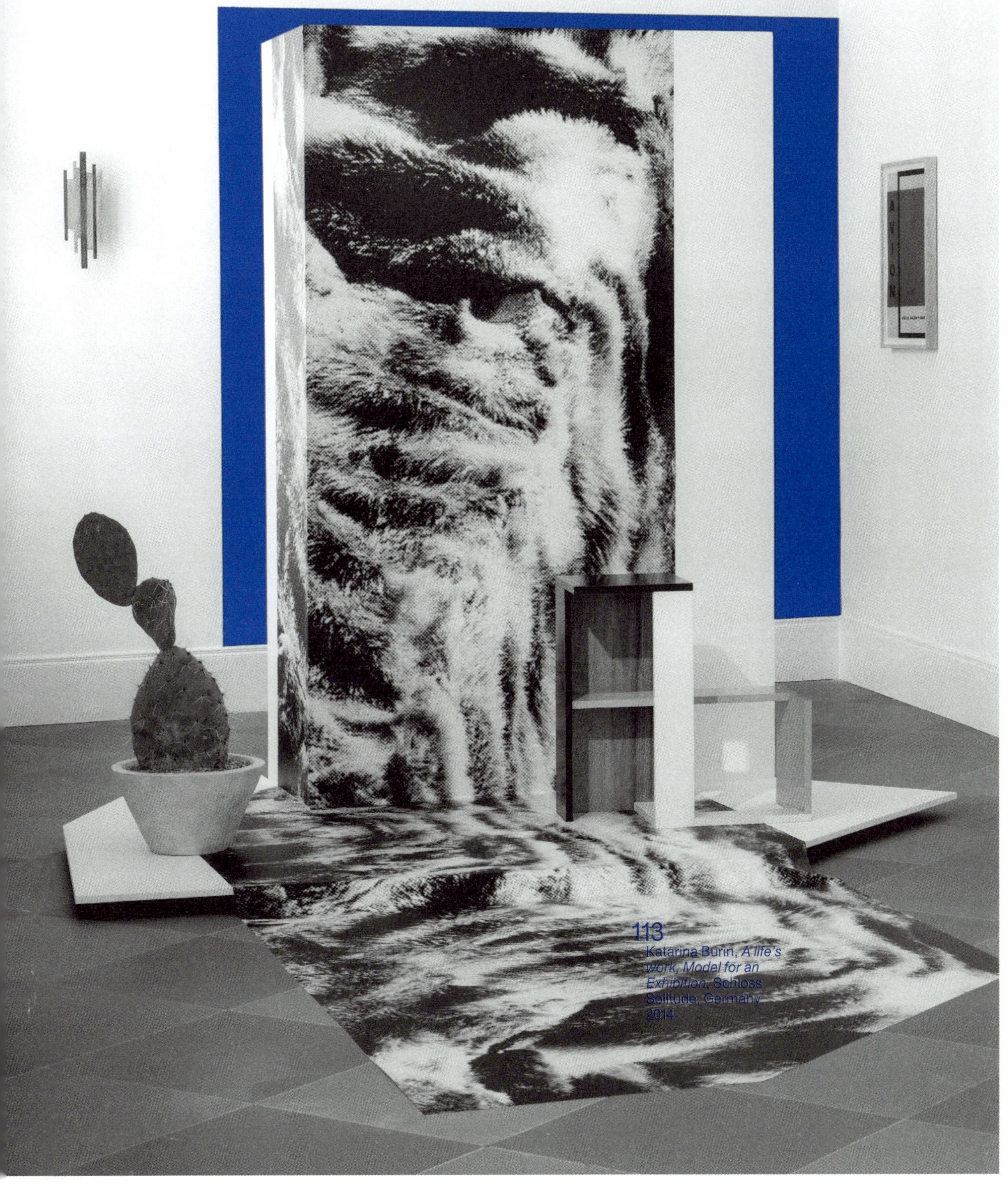

113
Katarina Burin, *A life's work, Model for an Exhibition*, Schloss Solitude, Germany, 2014

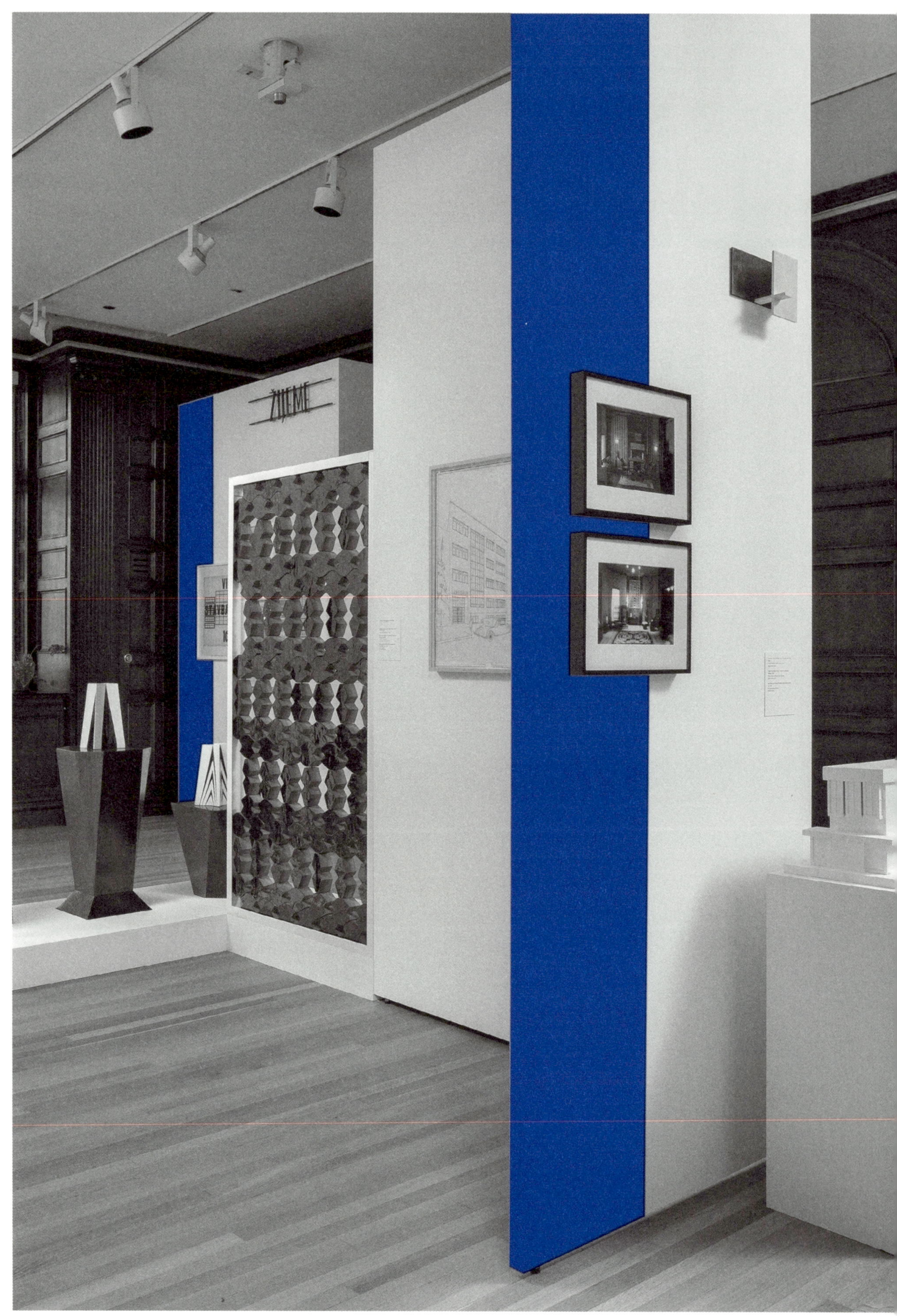

In 1932, a young Czechoslovakian architect named Petra Andrejova-Molnàr—known later as "P.A."—designed what was to become her signature interwar work: the *Hotel Nord-Sud*. To date, the best source of information on this building and its remarkable architect, who was active in the fertile period between the first and second world wars, is a slim volume entitled *Between Brno and Budapest: The work of Petra Andrejova-Molnár and her Contemporaries*, apparently published in 1976 to accompany an eponymous exhibition at the Architectural Association in London. Destroyed during the Second World War, the hotel was located on the Adriatic coast, near the city of Zadar in present-day Croatia. It contained fourteen cabin-like bedrooms and two suites, all with balconies, as well as an impressive lookout café on the third floor and an open restaurant and bar on the second. Nord-Sud's most arresting design elements comprised the remarkable terraces and large panes of glass that united interior to exterior, and its cantilevered design and extensive use of glass were complemented by custom-designed furniture and interior fittings.

Today, our knowledge of Petra Andrejova-Molnàr is largely due to the efforts of the Slovakian-born Canadian-American artist Katarina Burin, working at times in collaboration with a small coterie of friends and associates. The process of discovering and shedding light on the work of P.A. presented a daunting task for Burin—not only in creating the work itself (in the form of architectural drawings and models, graphic design, furniture, and "archival" photographs) but also the scholarly apparatus documenting P.A.'s contemporary rediscovery.

In the most recent chapter of this ongoing project, Burin has recovered and presented P.A.'s contribution to Josef Gočár's Czechoslovakian pavilion at the 1925 *Exposition Internationale des Arts Décoratifs et Industriels Modernes* in Paris. There, P.A.'s work appeared alongside that of other young architects such as Farkas Molnár, Jósef Fischer, Jaromír Krejcar, Bohuslav Fuchs, all of whom are actual

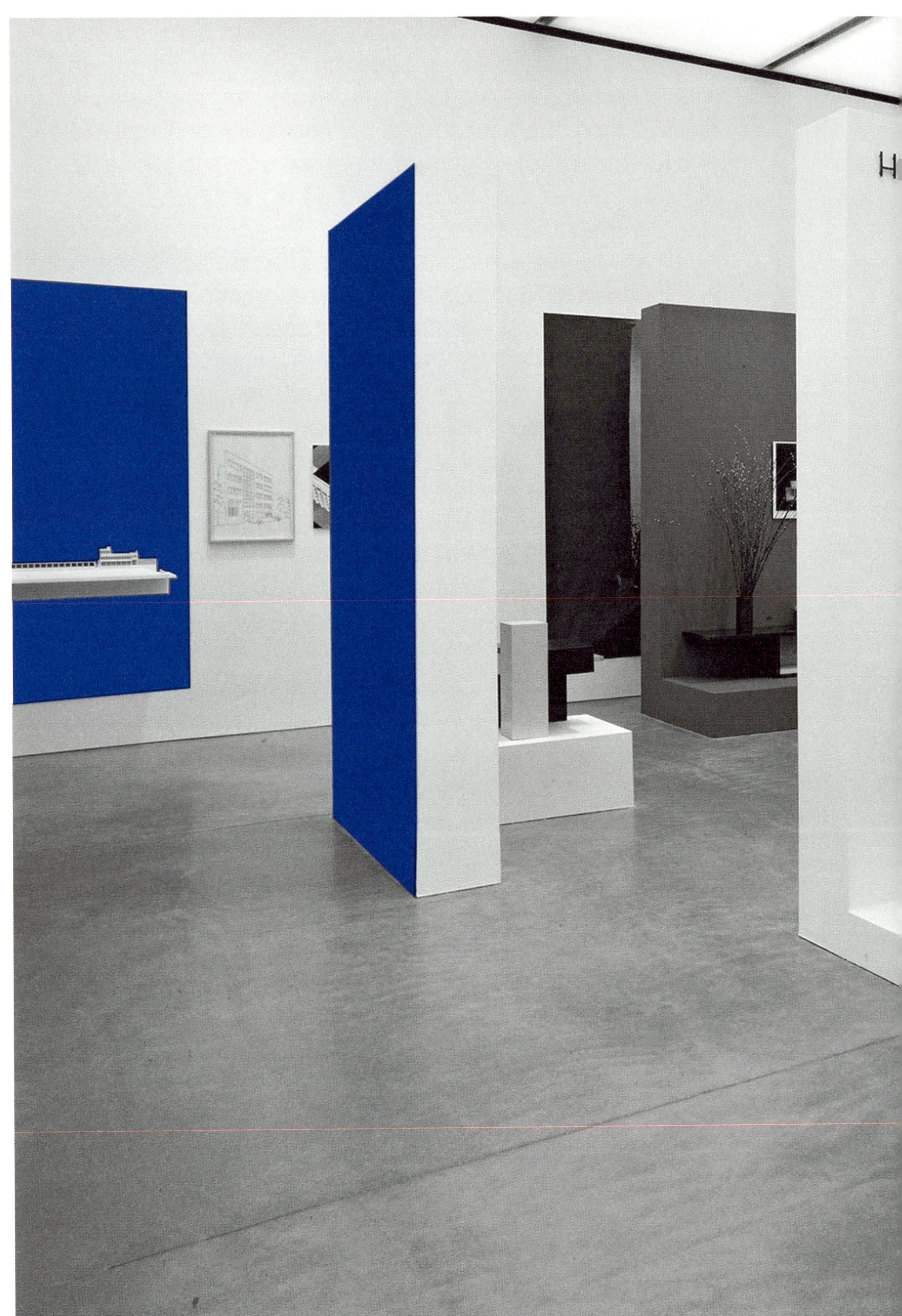

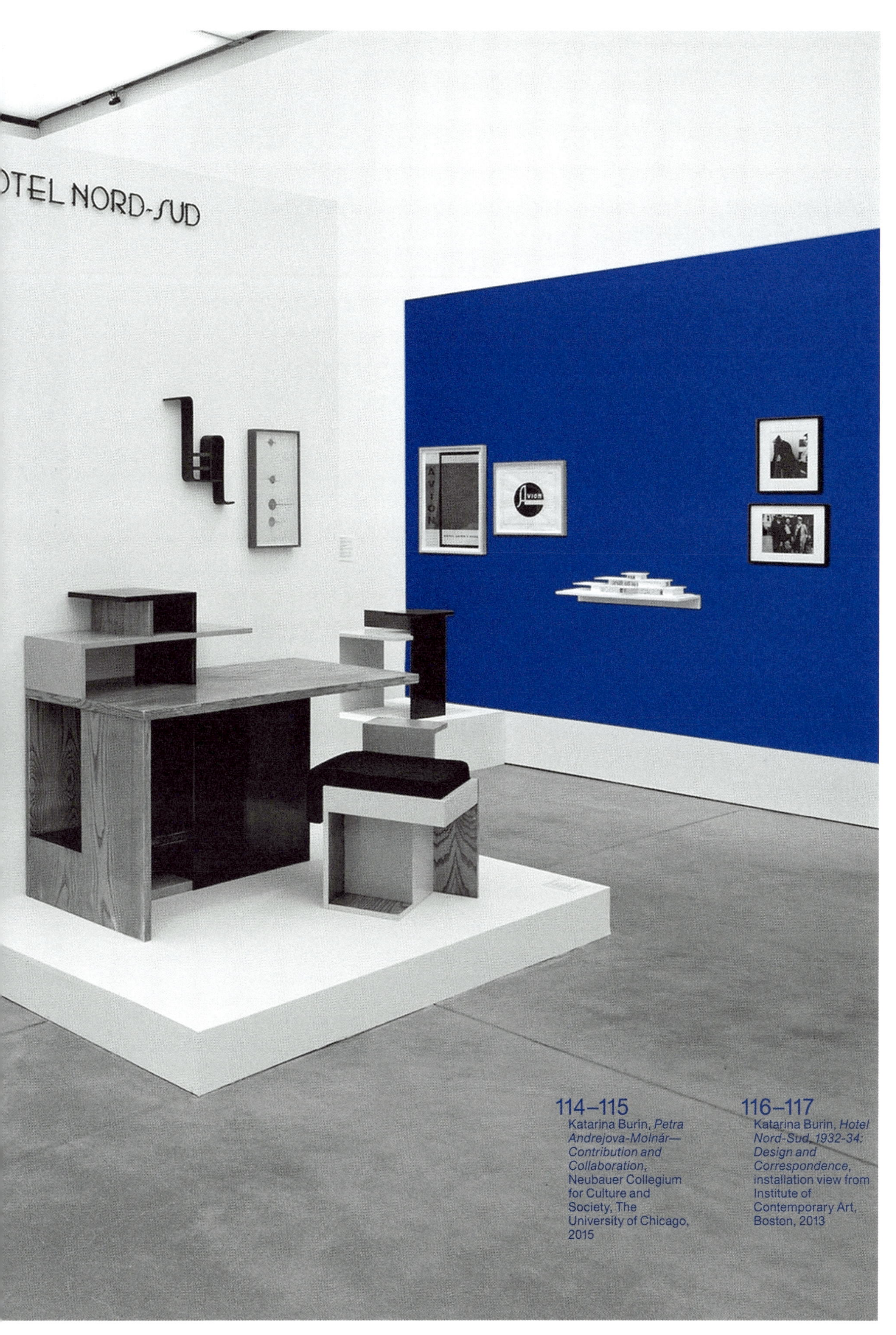

114–115
Katarina Burin, *Petra Andrejova-Molnár— Contribution and Collaboration*, Neubauer Collegium for Culture and Society, The University of Chicago, 2015

116–117
Katarina Burin, *Hotel Nord-Sud, 1932-34: Design and Correspondence*, installation view from Institute of Contemporary Art, Boston, 2013

historical figures—or, put differently, figures whose proper names have entered into the historical record.

In a sense, P.A. functions as what Alfred Hitchcock famously termed the MacGuffin—that is, the element in a film or story that serves to set the plot in motion and keep the action moving despite usually lacking intrinsic importance. In this way, the significance of P.A. and her narrative lies less in the specific story it tells than in the formal and conceptual moves that its structure makes possible. Part alter ego, part historical intervention, P.A. serves as a kind of cipher, allowing Burin to participate in the social, political, and aesthetic debates of an earlier historical moment.

Then and now, P.A. questions notions of authorship and authenticity, the relationship between gender and the archive, and the historical tension between national identity and internationalist aspiration. Alongside the production of P.A.'s works, Burin mobilizes the tropes and techniques of contemporary museological and academic discourse to establish the artistic persona of a figure who may not have actually existed but just as easily could have, pointing along the way to the mutability of the historical record itself. As Burin herself has noted, it is ultimately less important that P.A. is a fiction than that we encounter her as a previously unknown player in this historical milieu. In filling in for the figures we don't encounter in dominant historical narratives— those whose proper names are no longer available to us— she calls attention to their very real absence.

P.A. is also part of a long artistic and philosophical tradition of pseudonymous authorship. Of course, authors take on alternative identities for myriad reasons. In the literary realm, such considerations are often ones of practicality. An author with an established reputation in one genre may adopt a *nom de plume* when making a foray into another, or when it seems necessary to avoid the appearance of being *too* productive. In social and political contexts, pseudonymity may be the necessary corollary of anonymity, whether in order to

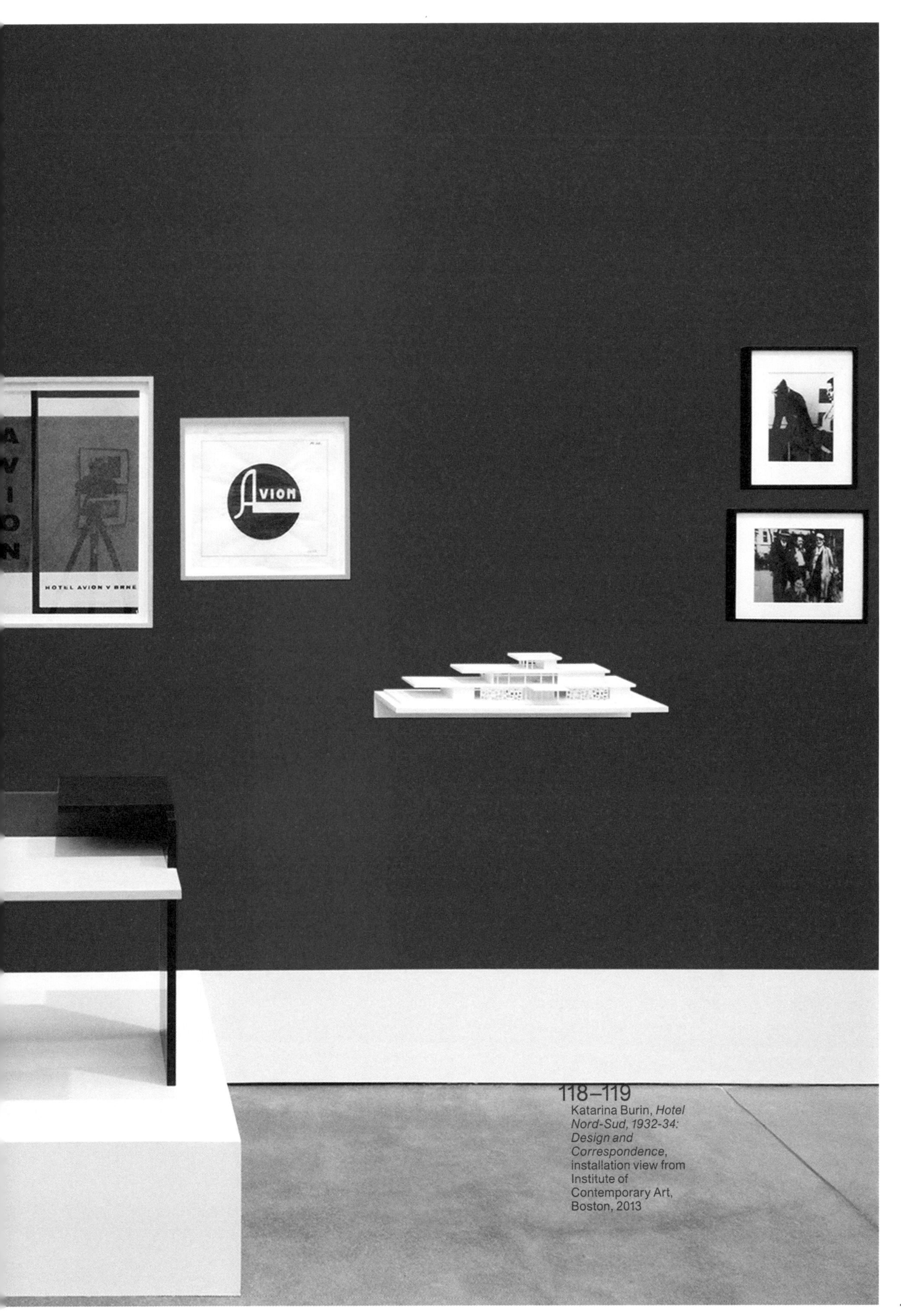

118–119
Katarina Burin, *Hotel Nord-Sud, 1932-34: Design and Correspondence*, installation view from Institute of Contemporary Art, Boston, 2013

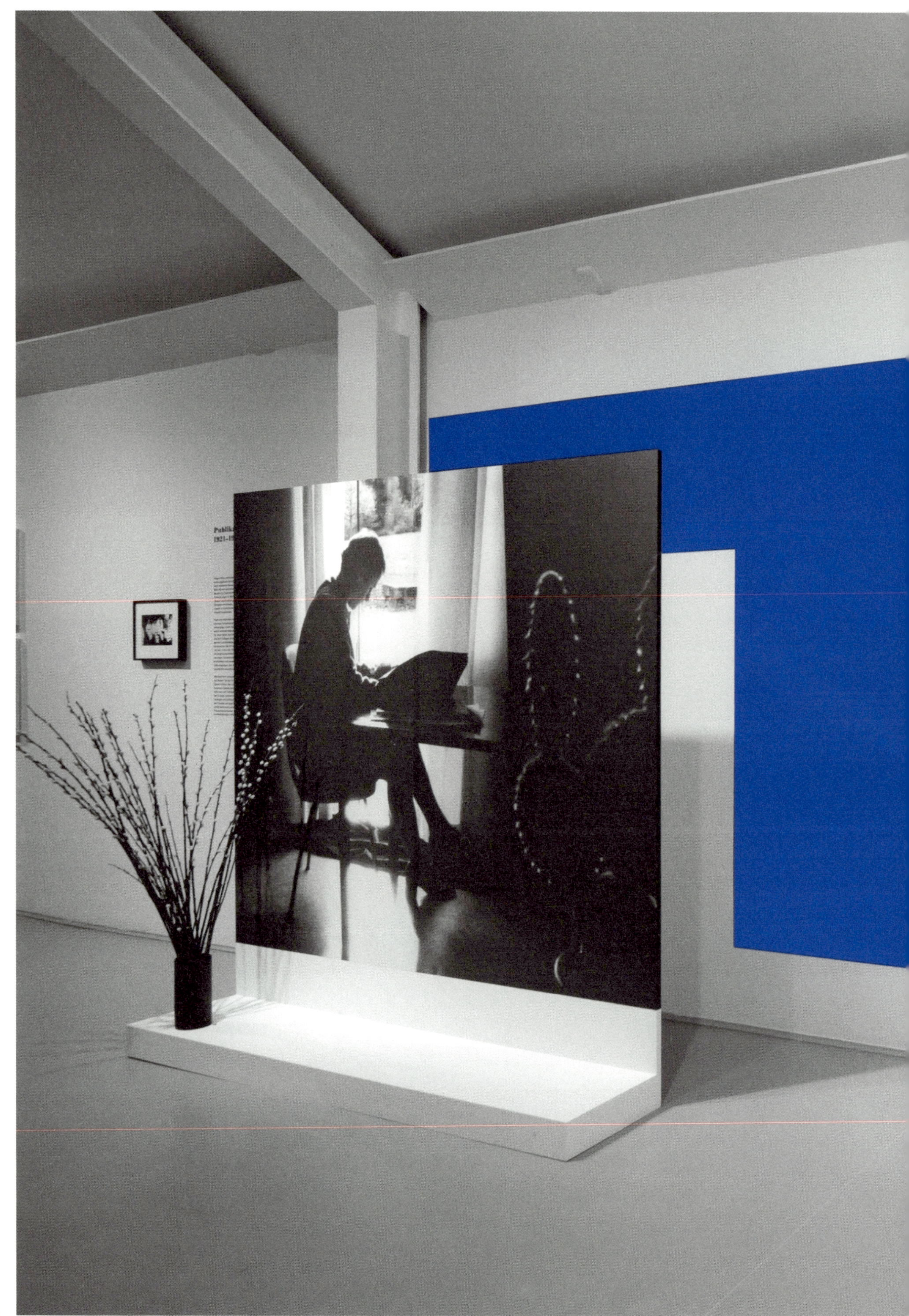

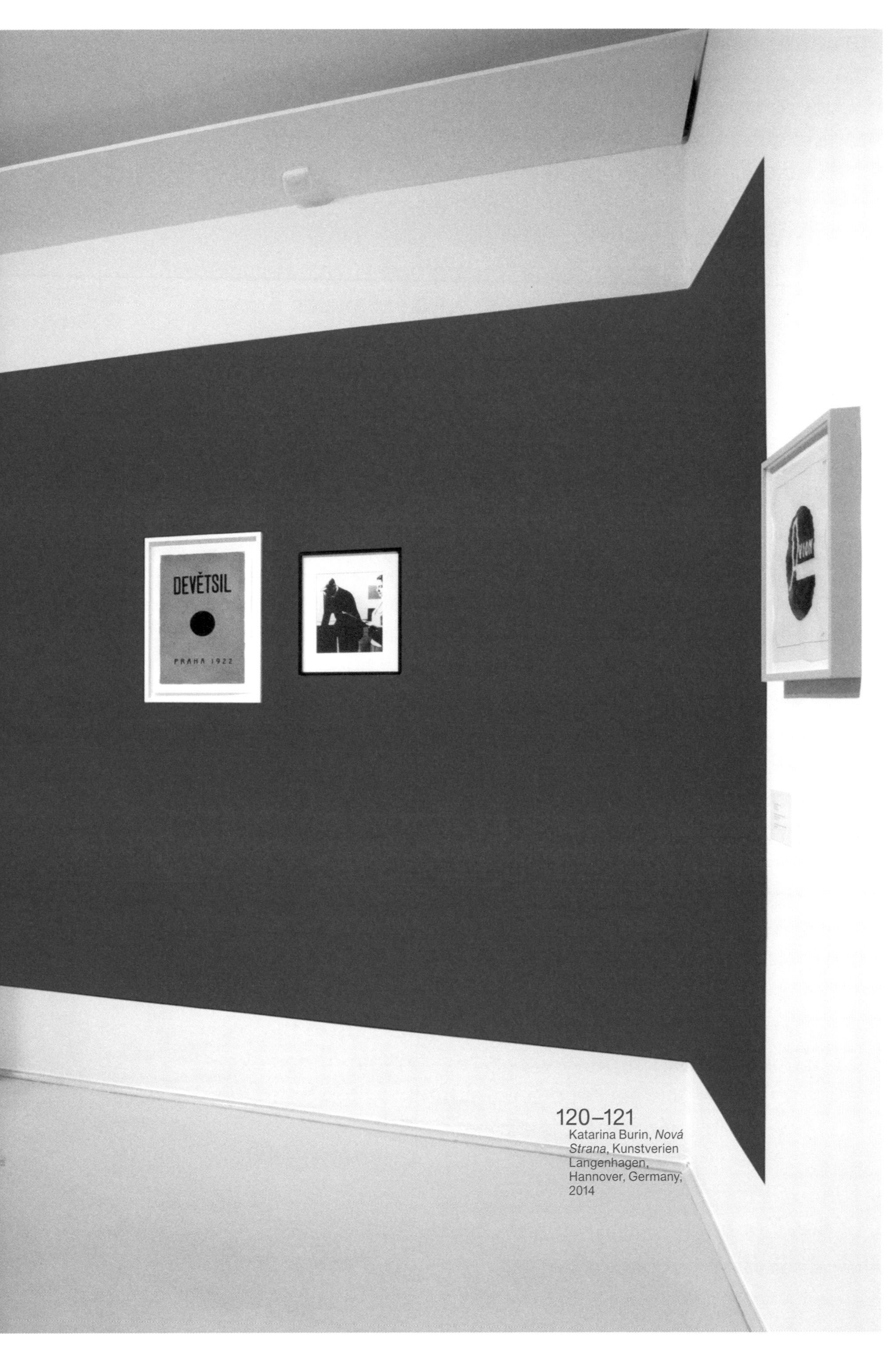

120–121
Katarina Burin, *Nová Strana*, Kunstverien Langenhagen, Hannover, Germany, 2014

preserve one's standing or to guard against physical harm or incarceration. Søren Kierkegaard adopted a long series of pseudonyms in order to explore complex philosophical problems from different perspectives. Closer to home, a vigorous anti-subjective drive can be traced through much twentieth-century art and music, with artists and composers devising a host of strategies designed to keep their own subjectivity out of their work and the compositional decisions that go into making it. Recent years have witnessed a vogue for invented, oftentimes collective, artistic identities that seek to interrogate corporate or quasi-state constructions of authorship.

None of these motivations, however, seem to adequately describe Katarina Burin's careful elaboration of Petra Andrejova-Molnár and her context. A more kindred spirit might be Pierre Menard, who in Borges's story writes and rewrites certain fragments of *Don Quixote*, with complete and utter authenticity, three centuries after Miguel de Cervantes first composed them. As with Menard, the ultimate aim of P.A. and her work is not to deceive, much less to parrot. But Burin's process is not quite that of Menard, either. In creating the work of P.A. and her contemporaries, Burin is not only making works that might exist elsewhere in the world, although that is sometimes the case. Rather, her particular combination of deliberate anachronism and erroneous attribution (to borrow terms from Borges) makes it possible to bring something new into the world, while at the same time prompting a re-thinking of what already exists.

We might say that to design the Hotel Nord-Sud in the early part of the twentieth century was a reasonable undertaking, necessary and perhaps even unavoidable; at the beginning of the twenty-first century, it is almost impossible.

— Jacob Proctor
Curator, Neubauer Collegium for Culture and Society, University of Chicago

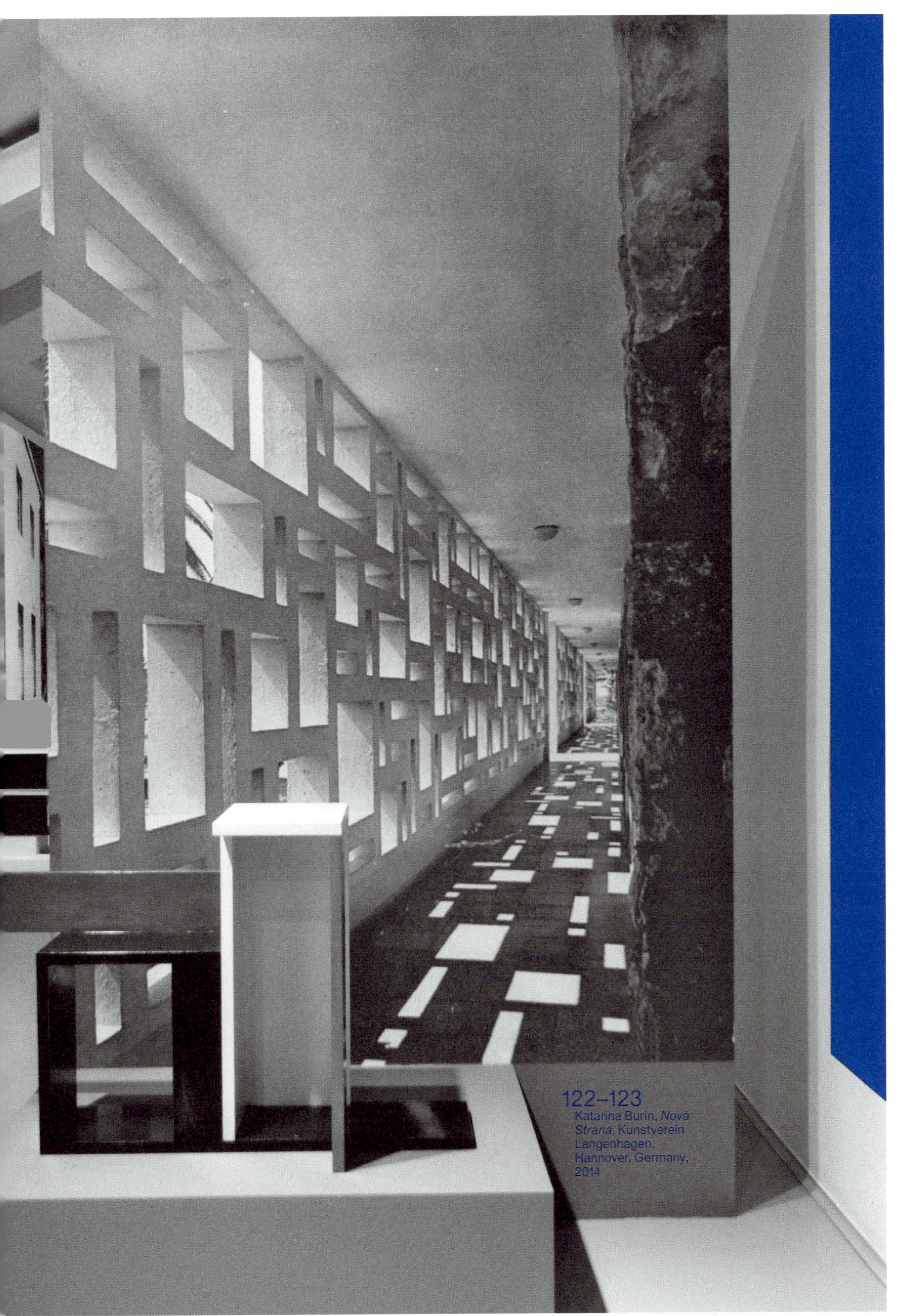

122–123
Katarina Burin, *Nová Strana*, Kunstverein Langenhagen, Hannover, Germany, 2014

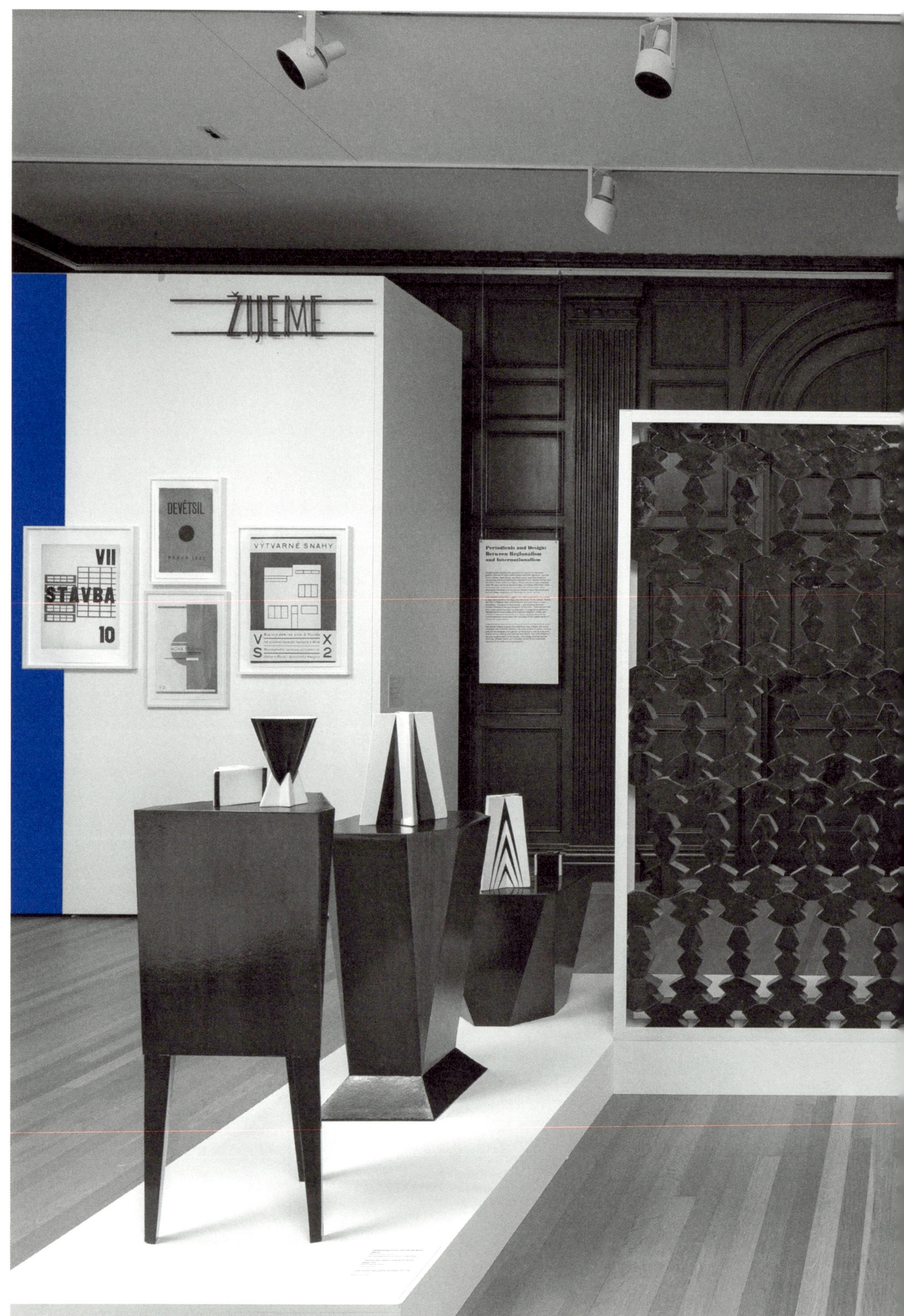
ŽIJEME
STAVBA VII 10
DEVĚTSIL
VÝTVARNÉ SNAHY
Periodicals and Design:
Between Regionalism
and Internationalism

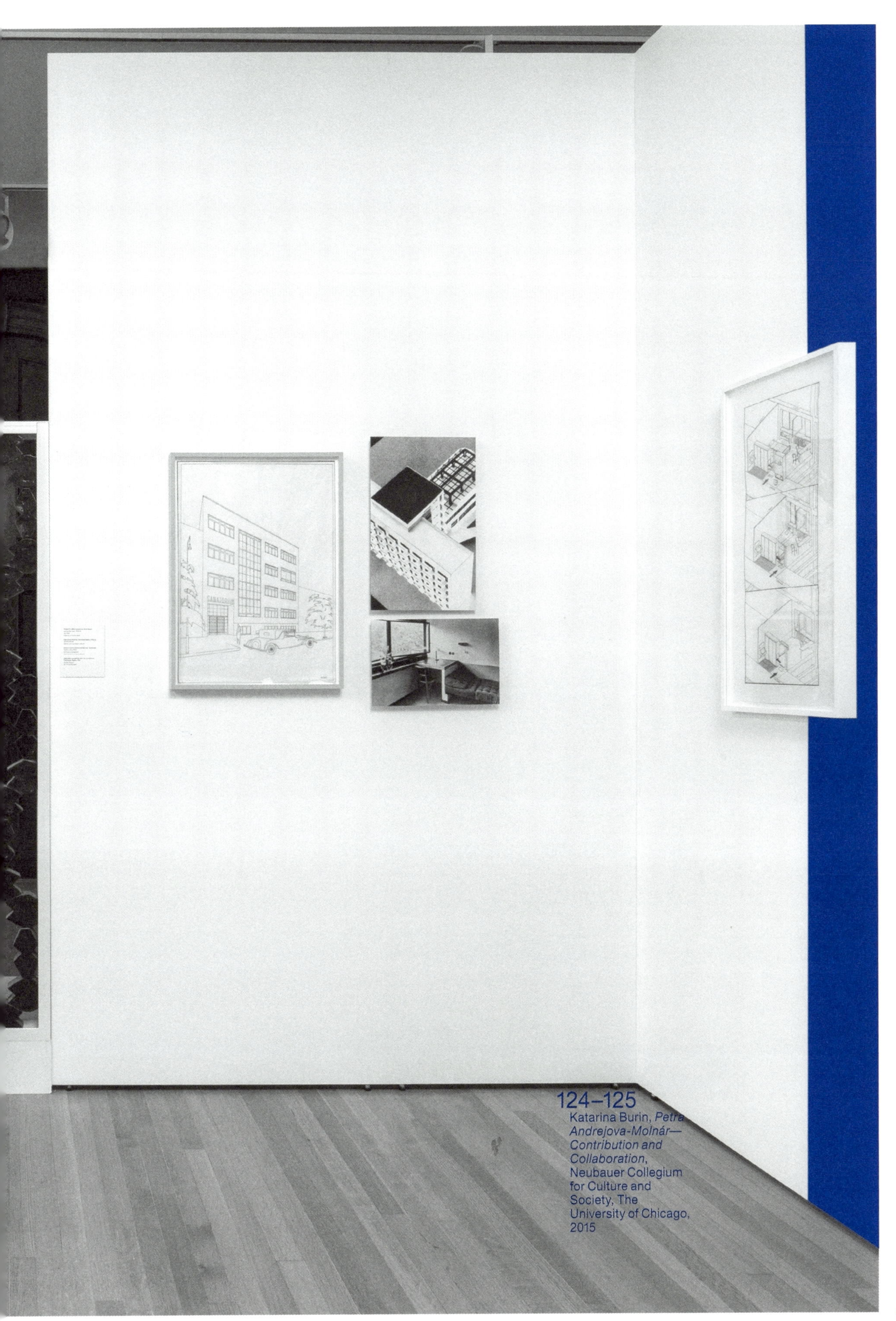

124–125
Katarina Burin, *Petra
Andrejova-Molnár—
Contribution and
Collaboration*,
Neubauer Collegium
for Culture and
Society, The
University of Chicago,
2015

Acknowledgements

This publication and the
exhibition at the Neubauer
Collegium was made possible
with generous support from the
Graham Foundation for
Advanced Studies in the Fine
Arts and coincided with the
Chicago Architectural Biennial.

Thank you to the curators,
writers, longtime collaborators
and early supporters of Petra
Andrejova-Molnár.

Jacob Proctor
Chris Perez
Helen Molesworth
Babette Richter
Nikifor Brückner
Prem Krishnamurthy
Ursula Schöndeling
Jean-Baptiste Joly
Dominic Eichler
Emma Astner
Valerie Chartrain
Andrew Sloat
Chelsea Haines
Francesca Grassi
Sybille Neumeyer
Amie Siegel
Jess Atwood Gibson
Sean Keller
Dominique Bluher
David Rodowick
Michel Ziegler
Nairy Baghramian
Luca Cerizza
Elizabeth Anne Watkins
Joel Seidner
Kevin Frances
Melissa Krok-Horton
Aimee Harrison
Joana Pimenta
Matt Saunders
Mark, Ines and Paul Burin

This catalogue is published on the occasion of the exhibition *Petra Andrejova-Molnár— Contribution and Collaboration*, at the Neubauer Collegium for Culture and Society, University of Chicago, September 16– November 13, 2015.

Design: Francesca Grassi
Proofreading: Sylee Gore
Lithography, printing and binding: Printmanagement Plitt Gmbh, Oberhausen, Germany

First published by Koenig Books, London

Koenig Books Ltd
At the Serpentine Gallery
Kensington Gardens
London W2 3XA
www.koenigbooks.co.uk

Printed in Germany

DISTRIBUTION
Germany & Europe
Buchhandlung Walther König, Köln
Ehrenstr. 4, 50672 Köln
Tel. +49 (0) 221 / 20 59 6-53
Fax +49 (0) 221 / 20 59 6-60
verlag@buchhandlung-walther-koenig.de

UK & Ireland
Cornerhouse Publications
HOME
2 Tony Wilson Place
UK – Manchester M15 4FN
Fon +44 (0) 161 2123466
Fax: +44 (0) 1752 202 330
publications@cornerhouse.org

Außerhalb Europas / Outside Europe
D.A.P. / Distributed Art Publishers, Inc.
155 6th Avenue, 2nd Floor
USA-New York, NY 10013
Fon +1 (0) 212 627 1999
Fax +1 (0) 212 627 9484
eleshowitz@dapinc.com

ISBN 978-3-86335-903-4